Historical Perspectives on Modern Economics

From new era to New Deal

Historical Perspectives on Modern Economics

General Editor: Professor Craufurd D. Goodwin,
Duke University

This series contains original works that challenge and enlighten historians of economics. For the profession as a whole it promotes a better understanding of the origin and content of modern economics.

From new era to New Deal

Herbert Hoover, the economists, and
American economic policy, 1921–1933

William J. Barber
Wesleyan University

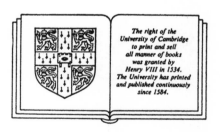

The right of the
University of Cambridge
to print and sell
all manner of books
was granted by
Henry VIII in 1534.
The University has printed
and published continuously
since 1584.

CAMBRIDGE UNIVERSITY PRESS

Cambridge
New York   New Rochelle
Melbourne   Sydney

Published by the Press Syndicate of the University of Cambridge
The Pitt Building, Trumpington Street, Cambridge CB2 1RP
32 East 57th Street, New York, NY 10022, USA
10 Stamford Road, Oakleigh, Melbourne 3166, Australia

First published 1985
First paperback edition 1988

Library of Congress Cataloging in Publication Data
Barber, William J.
From new era to New Deal.
(Historical perspectives on modern economics)
1. United States – Economic policy – to 1933.
2. United States – Politics and government – 1919–1933.
3. Hoover, Herbert, 1874–1964. I. Title. II. Series.
HC106.3.B27 1985   338.973   84–28545
ISBN 0 521 30526 8 hard covers
ISBN 0 521 36737 9 paperback

Transferred to digital printing 2002

To the memory of Louis O. Mink, Jr.

Contents

Preface

Scholars and statesmen have at least one characteristic in common: the projects they embark upon seldom materialize in quite the shape they anticipated. This study began as an inquiry into the way the Keynesian revolution was assimilated into the policy-making processes of the U.S. government during the presidency of Franklin D. Roosevelt. To set the stage for that discussion, an introductory chapter on the legacy of the Hoover administration to the New Deal seemed to be in order. What was originally intended to be a brief sketch of the bankruptcy of the economics of Hooverism has now become something else.

Most people below the age of sixty have been brought up to believe that the Great Depression was the watershed event of the twentieth-century history of the American economy and that all that went before is "premodern." Certainly the generation of economists acquiring professional status since World War II has been schooled in the view that a great burst of light broke through with the publication of *The General Theory of Employment, Interest and Money* in 1936 and that the intellectual era preceding it was largely one of darkness (or at least of very limited vision). The manner in which we report data on the aggregative performance of the economy reinforces this impression. All of the regular publications of the statistical services of the U.S. government begin their series with 1929. By implication, the economic world before that is of no interest.

There can be no question about the fundamental significance of the Great Depression in molding the institutional framework of subsequent economic life or about its ultimate impact in reshaping the thinking of economists and public officials. But, as this study will attempt to demonstrate, there are continuities as well as discontinuities between the theories and the policies of the 1920s and those of the 1930s. In the predepression decade, doctrines were being formulated which – in a number of respects – anticipated conclusions proclaimed by the "new economics" of the later 1930s. The form and timing of the ultimate absorption of the Keynesian ideas into American policy making cannot adequately be appreciated in detachment from an understanding of the economic debates of the 1920s. The chapters to follow take this story only up to 1933 with the transition from Hoover's presidency to the New Deal. Their sequel will have to wait a bit.

A work of this sort cannot possibly proceed without obliging the author to accumulate a host of debts. In particular, I should like to acknowledge the superb assistance provided by the staffs of the Herbert Hoover Presidential Library (West Branch, Iowa), the Franklin D. Roosevelt Presidential Library (Hyde Park, New York), and the National Archives (Washington, D.C.). I should also like to express my gratitude to numerous friends and colleagues who have read manuscript at various stages in its preparation: among them, Richard Buel, E. O. Golob, Basil Moore, Richard Miller, Richard Adelstein, William Parker, Burton C. Hallowell, and Richard Ohmann. They are, of course, absolved of responsibility for any errors of fact or interpretation which may remain. I am the grateful beneficiary as well of the secretarial skills of Marian Haagen and Joan Halberg and of support provided by the Trustees of Wesleyan University for faculty research.
    Above all, I wish to record my profound sense of indebtedness to Louis O. Mink, Jr., a friend, colleague, and constructive critic over many years. His penetrating comments on some early drafts played an important role in the further development of the argument. Had he lived to review the manuscript in its completed form, this would no doubt be a better book. To his memory, this study is respectfully dedicated.

Prologue: The Vision of a New Era in the 1920s

Many of the slogans attached to the decade of the 1920s solidify the view that – at least as far as economic thinking was concerned – this was indeed an antediluvian age. The "return to normalcy" that Warren G. Harding pledged in his successful campaign for the presidency in 1920 scarcely suggests that innovative economic thought was likely to find houseroom in official quarters. Support for the *status quo ante* was also apparent in America's rejection of Wilson's architecture for a League of Nations and in the isolationist attitudes that went with it. There was influential weight behind these positions, which were articulated at the highest levels in the pronouncements of Presidents Harding and Coolidge about the paramount importance of minimal governmental intervention in the economy, about the sanctity of fiscal responsibility and balanced budgets, and about the moral obligation of wartime allies to discharge their debts to the U.S. government on commercial terms. Coolidge pithily summed up a major strand of the mood of the time with his assertion that "the business of America is business." The unarticulated but self-evident corollary was that government should generally stand aloof from the functioning of the private market economy.

All of this rhetoric reflected an important component of the *Zeitgeist* of post–World War I America. But another strand of doctrine was also taking shape in these years – and it was one that took a quite different reading of the role of government in the economy. Much of the inspiration for a more interventionist approach to the economic process stemmed from the experience of economic mobilization during World War I. In those years of emergency, the American economy had demonstrated a capacity to produce at levels that had previously been held to be unattainable. This accomplishment had involved an unprecedented degree of governmental intervention in the economy in which leaders in government, in the business community, and in the economics profession had collaborated. Nothing quite like it had occurred during the lifetimes of the major participants, and the results had been impressive. Despite committing a substantial share of its resources to the prosecution of war and to the support of its allies, the nation had so enlarged its production that it could weather these years with little sacrifice in

1

current consumption by the civilian population. Clearly, the American economy possessed capacities far greater than had formerly been suspected.[1]

No one was prepared to argue that the instruments of control which had been deployed so successfully during war should be used to guide the economy in peacetime. Nevertheless, most of those involved in the management of economic mobilization were persuaded that this exercise had revealed truths that should not be forgotten with the cessation of hostilities. When terminating his work as chairman of the War Industries Board on November 19, 1918, Bernard Baruch expressed more than his personal view when he counseled President Wilson that it would be desirable "to continue the promotion of a better understanding between the Government and industry, (including in this term employers and employees alike), so that the problems affecting all may in times of peace be approached in the same spirit of helpful cooperation that has prevailed during the war."[2]

A similar note was struck by Irving Fisher in his presidential address to the American Economic Association in December 1918. Hundreds of professional economists, he noted, had temporarily abandoned the academy to lend their skills to "war work." He took it to be demonstrable that this public service by economists had made a useful contribution to the national cause. But this experience had also had a healthy effect in countering a tendency among economists – a tendency that he held to be all too prevalent – to "depend too much on books and official reports and too little on personally feeling the pulse of real events."[3] With the Armistice, the profession now faced a new challenge: to participate in shaping a "new world." Fisher admonished his colleagues as follows: "It is given to us as to no previous generation of economists to share in fixing the foundations for a new economic organization and one which shall harmonize with the principles of democracy." In his reading, the "great lesson" of war and its "miraculous achievements" was the success of the democratic method in "enlisting the active initiative, the enthusiastic interest and will to help, of the people."[4] The time was now ripe to ensure that cooperative endeavor for the common good would be sustained. To reach that goal, Fisher called upon his colleagues to join him in enlightening the public on the "fundamental principles" of economics and in campaigning for the creation of an economic research foundation (to be organized as a partnership of business, labor, and the economics profession) to generate the additional knowledge required to address the practical problems of a new day.

Management of the wartime economy had also taught a more immediate practical lesson: the value of comprehensive economic data for efficient utilization of the economy's resources. As a matter of necessity, the federal government had then mounted a statistical program on an unprecedented scale. This activity, in turn, had brought forth a wealth of information that had formerly been concealed from public view. Businessmen drawn to Washington to staff the economic mobilization agencies had observed at first hand the way these data could improve the quality of decision making. From their perspective, the moral of the tale was clear: pooled knowledge should be used as a tool for efficiency in peace as well as in war. Nor was the significance of wartime learning about the quantitative dimensions of the economy lost on the economists who had shared this experience. Wesley Mitchell (who had headed the Price Statistics Section of the War Industries Board) insisted in December 1918, for example, that it was reasonable to "cherish high hopes for the immediate future of social statistics," for they provided the tools for addressing "the gravest task that confronts mankind today – the task of developing a method by which we may make cumulative progress in social organization."[5] Mitchell also sensed the possibilities for a new breakthrough in economics, in which empirical studies could place the discipline on genuinely scientific foundations. American economics, he predicted, was on the threshold of "rapid theoretical development and of constructive application. . . . The grave problems of the war and of reconstruction will restore to economic theory the vitality it had after the Napoleonic wars."[6]

By the early 1920s another ingredient was added to the case for developing a new approach to the economic process – one that would be distinctively American. To many, there were lessons to be learned from the experience of peace making at Versailles which were fully as significant as those associated with the conduct of war. President Wilson had led Americans to expect that World War I would be "the war to end wars" and that adoption of his Fourteen Points would both minimize future international frictions and assure their peaceful resolution. To much of the American electorate, the realities of Versailles appeared to negate that expectation. Suspicion of the Old World and its ways, to be sure, had deep historic roots in the American consciousness. But this attitude was also reinforced in the early 1920s by the writings of the young Englishman John Maynard Keynes, who had resigned his position as a British Treasury delegate to the Peace Conference to publish a vitriolic denunciation of its proceedings. An American reader of this work might easily conclude that Europe was incorrigible as a breeding ground for nationalistic rivalries. Wilson, in Keynes's account, had been "bamboozled" by European statesmen bent on a peace of vengeance and their handiwork seemed likely to fertilize the soil for another war.[7]

From these ingredients, a doctrine began to emerge which held that the United States had both an opportunity and an obligation to chart a fresh and uniquely American course toward human betterment. Though professional economists assisted in its formulation, much of its content was contributed by the practical men in business and government. This view of a "new era" for the American economy and for American economics was not codified in any single document, nor was it expressed in the terms of formal economic theory. Nevertheless, a reasonably coherent implicit model was put in place during the decade of the 1920s. Its champions did not speak with a single voice on all points, but they did converge in support of three fundamental positions. In the first place, they challenged the orthodox view that economic activity was governed by immutable and universal "laws." To the contrary, they insisted that economic performance could be controlled and improved through informed manipulation. Second, they believed that the United States had a mission to serve humanity by demonstrating the superiority of a distinctive "American way." The patterns of Europe – which they associated with national antagonisms, class rivalries, and monopolistic combinations – were to be rejected. It was up to Americans to pioneer in setting higher standards that might ultimately be emulated in other countries. Third, they were in accord about the method appropriate to a new approach to economic affairs. It was to be one of full-blooded empiricism in which the facts were sovereign. Conclusions derived from deductive theorizing – built around preconceptions of human motivation and an idealized image of perfect competition – were instantly suspect. Not only were they held to be out of touch with reality; they were also tainted by their association with a discredited European intellectual tradition.

These were formidable claims indeed. It is hardly surprising that they were not accorded unanimous assent. Much of the academic orthodoxy could not be expected to find these propositions persuasive. Standard textbook teaching typically held that economic life was governed by laws of production, distribution, and exchange and that cyclical fluctuations in aggregate income and output were a normal and inevitable part of the economic system's behavior. From this point of view, it was heretical to suggest that these laws could be repealed by human intervention. Moreover, the assertion that the United States was a "special case" was, at best, dubious in the extreme. Presumably, the same laws of economics applied everywhere. Nor was this vision of a new era likely to win acclaim among public officials schooled in the belief that government should keep its hands out of private markets. Wartime planning, in this view of the proper ordering of affairs, was the exception, but not one from which any rules for the conduct of business in peacetime could be derived.

As a candidate for the leadership in the development of the new approach, one figure – Herbert Hoover – towered above all others. He was the example, par excellence, of the practical idealist. As a professional engineer, he had demonstrated outstanding talents as an efficiency expert and, by the age of thirty-five, had acquired a financial independence that would permit him thereafter to serve public causes with indifference to his compensation. As a relief administrator in war-torn Europe and as the director of the War Food Administration under President Wilson, he had displayed both his humanitarian concerns and his administrative skills. Nor could there be any doubt of his conviction that America should reject the way of the Old World and should blaze a fresh trail toward social betterment. This conviction had been sharpened by his experience at the Peace Conference in 1918 and 1919. With few kindred spirits other than John Maynard Keynes, Hoover had sensed the undercurrent of vindictiveness in the Versailles settlement and the unfortunate consequences it was likely to generate.[8] By 1920 no American in public life was regarded more highly for a capacity to form judgments on the basis of facts and without regard for partisan or personal advantage. Hoover's name was mentioned prominently as a presidential candidate by both major parties, and in the opinion of Franklin D. Roosevelt, then assistant secretary of the navy, no one was better qualified for the nation's highest post.[9]

Hoover brought this background to cabinet office when he joined President Harding's administration in March 1921. Strictly speaking, his assignment was to head the Department of Commerce, then one of the least prestigious of cabinet posts. This designation, however, did less than justice to his jurisdiction. As a condition of accepting this appointment, Hoover had insisted that he be given "a voice in all important economic policies of the administration," including matters pertaining to "business, agriculture, labor, finance, and foreign affairs as far as they related to these problems."[10] Once in office, he made sure that this presidential commitment was honored, proving himself to be a skillful bureaucratic infighter in the process. One of his official associates characterized Hoover's role in these years as "Secretary of Commerce and Undersecretary of all other Departments."[11] In view of his propensity to meddle, it is at least conceivable that a number of his cabinet associates might doubt whether Hoover could be satisfied as merely the *under*secretary of their departments.

With Hoover's vigorous sponsorship, the formulation of a "new economics" made considerable headway during the years 1921 through

1928. Its acceptance as an official theory of economic policy was, however, far from complete. Indeed, many of the recommendations Hoover championed encountered formidable resistance from the White Houses of Harding and Coolidge and from rival departments and agencies. Similarly, many of the academic economists were hostile to the tenets of the new doctrine. The election of November 1928 gave added significance to the vision of a new economics: the central figure in its shaping had become president of the United States. Though there was much unfinished business to be done, the performance of the economy during his years as secretary of commerce seemed to validate its major claims. In this spirit, a committee over which Hoover presided described the challenge of the years ahead as follows in February 1929:

To maintain the dynamic equilibrium of recent years is . . . a problem of leadership which more and more demands deliberate public attention and control. Research and study, the orderly classification of knowledge, joined to increasing skill, well may make complete control of the economic system a possibility. The problems are many and difficult, but the degree of progress in recent years inspires us with high hopes.[12]

CHAPTER 1

The ingredients of a model of a new economics

By the standards now applied by the editors of professional journals, the model of the economy worked out in the 1920s by Hoover and his associates would be judged to be deficient in rigor. It was not presented in technical language and was totally innocent of mathematical notation. Nor did it develop an explicit distinction between what would later be identified as macroeconomics, on the one hand, and microeconomics, on the other; that was to be an innovation of another time. Nevertheless, the doctrine of the Hooverites spoke to the issues to which economic theorists have long attended: the analysis of production and exchange, of the distribution of income, of the problems of economic stability and growth, and of the nature of international trade and investment. Not only did those who envisioned the emergence of a new age in the 1920s offer an account of the way these aspects of economic activity related to one another, they also posed the further question of how the observed functioning of the economy could be improved. Economics for them, as for Keynes, was "a dangerous science" in that part of its purpose was to challenge accepted patterns of thought and action.

Hoover had set out his views on the objectives of economic policy before he began his duties at the Commerce Department. In November 1920, in his capacity as president of the newly formed American Engineering Council, he commissioned an investigation into waste in industry. This was the first inquiry of its kind and those conducting it were charged to report their findings with dispatch. Hoover's introduction to the report (which was published in June 1921) summarized its message. Americans had tolerated a major shortfall of potential output, which represented "a huge deduction from the goods and services we might all enjoy . . ." The responsibility for this outcome could not be assigned uniquely to any single cause. In part the results were attributable to the unsatisfactory functioning of the microeconomic system (in deficiencies in managerial skills and practices, in labor–management frictions); in part they were traceable to macroeconomic phenomena ("the wastes of unemployment during depression; from speculation

7

and over-production in boom"). The task of the future was "to do a better job of it."[1] Inefficiency, whether writ large or writ small, was the enemy.

The role of economic information

In the new way of thinking, the first step in closing the gap between actual and potential production required an attack on economic ignorance. For his part, Hoover subscribed fully to Bacon's dictum that "knowledge is power," but he was prepared to add that government had a crucial part to play in gathering and distributing relevant economic facts. One of his first acts as secretary of commerce was to appoint an Advisory Committee on Statistics, with Mitchell as one of its members. Others invited to join this group were Edwin R. A. Seligman (of Columbia University), Allyn A. Young (Harvard), Walter F. Willcox (Cornell), Carroll W. Doten (Massachusetts Institute of Technology), Edwin F. Gay (then president of the *New York Evening Post*, who had formerly served as the first dean of the Harvard Business School), and William S. Rossiter (formerly the head of the U.S. Census Bureau). This was a formidable assemblage of talents which embraced some of the most respected names in American academic economics. But it was surely no accident that the membership was leavened by veterans of wartime work in government.[2] Nor could it have come as a surprise to Hoover when this group presented "urgent recommendations" in June 1921, that the statistical services of the government should be strengthened, that they be consolidated under the jurisdiction of the Department of Commerce, and that timely data on the activities of the economy's key sectors should be published regularly.

In Hoover's view, the rationale for this statistical program was compelling. In the first instance, it was a resource to aid businessmen in reducing the costs of their operations. But, in his judgment, prompt availability of reliable economic statistics also served larger social purposes. The intermediation of government in ensuring equal access to information would itself tend to perfect the market. No longer would larger firms (with a capacity to finance their own economic intelligence services) enjoy a differential advantage over their weaker rivals. Moreover, Hoover maintained that "prompt and comprehensive monthly publication of fundamental data . . . would contribute greatly" to stabilizing macroeconomic activity. Accurate information would tend "to prevent over-expansion and over-speculation, over-stocking of foreign goods, etc. At the same time it gives courage in times of depression as it tends to correct public psychology by giving a properly weighted idea of the very large continuing activities often overlooked in the midst of pessimistic outlook."[3] But this was not the end of the benefits that could be foreseen. Consumers as well as producers stood to gain. As Hoover saw matters: "competition based on fair and equal information of existing conditions would more likely result in lower prices to the consumer than competition based on uncertainty, in which each dealer must add something to his price to cover unforeseen eventualities."[4] With such arguments to commend it, a new monthly publication – the *Survey of Current Business* – was launched by the Department of Commerce in August 1921. In introducing it. Hoover stated that its purpose was "to aid the individual business firms in basing their policies upon fact, and to stabilize business in general through proper coordination of production, prices, stocks, etc."[5]

This was a modest beginning. Initially, the coverage of the *Survey of Current Business* fell far short of what Hoover hoped it would be. Not all important sectors were represented and only partial treatment could be given to many of those that were included. Hoover aspired to embrace the entire economy within his statistical network, including activities (such as agriculture and mining) which were held to be within the preserve of other governmental departments. The outputs of these sectors, once produced, were, he maintained, primarily of "commercial interest" and thus properly within the jurisdiction of the Department of Commerce. Resistance from the Departments of Agriculture and of the Interior frustrated the full realization of his ideal. But even within the more limited domain of manufacturing, distribution, transportation, and construction – activities over which the Department of Commerce could assert oversight without risk of being charged with bureaucratic encroachment – Hoover's grand design met resistance.

Within the business community, no one would contest the functional importance of economic information. But questions remained about how it should be acquired, to whom it should be made available, and about which parties should bear the costs of its collection and dissemination. By contrast with the situation during the war, when government could commandeer the information it required, government in the 1920s lacked the authority to obtain data now deemed to be essential to improved productive performance. Most of the raw material for the statistical base that Hoover sought to put in place was instead in the hands of private trade associations. From the point of view of members of these groups, such information was proprietary and inherently privileged. After all, who could reasonably argue that those who bore the costs should share the benefits with freeloaders (including departments of government)? If public officials attached importance to open access to economic data but were not equipped to produce them themselves, it was essential for government to establish an understanding with those who controlled the primary sources. This was not the least of the considerations that led Hoover to support the statistical work of trade associations and to stimulate the further growth of these organizations.

Hoover's enthusiasm for the trade association movement was not shared by the Department of Justice in the early 1920s. Indeed the very legality of the activities that he sought to encourage was challenged by its Anti-Trust Division. The existence of a potential problem had long been recognized. Bernard Baruch, for example, had advised Hoover early in his tenure of office at the Commerce Department that it was essential for the government to work out a mechanism for "supervision of industry which would permit a closer cooperation than now permitted by the Sherman Anti-trust Law," and that government should act as "a constructive and not alone a critical body."[6] Expert opinion within the Commerce Department favored the creation of a public authority empowered to pass judgment, before the fact, on the legitimacy of proposed trade association activities. Such a mechanism, it was noted, had been a part of the original conception of the act creating the Federal Trade Commission in 1914, but the language which would have conveyed this power to the commission had been stricken from the bill ultimately enacted.[7]

Within the existing legal framework, the Department of Justice was charged to police compliance with antitrust legislation and it was not prepared to endorse the collection of data by trade associations on production, shipments, inventories, and prices unless two conditions were satisfied: (1) that such information was transmitted exclusively to a government agency and not submitted to member firms and (2) that the data were presented at a level of generality that would preclude identification of the operations of individual firms. These safeguards were necessary, in the opinion of Attorney-General Daugherty, because the practice of many of these associations effectively meant that "each member reveals the details of his entire business to every other member," a situation held to be "entirely inconsistent with the normal attitude of real competitors." In his view, "the spirit of comradeship created by the confidential exchange of information of this character necessarily prevents the free competition between them which would otherwise prevail." In addition, he observed that trials of cases involving trade associations had revealed that "the members first agreed upon prices; but such a plan did not work because the members could not be relied upon to keep the agreement; and the system of exchanging statistics was adopted because it was found to be the only effective way to procure cooperation as to prices and production; and such co-operation could thus be procured even in the absence of any positive agreement."[8]

From Hoover's perspective, the proposed conditions were entirely unworkable: trade associations would no longer be willing to cooperate with the Department of Commerce in the gathering of socially useful statistics. "They would not go to the expense of collection," he noted, "if the only use that can be lawfully made of them is to transmit them to some governmental department."[9] He recognized that there was a latent danger in trade associations if members abused the information at their disposal to engage in price-fixing conspiracies, but he regarded this risk to be minor and, in most instances, likely to be neutralized by the disclosure of data to the public. In April 1922, for example, he reported that a canvass of nearly 2,000 trade associations showed that "only a small minority were engaged in those functions which lay the foundations upon which restraint of trade is suspicioned."[10] Those who took advantage of "the benevolent purpose of trade association work as a cloak to create combinations" should, he insisted, be dealt with by the full force of the law. The "real problem," as he saw matters, was "to avoid destroying the good in uprooting the evil. Men have murdered with brickbats but that is no reason for prohibiting brick houses."[11] In his considered opinion, the social benefits arising from a pooling of economic information far outweighed the likely social costs. As Hoover argued in his correspondence with Daugherty: "If business be compelled to operate without such vital information, it will naturally be forced into unscientific and highly speculative avenues."[12]

Though this controversy did not die, the discussion of the issues at stake took a different turn after June 1, 1925. On that date, the Supreme Court, in cases involving trade associations in the maple flooring and cement industries, ruled that exchanges of information among trade groups did not in themselves represent unlawful restraint of commerce. Hoover would have preferred a ruling with an added stipulation: that the data distributed to association members be made available simultaneously to a responsible government department. The court did not attach this condition, but he still counted its decision as a validation of his position.

Even so, some intricate questions remained. The Supreme Court continued to hold that attempts to reach agreements on common price and production policies were unlawful. Hoover was in full accord with this doctrine. Collusive price making was antithetical to his concept of a healthy economic order. As a practical matter, however, it was seldom easy to distinguish the impact on price formation when firms apparently acted independently (but with shared information on production and inventories) from cases in which explicit agreements on pricing policies were reached. At the level of economic theory, there was also a puzzle. The equilibrium conditions produced in a regime of perfect competitors and by a tightly organized cartel would yield one result in common: all producers would sell at the same price. Hoover was certainly aware that the lines dividing legitimate from illegitimate activity were blurred and that judgments should be based on careful investigation of the circumstances surrounding individual cases. At the same time, he left no one in any doubt about his principled opposition to price fixing. His most forceful applications of this principle, however, were in cases that he regarded as unambiguous, those in which governments were parties to price making. On this basis he vigorously opposed the practices of foreign governments in encouraging collusion among producers of raw materials that the United States imported. The same argument was invoked to attack proposals that the U.S. government should intervene in setting prices of American agricultural products.

But it was also asked whether the license accorded to trade associations might not foster greater industrial concentration and produce a structure that was incompatible with effective competition. Hoover steadfastly denied that this was the case. When challenged in June 1925 that his policy seemed calculated to accelerate the trend toward bigness, he responded: "It certainly is not. It is exactly the reverse of the truth. ... [T]he whole work of this Department ... is for the purpose of giving the small unit the same advantages which are already possessed by big business."[13] The duty of the department was to assure an open door to information for all market participants. If this could be accomplished, the competitive environment would be strengthened. This did not mean that larger units should be inhibited by virtue of their size alone. If economies of scale could be achieved by large firms which were not available to small ones, it was to be expected that the more efficient would prevail. Society had much to gain from the promotion of efficiency. But the efficient would have to win in a fair fight: one that was free of any suspicion of collusion or conspiracy.

In view of the high social yield Hoover and his associates expected from an improved flow of knowledge about the economy's performance, it is at first glance surprising that they did not extend their statistical efforts even further than they did. The latter-day observer is likely to be as struck by what was left undone as by what was done. The absence of data on the aggregative behavior of the economy, for example, is particularly noteworthy. The technique of national income accounting was, of course, then in its infancy. Hoover acknowledged that the preparation of such data was intellectually interesting and endorsed such work by private scholars.[14] It did not figure, however, among his priorities for the Department of Commerce.

The technocratic aspect of the attack on waste

As a catalyst to efficiency, government – in Hoover's judgment – had an obligation to lead the fight against wasteful practices in the production process as well as to counter deficiencies in market intelligence. The inquiry into *Waste in Industry* which he had commissioned in his capacity as president of the Federated American Engineering Societies had spoken eloquently about the costs in forgone output arising from unnecessary product differentiation and from the failure of many manufacturers to apply "best-practice" methods to the production process. The implication for governmental policy was clear: it should encourage the adoption of standardized specifications covering a wide range of industrial products and should promote productivity consciousness among manufacturers.

In Hoover's reorganized Department of Commerce, a central place was assigned to a newly created Division of Simplified Practice. In staffing it, he could tap a stream of talents flowing from Frederick Taylor's campaigns for scientific management. The charge to this unit was to develop, in consultation with representative groups from the relevant industries, a series of recommendations on steps to eliminate avoidable waste. Once agreed positions had been formulated, the department sponsored conferences and distributed pamphlets to promote their adoption. By the time Hoover left the Department of Commerce, some eighty-six such recommendations had been promulgated with results that appeared to be impressive. In the judgment of officials in the department, a "general estimate" of proved savings in "material, time, labor, and money" came to $600 million a year.[15] In an economy in which value added in the manufacturing sector was of the order of $18 billion annually, this was not a trivial sum.[16] Some of the enthusiasts for "industrial rationalization" even claimed that the new approach, if pressed to the full, could raise living standards by 20 to 30 percent.[17]

Much of this work was undramatic and largely uncelebrated. Such activities as standardizing the sizes of electrical fittings, homogenizing the threading of firehose couplings, or determining optimal radio frequencies seldom grabbed the headlines. Nevertheless, these steps toward the elimination of waste have made a major, though unquantifiable, contribution to the adaptability and the technical dynamism of the

American economy and have become part of what we now take for granted. The significance of this strand of Hooverism is perhaps better appreciated in countries that did not experience a similar technocratic intervention in the 1920s than it is in the United States.[18]

The advantages of this type of governmental intervention were not universally regarded as compelling by the business community in the 1920s. Though businessmen could readily grasp the merit of improved practices that reduced their costs, governmental guidance on the specifications of their outputs was not necessarily welcome. After all, captive markets are much easier to develop and to sustain through product differentiation than through product standardization. It is not clear whether or not Hoover was acquainted with the writings of Thorstein Veblen, who had argued that there was an inherent conflict between the engineers (whose objective was to maximize efficiency) and businessmen (whose objective was to maximize profits).[19] In light of some of the battles in which he was engaged, Hoover would have understood this point, whether informed by Veblen or not. When addressing business complaints about excessive governmental meddling in the technical details of their operations, Hoover always insisted that he neither had nor sought power to compel industrialists to adopt the Commerce Department's recommendations. At the same time he supported using government's leverage as a purchaser to encourage compliance. As one of his aides put it: "The Federal Specifications Board promulgates specifications for the government purchases and although there is of course no pressure being brought by the Department for the adoption of these by industry, nevertheless there is manifest a tendency to so adopt them by state and municipal organizations and to an increasing degree by industry."[20] The payoff to the economy at large from this effort was expected to be considerable. In the tire industry alone, for example, it was estimated in 1928 that the reduction in the number of standard tire sizes from twenty-four to sixteen would represent a savings of $25 million per year.[21]

The technocratic effort to promote cost-minimization, in Hoover's judgment, might properly take a somewhat different form in the sectors of the economy which were subject to public regulation. Here the hand of government could be more visible. Great gains were possible, he maintained, through rationalization in the railway network (which was subject to the jurisdiction of the Interstate Commerce Commission), particularly if weaker lines were merged with stronger ones. Similarly, economies were there for the taking if the Federal Power Commission could promote linkages of electric utilities into interstate grid systems.

There was thus an enlarged role for government in bringing these desirable improvements about. Moreover, government could contribute directly to making low-cost power available by using public monies to harness the water resources of interstate river systems. In such cases, the federal government could legitimately be a producer of marketable outputs, though the final step in the transaction – the distribution of electric energy to ultimate consumers – should be assigned to others (private utilities, municipalities, or cooperative associations).

Hoover's vision of the elimination of unnecessary waste embraced all of these matters. Little of the latter part of this grand design was accomplished, however, during his years at the Commerce Department. The established federal regulatory bodies preferred to operate with their procedures and at their own pace, without benefit of instruction from the secretary of commerce. Nor was Hoover successful in moving Coolidge to take action on these matters. In advance of each congressional session, Hoover proposed that the president should request legislative action to give greater authority to the Interstate Commerce Commission and to the Federal Power Commission to spur consolidations and he pressed also for federal appropriations for power production on interstate waterways at sites such as those available on the Colorado River. These proposals fell on deaf ears at the White House.

The design of an economic stabilization strategy: new dimensions of fiscal policy

To people of Hoover's persuasion, it was axiomatic that a systematic campaign to push production to its full potential called for the mitigation, if not the elimination, of cyclical disturbances. Downturns in economic activity represented a wastage that should not be tolerated in a well-ordered system. But could intelligent economic management banish such fluctuations? It was expected that an improved flow of information to producers about business conditions would itself tend to stabilize the economy by minimizing speculative excesses. But it was also maintained that this strategy could usefully be reinforced with other measures. Hoover believed that human manipulation could triumph over any alleged "laws" of economics. As he stated his position in 1923: "We are constantly reminded by some of the economists and businessmen that the fluctuation of the business cycle is inevitable; that there is an ebb and flow in the demand for commodities and services that cannot from the nature of things be regulated. I have great doubts whether there is a real foundation for this view." [22]

The importance of a technique for taming the business cycle was driven home forcefully early in Hoover's career as secretary of commerce. The year 1921 witnessed a sharp downturn in economic activity, which was accompanied by a disturbing increase in unemployment. Hoover's reaction to this situation was to convene a gathering of business and labor leaders and government officials in Washington to consider remedies for the recession. Though officially styled the President's Conference on Unemployment, it was organized on Hoover's initiative and he chaired its proceedings. Crucial to the deliberations of the conference was the groundwork laid by an economic advisory committee appointed by the secretary of commerce. Its advance report set the agenda for the subsequent discussions.[23] The primary conclusion of the economic advisers was that spending on public works, if properly timed, could smooth much of the fluctuation in business activity and employment.

A novel concept was central to an understanding of the argument supporting this finding. The impact on the economy of an accelerated public works program in times of depression, it was maintained, would be much greater than the direct stimulation it would give to incomes and jobs in the construction industry. Indirect effects would also be felt throughout the system when this added purchasing power augmented the demand for consumer goods. Nor would the expansionary effects end there. Still more jobs and more income would be created when the producers of consumer goods began to spend their enlarged incomes. The leverage for lifting the economy via public works spending was graphically depicted in charts designed to show the "multiplying effects" on employment and income which it could generate. (See Figures 1.1 and 1.2.)

In recommending this strategy to deal with depression, the committee insisted that "only necessary public works should be undertaken," projects that "would ordinarily be executed at some future time." And it added: "Public works must be on a 'commercial' basis, not a 'relief' basis, otherwise waste will result. On a 'commercial' basis men fit for the work are engaged at usual rates and wages and unfit workers are discharged. On the 'relief' basis the workers are chosen primarily because they are in need and retained whether fit or not."[24] In other words, a sound public works program would be required to satisfy the usual tests of efficiency and its purpose was to provide jobs, not handouts.

This line of thinking owed much to the work of Otto T. Mallery, a member of the Pennsylvania State Industrial Board and secretary of the state's Emergency Public Works Commission. In January 1919 Mallery had called for the development of a national policy to set aside one-

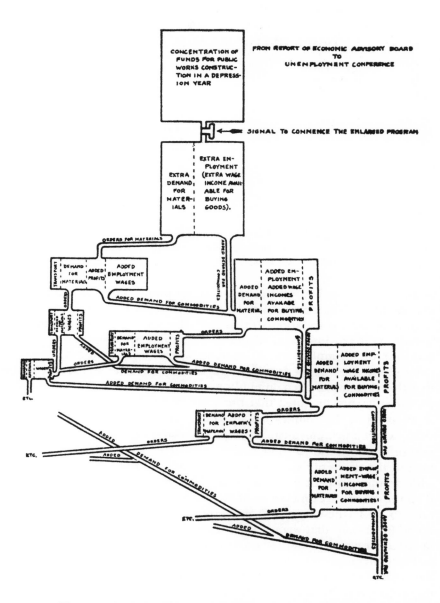

Figure 1. Aggregate stimulus to private industry caused by pressure of concentration of public works construction in depression years. Reprinted from *Report of the President's Conference on Unemployment*, 1921, p. 102.

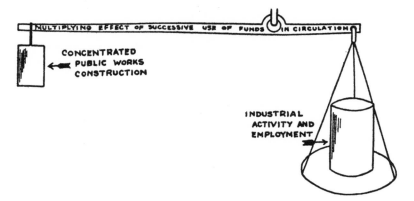

Figure 2. Manifold power of concentrated public works construction to sustain and revive industry. Reprinted from *Report of the President's Conference on Unemployment*, 1921, p. 103.

tenth of the normal volume of spending on public works as a reserve that could be drawn on to cushion a downturn in economic activity. According to his calculations at that time, five years of reserve accumulation would provide a sum adequate to "employ 800,000 workers in a bad year of unemployment at average wages for a period of three months." In view of the fact that roughly two-thirds of the total construction then undertaken on public account was performed by municipal governments, he noted that this strategy would reemploy workers in all parts of the country, and particularly in the larger industrial cities, where unemployment was typically concentrated.[25] In elaborating his version of an income and employment "multiplier," Mallery likened the effects of expenditures on public works to those associated with dropping a pebble into a pond: "the ripples . . . extend farther than the eye can see and circles of motion widen and move in all directions to the farthest shores."[26] His recommendations, he insisted, were sound for reasons that went beyond their effect in offsetting downturns in economic activity; they were also supported by considerations of elementary financial prudence. Construction undertaken in a period of slack, when prices of materials were likely to be softening, would mean that costs would be lower than otherwise would be the case.

This general strategy was endorsed by the President's Conference on Unemployment when it issued its own report in October 1921. The doctrine that the federal government should act as a catalyst to economic activity thus took on further meaning. The federal government, to be sure, was not expected to be a major spender on public works in

its own right. Normally, the federal government accounted for only
about 10 percent of construction spending undertaken in the public
sector. In keeping with public attitudes of the time, that was the way
things should be. The bulk of the capital facilities for which a genuine
need was envisaged were properly in the domain of the states, counties,
and municipalities. They provided the schools, streets, water and sewer
systems, and most of the roads and bridges. The central government's
role, on the other hand, was restricted to projects that were interstate
in character and to those over which it had a constitutional mandate
(such as capital expenditures for national defense and for a postal system). This allocation of responsibilities was clearly reflected in the
weights of various levels of government in construction spending within the public sector: in the years 1921 through 1928, state and local
governments were consistently responsible for more than 90 percent of
total public sector outlays.[27] This type of mix was held to be the only
one compatible with the ideals of American federalism. In the nature
of things, state and local governments were thus necessarily expected to
be the main actors in the deployment of public resources for capital
projects.

But the federal government was still the vital force in the implementation of this strategy for macroeconomic stabilization. Its most important assignment was to guide other echelons of government on the
appropriate timing of their construction work. Further, it was desirable
for the central government to educate the private sector on the merits
of phasing its capital spending countercyclically. In the words of the Report of the President's Conference on Unemployment:

it should be possible in some measure to control the expansion of the national
plant and equipment. If all branches of our public works and the construction
work of our public utilities – the railways, the telephones, etc. – could systematically put aside financial reserves to be provided in times of prosperity
for the deliberate purpose of improvement and expansion in times of depression, we would not only greatly decrease the depth of depressions but we would
at the same time diminish the height of booms. We would in fact abolish acute
unemployment and wasteful extravagance. For a rough calculation indicates
that if we maintain a reserve of about 10 percent of our annual construction for
this purpose, we could almost iron out the fluctuations in employment.[28]

This was a call for indicative planning on a grand scale. The freedom
of private businesses and state and local officials to make their own decisions was not to be compromised. But an audible voice, if not a visible
hand, should assist them. These considerations in turn strengthened the
case for improving the statistical services of the federal government.[29]

Though the group called to Washington for the President's Conference on Unemployment adjourned its plenary sessions in October 1921, it did not disband as an organization. The Conference charged a standing committee to direct further studies of economic stabilization, with particular attention to the place of public works in the strategy. Under its auspices, the National Bureau of Economic Research was commissioned to launch a major research program on this problem.

As the discussion of this issue evolved during the 1920s, opinion gradually shifted away from the original notion that public works should be funded from contingency reserves set aside in periods of prosperity. To many, it seemed preferable to keep the borrowing authority of various echelons of government in a state of readiness, rather than to accumulate surpluses for use in contingencies. If the machinery were already in place, governments could turn to capital markets without delay in a period of downturn when there was no risk of "crowding out" private borrowers. Implicit in the general understanding of the way things should work in a federal system was a notion that various echelons of government were subject to different rules in the financing of public works. State and local governments were normally expected to borrow to cover such expenditures and the federal government encouraged this practice by exempting the interest received by holders of state and municipal bonds from its income tax. Borrowing by the central government, on the other hand, was thought to have quite different significance. Historically, deficit financing by the federal government had been associated almost exclusively with expenditures for war. Unlike state and local debt issues for public works, such borrowing left nothing useful behind to show for it. Deficits at the federal level were also dubious for another reason: there was always suspicion that they might be covered through the irresponsible creation of new money, a financing device not available to state and local governments. Even so, there was some elasticity in interpreting what a "balance" in the federal budget really meant. Legislation in 1921 had stipulated that the Treasury should henceforth earmark a portion of each year's tax revenues to the retirement of the war-swollen national debt. This "sinking fund" transaction was charged in the Treasury's accounts as an "ordinary expenditure" of the federal government. This accounting convention meant, however, that an administrative budget which was nominally in balance was actually in surplus. It also suggested, as a number of economists (most notably F. G. Dickinson of the University of Illinois) were to point out, that funding required for an accelerated program of federal public works could be found internally if the central government temporarily suspended retirement of public debt when the economy could use a stimulant to spending.[30] Though the federal government was still not to be the big spender on public works, it still had latitude to spend more when the economy needed a bit of needle and it could do so within the framework of a balanced budget (if appropriately defined).

In these years, much discussion also centered on the procedure for identifying the circumstances in which an increase or a decrease of spending on public works was warranted. Most commentators favored the use of an objective indicator as the triggering mechanism. But which index and what magnitude of variation in it should be specified? Various possibilities were canvassed: an index of construction activity (favored by the sponsors of the Jones Bill submitted in the Senate in 1928), an index of employment (supported by F. G. Dickinson), or an index of general business activity (which was apparently the preference of Secretary Hoover). Most of the enthusiasts for this type of intervention favored mechanisms for the control of public works spending which would be neutralized from partisan influence and insulated from the pressures of pork-barrel politics. The task of advising public officials when they ought to sell bonds and let contracts could, in the judgment of one commentator, be assigned to a first class clerk in the Bureau of Labor Statistics in Washington.[31] Others preferred to entrust this responsibility to a nonpartisan board. Though tastes differed on the choice of administrative instrument, all could agree that success depended on the preparation of a backlog of worthwhile projects. Once this logistical planning was in place, it was widely held that the decisions on when to activate the strategy and on what scale could be left to the judgment of experts.

With Hoover's encouragement a major lobbying effort was mounted in the 1920s to win congressional endorsement for the principle of countercyclical phasing of public works. Mallery was the point man in this campaign, and by 1928 he had won support from the American Engineering Council, the Associated General Contractors of America, and the American Association for Labor Legislation.[32] Mallery and his associates could rightly draw satisfaction from some impressive achievements in reshaping public and congressional attitudes on this issue. Despite their best efforts, however, these activities produced no legislative results in the 1920s. In part, this disappointment could be attributed to a lack of consensus among the sponsors about the detailed provisions of proposed legislation. But much of the foot dragging by politicians stemmed from their reluctance to cede spending powers of government to experts and to formulas. The "weakest point" in the salability of the general scheme, as Mallery came to understand it, was that "it will not get votes. . . . Spending public money is good politics at one time; economy is better at others. These times may not coincide with the need to stabilize employment."[33]

Even in the absence of new legislation, it was still possible for the federal government to perform many of the functions called for by the new strategy of fiscal stabilization. The message sent out from the Conference on Unemployment the autumn of 1921 had itself produced a salutary effect. In the months that followed, bond issues for local public works broke all existing records.[34] Meanwhile Hoover had persuaded Harding to urge federal departments "to advance any work that they may have available . . . without expanding the expenditure of government funds beyond what would take place in any event"; and he added that "we should make this visible demonstration to the mayors and governors of the anxiety of the Federal government to pursue the matter with the same earnestness that they are already doing."[35] In 1923, when the economy had showed signs of overheating, Hoover had intervened to turn the expenditure dials in the opposite direction. He then sent an open letter to President Harding, calling for a slowdown in public works "'until after there is a relaxation of private demands for labor in construction. . . . We can by this means contribute something to a more even flow of employment, not only directly in the construction work but in the material trades."[36] This recommendation was supported by the president of the American Construction Council, Franklin D. Roosevelt. In the judgment of contemporaries, this type of intervention made a healthy contribution to dampening the upswing of the cycle.[37]

The general design of a fiscal strategy to counter fluctuations in aggregate economic activity was thus shaped during Hoover's years at the Commerce secretariat. Even without any extension in congressionally sanctioned executive authority, the experiments with this scheme which were run in the early 1920s seemed to have produced gratifying results. Moreover, public consciousness of the possibilities for taming the business cycle had been raised to a point at which even more ambitious planning was entertainable. Shortly after his election as president in November 1928, Hoover gave his blessing to a trial balloon to be floated by Governor Ralph O. Brewster of Maine before the Conference of State Governors in New Orleans. The scheme Brewster proposed called for various units of government to approve advance authorizations for public works, on a scale amounting to $3 billion for the nation as a whole, which could be activated without delay to buffer a downturn in employment. This was a far cry from the original notion that contingency reserves should be accumulated from budget surpluses before the tap controlling spending on public works could be turned on.[38]

Puzzles over the place of monetary policy in macroeconomic stabilization

The Hooverites did not doubt that the terms on which money and credit were available had an important bearing on the prospects for achieving their goals of economic growth and stability. Strictly speaking, primary responsibility for monetary policy was assigned to the Federal Reserve System, which was constitutionally insulated from the jurisdiction of officials in the executive branch of government. Hoover understood well the institutional factors that limited his influence over the management of monetary affairs. At the same time, he held strong views about how a properly ordered banking system should behave. Its primary job, in his judgment, was to channel the flow of credit in ways that contributed to macroeconomic stabilization. This understanding of matters did not necessarily coincide with the views of central bankers. The language of the Federal Reserve Act of 1913 had charged the monetary authorities "to serve the needs of commerce and business." Most of the central bankers interpreted this mandate to require them, for example, to make the appropriate accommodations in periods of expanding demand for credit. Such monetary ease in periods of expansion, however, might not be compatible with the objective of dampening macroeconomic fluctuations. Indeed, considerations of "accommodation" and "stabilization" might well yield quite divergent recommendations for monetary policy. Though leaders in the Federal Reserve System were sensitive to the importance of regulating the money supply in ways that would keep the United States competitive in international markets, the notion that they should "lean against the wind" in the domestic economy was far from fully accepted.

A further source of tension about the conduct of monetary policy was latent in the structure of the Federal Reserve System as it existed in the 1920s. Lines of authority were then systematically blurred. Though the nominal apex of the system was the Federal Reserve Board in Washington, D.C., the effective powers of this body were limited. The dozen Federal Reserve District Banks dispersed throughout the country retained wide latitude to carry on their business as they saw fit, with little regard for whether or not their actions were consistent with recommendations from the center. For practical purposes, the most powerful single figure in the system in the 1920s was Benjamin Strong, governor of the Federal Reserve District Bank of New York. His primacy reflected both the force of his personality and his situation as the central banker whose operations were located in the nation's financial center.[39]

In the 1920s considerable confusion also surrounded the nature of the control instruments the monetary authorities could effectively deploy. The original design of the Federal Reserve Act in 1913 empowered the various district banks to influence the lending capacity of member banks with two devices: (1) variation in their required reserve ratios and (2) variation in the rate of discount on eligible paper presented as collateral by banks making use of "lender of last resort" facilities. Almost by accident, the central bankers discovered that another form of leverage over commercial banks was potentially at their disposal. The act of 1913 had authorized the Federal Reserve Banks to hold securities on their own account with the expectation that the earnings from this portfolio would cover the operating expenses of the system. In 1921 and 1922 the Federal Reserve Banks undertook a program of portfolio switching with an eye to increasing their earnings. A statistical postmortem on this activity yielded a striking and unexpected finding: that acquisitions of government securities by Federal Reserve Banks were associated with reduced borrowings by member banks from the Federal Reserve. Conversely, reductions in Federal Reserve security holdings were correlated with increased use of "lender of last resort" facilities by member banks.[40] It thus appeared that purchases and sales of securities by the central banking system had a direct impact on the reserve positions of commercial banks. A promising new technique, "open-market operations," for influencing the lending capacity of banks (and thus for exercising greater control over the terms and the availability of credit) appeared to be at hand.

Though officials of the Federal Reserve System were initially uncertain about how effective this instrument might be, Irving Fisher of Yale University entertained no such doubts. At this point in his career, he had disengaged himself from most of his university duties and spent a substantial portion of his time directing an Index Number Institute (which sold its services to businessmen) and to campaigning for public causes. One cause close to his heart in these years was economic stabilization through scientific management of the money supply.[41] Fisher was the intellectual inspiration for the Goldsborough Bill (first introduced in the Congress in 1922 and discussed in various versions for the next decade) which provided that "all of the powers of the Federal Reserve System shall be used for promoting stability in the price level." In his analytic scheme, however, price stability was an instrumental objective, not a final one. It was Fisher's claim that success in achieving price stability would effectively eradicate cyclical fluctuations. This conclusion, he maintained, was supported by statistical evidence that the rate of change in the general price level was highly correlated with variations in the volume of trade. The relationship, to be sure, was not instantaneous. His empirical investigations suggested a lag of approximately seven months between the turning point of the rate of change of prices and changes in the level of aggregate economic activity. Even so, he was satisfied that his results demonstrated conclusively "that a rising price level temporarily stimulates trade and that a falling price level depresses trade."[42]

If variation in the general price level was responsible for the ups and downs of business activity, how then might it be controlled? Fisher's answer was informed by a "quantity theory of money," which holds that the money supply multiplied by the velocity of circulation (the number of times the money stock turns over in a period of, say, a year) would necessarily be equal to the total number of monetized transactions multiplied by their average price. There was nothing new about this theory itself; in some form it had been a part of economic discourse for at least a century and a half.[43] Fisher had first restated it as the "equation of exchange" in 1911. In England Alfred Marshall had kept this tradition alive, though with slightly different nomenclature, and one of his pupils, John Maynard Keynes, had expanded on it in his tract *Monetary Reform*, published in the United States in 1924.

In the America of the 1920s, Fisher maintained that this venerable doctrine could be given a fresh vitality. It was now possible, for the first time, to give it precise operational content. Technical refinements in the construction of index numbers showing the behavior of the general price level now meant that monetary policy could be conducted on a scientific basis. "Prior to the advent of the index number as an instrument for measuring," Fisher wrote, "even the concept of a stable buying power of money was too vague to form the basis of reform."[44] With the aid of this tool, the dream of economic stabilization now "approached realization." Attitudes of "monetary fatalism" could confidently be pushed aside. "[N]early all inflation and deflation are man-made . . . Why," Fisher asked, "should we not therefore have a man-made stabilization?"[45]

To achieve this happy result, all that was needed was an instruction to the Federal Reserve System to use its discretionary authority to vary the money supply as needed to stabilize prices. In Fisher's view, it was adequately equipped for this task. Not only could it deploy its control over discount rates and require reserve ratios to influence the volume of bank lending; it now also had an effective tool in the form of purchases and sales of securities in the open market. Fisher was convinced that the powers of the Federal Reserve System, if "rightly used," could make it "the greatest public service institution in the world."[46] Scientific management of the money supply offered the prospect of producing a stable general price level and this, in turn, would tend to iron out fluctuations in aggregate economic activity.[47]

While stabilization of the economy was the primary objective of Fisher's monetary proposals, he insisted that other social benefits would flow from the adoption of his recommendations. In the first place, steps assuring that the dollar had stable purchasing power would eliminate a major source of social friction. As he stated his case before a congressional committee:

Whenever there is inflation you will find socialism thrives, because the socialist, with his suspicious mind, believes that the great corporations are grabbing, and thus you have the word "profiteer" and other nicknames applied to people into whose laps fall the profits which inflation takes away from others; and, on the other hand, you will find when there is deflation the farmers and others blaming Rockefeller and Morgan and others personifying Wall Street as the cause of their troubles when as a matter of fact the cause is an impersonal one. Out of these unjust accusations that the creditor class controls the price level, or the debtor class, you have the evils of distrust and suspicion and ill feeling and class warfare and sometimes bloodshed.[48]

Similarly, much of the difficulty faced by farmers in the 1920s stemmed from failure to stabilize the general price level in the immediate postwar years. In Fisher's estimate at least 50 percent of the "evils of farmers" were "left overs of the deflation of 1919 and 1920."[49]

Fisher's monetarist approach to macroeconomic stabilization was clearly in the spirit of "new era" thinking. In company with the Hooverites, he proclaimed faith in the capacity of informed intervention to serve the public good. Though they shared a common style and sense of purpose, they differed in the emphases they assigned to particular strategies of macroeconomic stabilization. Fisher accepted that intervention to adjust the timing of spending on public works could play a useful role, but he gave greater weight to monetary than to fiscal interventions. The Hooverites, while prepared to give a sympathetic hearing to suggestions on the way the conduct of monetary policy could be improved, looked primarily to countercyclical spending on public works as the primary tool in a strategy of stabilization.

Though Hoover stopped short of giving his formal endorsement to Fisher's legislative proposals, he was not reluctant to offer unsolicited counsel to the Federal Reserve System on the way it should manage monetary policy. He understood that this was not part of his official prerogative. Nevertheless, he usually made his views known through an intermediary. Senator Irvine Lenroot (a member of the Senate Committee on Banking and Currency), for example, performed this function in 1925 and 1926. At that time, Hoover took exception to the Federal Reserve's policy of monetary ease, a policy that he feared was both allowing the economy to overheat and fueling speculative activity by financing the purchase of stocks through loans to brokers.[50] And he was sharply critical of the Federal Reserve's failure to work out arrangements to discourage banks from lending for stock market transactions. As Hoover's surrogate, Lenroot obligingly pressed the Federal Reserve on these points, though to no avail. The Federal Reserve steadfastly defended its right to pursue a course of its own choosing and took particular exception to the suggestion that it could or should require banks to police the ultimate uses to which creditworthy customers put borrowed funds.

At times Hoover was also prepared to go over the heads of the Federal Reserve officials by calling directly on commercial bankers to conduct their affairs in a manner consistent with macroeconomic stabilization. In this vein, the final report of the President's Conference on Unemployment in 1921 had admonished bankers to display "courage" in periods of high economic activity by denying loans to creditworthy customers. Even though it was not in the narrow self-interest of bankers to do so, they would thereby be serving the larger public good by dampening inflationary pressures. This was a theme that was to recur in Hoover's later pronouncements from the White House. In his view, the banking community should recognize its social responsibilities and, should profit maximization and the public interest be in conflict, the latter should guide their conduct.

New era doctrine on wage determination and income distribution

Though innovative approaches to production and its stabilization took precedence in the formulation of a model for a new era, they were closely linked with a no less arresting set of ideas about the way income should be distributed. Indeed, these strands of thought were mutually reinforcing. The expansion in output promised by the reorganization of production quite naturally invited questions about the capacity of consumers to absorb an enlarged volume of goods and services. At the same time, realization of the economy's full productive potential required that frictions between labor and management which interrupted the flow of output should be minimized.

The champions of the new era proclaimed a doctrine of high wages as the solvent to both of these potential difficulties. This view stood in direct conflict with the theory that some "iron law" necessarily imposed a low ceiling on the income of workers. It was now asserted that a national commitment to a regime of high wages should be the centerpiece of a distinctive American approach to a new economic order. Not only would high wages promote efficiency and sustain high levels of consumer demand; they would also mitigate social class differentiation. In addition, it occurred to some that this strategy could blunt the attractiveness of trade union membership and the threat it might pose to the development of a harmonious partnership between capital and labor.

Strictly speaking, matters of wage policy and labor relations were within the province of the Department of Labor, not the Department of Commerce. Hoover felt under no obligation to live within these jurisdictional boundaries, however. As the prime mover in the President's Conference on Unemployment in 1921, he won the endorsement of those assembled for the principle of high wages and for the view that wage cutting should be resisted in periods of recession. And he took the lead in pressing for reductions in the length of the working day, arguing that practices such as those in the steel industry (in which the twelve-hour day and the eighty-four hour week were standard in the early 1920s) were both inefficient and inhumane. When leaders of the steel industry rejected his recommendation to adopt an eight-hour day and a six-day week, he ultimately brought them into line by mobilizing public opinion.[51]

In Hoover's grand design, a fundamental change in institutions and attitudes was called for. Even before taking up his post at the Commerce Department, he had indicated the direction of this thought in correspondence with Samuel Gompers, president of the American Federation of Labor. In October 1920 he stated his conviction that "an increased production of anything from 5 to 30 percent could be obtained if the mental and physical attitude of the worker towards his work could be enlisted and re-aligned and if interruption by strike and lockout could be minimized." But he recognized that this desirable goal could not be reached if workers associated improvement in productivity with hardship for themselves. Though he was persuaded that the ultimate result would be improvement in living standards and an increase in the number of jobs, some mechanism was needed to allay the understandable fears of workers that they would bear the costs of transitions generated by productivity improvement. Hoover proposed that collective agreements be struck between labor and management providing that gains arising from increased efficiency be allocated to "the provision of unemployment and sickness insurance and on an adequate scale." He suggested, in addition, that these funds should be "administered through the major voice of organized labor."[52]

Though few of the leaders in the business community were prepared to follow Hoover in his sympathies for organized labor, some were prepared to outdo him in their enthusiasm for the doctrine of high wages. The experience of Henry Ford – who had taken the unprecedented step in 1914 of paying his workers a minimum of $5.00 a day, when he could have hired all the labor he needed at half that wage – seemed to provide dramatic testimony to the soundness of this approach. The Ford Motor Company had subsequently prospered and its owner commended his example to his colleagues in the business community. Ford insisted that a high wage policy was not altruism, but simply good business, and that it more than paid for itself through increased productivity, improved industrial relations, and expansion in markets.[53] At least one member of the business community was sufficiently impressed by this experience to recommend that the conventional objections against the use of governmental powers to set prices be waived. Edward A. Filene, the innovative Boston retailer, spoke eloquently in 1923 in favor of raising the price of labor by concerted action of state governments in fixing minimum wages. Such intervention in the labor market was essential, he maintained, in order to protect the enlightened employer from the "meanest and most short-sighted" who would attempt to gain a competitive advantage at the expense of their workers. This unscrupulous practice should be outlawed. Moreover, high wages would advance the cause of efficiency by compelling management to improve its performance. But there was yet another consideration: the climate created by high wages would induce businessmen to take their community responsibilities more seriously. In particular, it would alert them to their stake in supporting improvements in public education which would raise the quality of the labor force.[54]

But a question remained: Was it not likely that a strategy to push wage rates above the market equilibrium level would induce employers to reduce the volume of employment they would be prepared to offer? The advocates of the high-wage doctrine generally satisfied themselves that no problem of unemployment would follow the adoption of practices they recommended. The marginal product of labor, they insisted, would be increased by at least enough to offset the increment in the costs of labor. High wages were themselves expected to spur superior managerial performance to raise productivity. In addition, it was argued that a powerful reinforcement to sustained improvement in labor productivity had been built into the American system with the passage of a constitutional amendment in 1918 outlawing the sale of alcoholic beverages. Prohibition was frequently cited as responsible for enhancing on-the-job effectiveness and for reducing absenteeism.[55]

It was also recognized that government had further responsibilities to discharge if the full benefits of high wages in the United States were to be realized. In the first instance, it should design and administer the immigration laws to prevent "irresponsible" employers from eroding American standards by importing cheap labor. From this perspective, the tightening of immigration restrictions (particularly against peoples from Southern and Eastern Europe) in the 1920s was deemed to be altogether right and proper. The defense of high wages also implied that governmental intervention in setting the terms of international commerce was justified. The "cheap foreign labor" argument could be invoked to support protective tariffs and, on occasion, a case for governmental subsidies could be built on similar reasoning.[56]

By 1926 Hoover was generally satisfied that the nation had moved well along the road toward the desired goals. As he then summarized his views:

The very essence of great production is high wages and low prices, because it depends upon a widening range of consumption only to be obtained from the purchasing power of high real wages and increasing standards of living . . . The acceptance of these ideas is obviously not universal. Not all employers . . . nor has every union abandoned the fallacy of restricted effort . . . But . . . for both employer and employee to think in terms of the mutual interest of increased production has gained greatly in strength. It is a long cry from the conceptions of the old economics.[57]

A voice from the academic community spoke with much less restraint. Thomas Nixon Carver, professor of political economy at Harvard, surveyed the American scene in 1925 as follows:

To be alive today, in this country, and to remember the years from 1870 to 1920 is to awake from a nightmare. Those were the years when our ideals were all but obscured by floods of cheap laborers upon whose cheap labor great fortunes were made, and by floods of abuse because we were not instantaneously solving all the social and economic problems these newcomers were inflicting upon us. Those were the years of slums and socialist agitators, of blatant demagogues, and social legislation. We are now emerging into a period when we can give our own ideals a chance to work.[58]

When the doctrine of the new era was proclaimed in this fashion, it seemed plausible for its enthusiasts to believe that the American story was indeed different. Orthodox teaching that high wages would simply price labor out of the market and lead to unemployment could now be dismissed. Nor did the view that class antagonisms were an inevitable part of capitalism deserve to be taken seriously. The American economic system was in the process of producing its own revolution, but it was to be a classless and a bloodless one.

Defining America's position in the international economic system

The champions of a new economics in the 1920s were in accord about their aspirations to build a new Jerusalem in America and in their willingness to invoke powers of government in this task. But they were also aware that the pattern of economic relationships established with the outside world would have a bearing on whether or not their goals could be reached. This part of the agenda presented problems of extraordinary complexity. In their struggles to resolve them, the Hooverites could converge on a general proposition: that the test of adequacy of foreign economic policy should be its contribution to growth and stability in the domestic economy. On matters of detail, however, the ranks were not always united.

It was hardly surprising that confusion abounded in the discussion of international economic affairs. The First World War had transformed America's position in the world economy. Almost overnight, the nation's status had shifted from that of an international debtor to that of a leading international creditor. In the process the United States had accumulated a substantial share of the world's monetary gold stock; by 1923 America held about 45 percent of the total. No one doubted the importance of rebuilding the international economic system, which had been shattered by war, if healthy conditions for world trade and investment were to be re-created. Nor was there any question that the United States had a stake in the outcome. But what model should guide this enterprise? Should the United States pursue the course Britain had charted in its period of international economic supremacy in the late nineteenth century by espousing the reduction, if not the elimination, of barriers to movement of goods across international boundaries? What should be the role of the United States as an international lender? And what were to be the likely implications of the overhang of intergovernmental obligations generated by war for the reconstruction of the international economy?

As was the case with other aspects of economic policymaking, Hoover participated forcefully in the discussion of international economic relations in the 1920s. When taking office as secretary of commerce, however, he felt less than secure in his command of the technical intricacies of international trade and finance.[59] Nevertheless, his ideas were already well formed on the fit to be sought between economic progress at home and foreign trade and investment. The requirements of the domestic economy had overriding priority.

In relation to aggregative economic activity, foreign trade was far less important to the United States than it was to the major European countries with which people of the 1920s frequently made comparisons. Nevertheless, it was in America's interest to be an active participant in the international economic system. Foreign markets for American goods could make an obvious contribution to sustaining U.S. prosperity. Moreover, the nation was dependent on foreign sources for a number of inputs required by its productive machine (notably rubber, nitrates, and potash) and for some of the consumption items associated with the American standard of living (such as coffee, tea, and silk). Though the United States might outdo its major rivals in its capacity to approach self-sufficiency, the terms on which international transactions were conducted still touched the domestic economy at a number of sensitive points.

Hoover was persuaded that a major campaign to promote American exports was essential. In mounting this exercise, he was certainly not unmindful of the importance of foreign markets to farmers. In the peak year for agricultural exports, 1919, foreign sales absorbed more than a quarter of the nation's total farm production.[60] Similarly, farmers were important as contributors to the aggregate volume of U.S. export earnings. In 1921, for example, more than half of the value of domestic exports was generated by producers of primary products and the growers of wheat, cotton, and tobacco were responsible for approximately three-quarters of foreign exchange earnings in this category.[61] Once Europe had recuperated, there appeared to be little prospect that the remarkable export performance of American agriculture during the war and the immediate postwar years could be sustained, let alone increased. Accordingly, it seemed altogether appropriate that a strategy of export promotion should focus primarily on finding new market space for U.S. manufactured goods. Hoover set about this task by expanding the network of commercial attachés stationed in embassies and consulates throughout the world. The market intelligence they gathered was in turn transmitted to the business community through the Commerce Department's field offices at home.

In the official view, the payoff from this strategy could be readily observed in the impressive growth in exports of manufactured goods. Between 1922 and 1927 this category of exports expanded by 55 percent (in contrast to a 2 percent growth in exports of crude materials and foodstuffs). Meanwhile the American share of total world trade had grown despite "extremely keen competition from other industrial nations."[62] These gratifying results appeared to provide further demonstration of the success of the new approach to economic management.

As Hoover reported, the United States had shown its capacity "to sell goods of high quality, produced under the highest real wages in the world, in competition with goods produced under lower standards of living."[63]

But government, in Hoover's judgment, also had a responsibility to assure that imports were acquired on the most favorable terms. In the first instance, it was its duty to defend American producers and consumers from price gouging by foreigners who controlled the supplies of commodities that could not be produced in adequate volume at home. By 1926, according to Julius Klein, director of the Bureau of Foreign and Domestic Commerce, "no less than 20 per cent of the total value of our imports, comprising nearly $900,000,000, [were] represented in such price-fixing controls . . ."[64] The principal commodities in question were rubber (from British territories in Asia and subject to production controls authorized by the British Colonial Office); potash (controlled by Franco-German price and production agreements); nitrate (subject to production controls in Chile); and coffee (the price of which was controlled by restrictions on marketing in Brazil). Hoover led the campaign against such manifestations of "monopolistic pricing," which, it was alleged, extracted hundreds of millions of dollars from American pocketbooks. Buyers were urged to cut back their purchases of controlled items and to practice conservation in their use. Business was encouraged to seek out alternative sources of supply which would be more amenable to American influence (if not directly under American control) and, where feasible, to spur research on synthetic substitutes. In addition, government urged the banking community to dissociate itself from loans aiding those engaged in price and production controls. To put further pressure on the raw material "monopolists," Hoover supported legislation that would authorize the formation of American import buying pools to offset the market power of foreigners if the secretary of commerce determined that the national interest was threatened by price fixing. When the British government terminated the rubber control scheme (known as the Stevenson Plan) in 1928, Hoover and his colleagues congratulated themselves on this outcome.[65] (It should be noted, however, that the primary cause of the collapse of the Stevenson Plan arose from its inability to curtail rubber growing by peasant producers in Asia; production quotas could be effectively monitored only for the outputs produced by plantation methods.)

Though Hoover insisted that the prices of commodities that the United States needed to import should be determined competitively without governmental interference, he did not apply the same principle to other categories of imports. The American government, in his view, had an obligation to reinforce "high standards of living amongst our working people by protecting them so far as we can from underpaid subnormal living conditions of competitive countries in manufacturing industries."[66] In short, he was a staunch believer in the "cheap labor" argument for tariffs. His commitment to the high-wage doctrine for America was not to be sacrified on the altar of free trade.

In a decade that set great store on novelty, this approach to the management of the merchandise account of the balance of payments was far from new. In one respect, however, Hoover's brand of mercantilism added a note of sophistication to earlier statements of this position. The conclusions as he presented them in the 1920s were allegedly validated by statistical "facts." He invited the skeptics to consider what would happen if the tariff protecting the clothing, pottery, and domestic hardware and tool industries were removed. These industries, in combination, had an annual production of about $3.9 billion and offered direct employment to roughly 600,000 workers. In addition, at least another million workers were dependent for their livelihood on the activities of these industries as suppliers of raw materials and distributors of their final products. Abolition of protection on these commodities would, he maintained, lead to either of two results, both of which were bad. On the one hand, it might force down American prices to European levels: a reduction of 30 percent (the average amount of the tariff on the relevant items) could be anticipated. This would initially mean a debasement of American wage standards in the industries directly affected. But the impact of reduced purchasing power in these sectors would soon be felt throughout the economy. As Hoover saw matters: "A reduction in the buying power of the American workers results at once in the elimination of those items in the standard of living which they can do without and still subsist. . . . Decreased buying power also eliminates at once the whole of those distinctive contributions to the American standard of comfortable living such as the automobile, radio, phonograph, high grade periodicals, movies, etc."[67] But elimination of the tariff might also lead to a reduction in employment, rather than an initial wage reduction in the exposed industries. The ultimate outcome, however, would be the same. Those laid off would soon compete wage standards downward throughout the system.

Within the framework of standard textbook teachings on the theory of international trade, this defense of protectionism was wrong in principle and self-defeating in practice. After all, would it not be reasonable to expect the prospects for American exporters to be dimmed when the ability of foreigners to earn dollars was restricted by the actions of the

U.S. government? Hoover steadfastly denied that there was any incompatibility between his advocacy of export promotion, on the one hand, and his support of U.S. tariff policy on the other. In his view, the world – and not just the United States – had a stake in American prosperity. High incomes and high wages increased the demand for imported raw materials which, for the most part, entered the country duty free. In addition, prosperity in the United States tended to swell the flow of dollars abroad through tourism and remittances. In short, the reinforcement to American income levels provided by the right kind of tariff program created the conditions that would permit foreigners to acquire more dollars.[68] A skeptic could readily point out that other countries might be tempted to use similar arguments to justify protectionist measures of their own. As Hoover developed the case, however, the argument was not generalizable. The circumstances of the American economy, it was suggested, made it special. By virtue of its structure, demand for imports in the United States was highly elastic with respect to national income, but not particularly sensitive to changes in the prices of imported goods.

But America's position as an international lender also required definition. People of the 1920s expected that the United States would be asked to play a significant role in financing European recovery from war. As Hoover put it in 1922, "America is practically the final reservoir of international capital."[69] But by whom and on what terms should this financing be arranged? Agreement on the answers to these questions was not easy to reach.

Hoover insisted that lending by Americans to foreigners should be undertaken only when two conditions were satisfied. First, it should be financed exclusively from private sources; there was no place for public monies in such activities. During the war and immediate postwar years, the U.S. Treasury had extended sizable credits to foreign governments, an experience that had not been altogether happy and should not be repeated. Second, foreign lending should be permitted only when used for "reproductive" purposes. In Hoover's vocabulary, this meant that American resources should not be used to help foreign governments cover budget deficits or to maintain military establishments. It was up to Europeans to put their internal houses in order first. When this had been done, private American capital could assist them in enlarging their productive base.

But was it reasonable to expect that private American financiers, if left entirely to their own devices, would channel funds abroad properly? Hoover doubted that this would be the case. In this sphere of economic activity, as in others, government had a duty to lead. At the minimum, it should educate bankers and the general public about the standards that should guide the flotation of foreign loans.

In 1921 and 1922 Hoover pressed hard to win support for proposals to regulate foreign lending. Unless American capital were to be deployed for "reproductive" purposes, he saw "little hope for economic recovery." He recognized that a "destructive use of capital" – that is, "in the maintenance of unbalanced budgets or the support of armies" – might bring "temporary values to the lender of the money, or the exporter of goods." But such action was shortsighted and, in the long run, self-defeating. "[I]t makes no contribution to the increase of economic stability and in fact contributes directly toward the continuation of instability, and thus indirectly robs both the lender and the exporter of goods of the real benefit that would otherwise accrue." In addition, government had a moral responsibility to alert the public to the riskiness of unsound foreign lending. "Our citizens," he noted, "have had but little experience in international investment."[70] They usually lacked the information needed to appraise these propositions properly. Certainly, they should be made aware that loans to countries already deeply in debt to the U.S. government might never be repaid.

Hoover was skeptical about the merits of unsupervised lending abroad for a further reason. In the absence of official surveillance of these practices, a conflict between capital exports and investment needs at home might well arise. Foreign government debt issues placed in the U.S. market, he noted, typically carried interest premiums of 2 to 3 percent over domestic issues. This suggested that U.S. savings were being diverted abroad – for uses which he suspected were of questionable value – at the expense of productive capital formation at home. In addition, he believed it to be prudent to defend American exporters by requiring foreign borrowers to spend the proceeds of loans financed from U.S. sources on American goods. The practice of "tied loans" was, he recognized, "undoubtedly bad economics," but it was consistent with the behavior "of British bankers and others."[71]

This brand of paternalistic interventionism found little favor at the departments of state and treasury or among the central bankers. Benjamin Strong, governor of the Federal Reserve Bank of the District of New York, was especially adamant in his opposition. In his opinion, governmental screening of foreign issues in the domestic capital market was not only an impracticable intrusion on the market's judgments, it was also likely to create more problems than it solved. "If our government," he asked, "undertakes to pass upon the goodness of a loan, even in a minute degree, does it not inaugurate a system of responsibility to which there may be no termination except by the assumption of full responsibility?"[72] In those years no one could comfortably contemplate a situation in which the federal government became a guarantor of private transactions.

From these controversies in the early 1920s, a compromise position emerged, though it fell far short of what Hoover wanted. In March 1922 President Harding announced that henceforth the American financial community would be requested to consult the State Department on contemplated public offerings of foreign securities and to give government officials an opportunity to express an opinion. This review mechanism had no teeth, however. The bankers were not obliged to seek an official judgment, nor were they under any obligation to be guided by one. Moreover, the scope of the request for cooperation was itself limited. Only public offerings of foreign securities were covered; private placements were outside the review mechanism altogether. Save for a few exceptions, Hoover's scheme for controlling foreign lending was frustrated. One was the application of official pressure to deny access to the U.S. capital market to foreign governments that had not yet worked out a program for settlement of their war debts to the United States. This tactic was effective in speeding negotiations on this troublesome matter.

Despite the rhetoric, American lending to foreigners in the 1920s was largely unregulated. Meanwhile the volume of this activity underwent a major expansion. By 1927 the sums raised in public offerings of foreign capital issues were about three times greater than they had been in 1921.[73] The 1927 magnitudes for foreign financing, in turn, represented more than one-sixth of the total placements of capital issues offered to the public. The American capital market had indeed reached a position of primacy in international finance. As a supplier of funds to the rest of the world, the United States had far outstripped its main rival, Great Britain. In the years from 1924 through 1928, for example, U.S. capital exports were approximately twice those of Britain.[74]

While the data on public subscriptions to foreign issues provided a clear indication of the dominant position the United States had acquired in international finance, they did not tell the full story. American firms were also providing dollars in substantial quantities to the rest of the world through direct investment. The magnitudes involved, however, were less susceptible to precise measurement. One estimate suggested that some 200 American manufacturers (with 4,000 foreign branches) had placed $1.3 billion in factories abroad by 1929.[75] Hoover was not pleased by this activity, though it presumably satisfied the condition that American funds were being used productively. His reservations turned on the fear that it might lead to a sacrifice in American jobs. Would it not be better, officials in the Department of Commerce asked, to export goods produced in factories at home than to build factories abroad to serve foreign markets? A case could be made for direct investment in branch plants when this was the only way to get behind the foreigner's tariff walls. Otherwise, American firms should create jobs at home and ship their products abroad.

But the most vexed problem in international economic relations in the 1920s concerned the treatment of the overhang of intergovernmental obligations generated by the war and its aftermath. The essential facts were not in dispute: American official lending to Allied governments amounted to more than $10 billion, a sum accounting for more than two-fifths of the increase in the U.S. national debt between the fiscal years 1916 to 1919.[76] Intense passions were aroused about the way this matter should be handled and about what its resolution implied for the prospects of international economic reconstruction.

From a European perspective, the debts of Allied governments to the United States should ideally be waived altogether on the ground that Americans should regard this financing as a contribution to the common cause. Keynes, for example, wrote eloquently in support of this position, arguing that American insistence on repayment imposed intolerable burdens on debtor countries and precluded a satisfactory rebuilding of the international economic system. Alternatively, in the view of the leaders of the Allied governments, repayments to the United States should be linked to their own receipts of reparations from Germany.

Official opinion in the United States rejected both of these approaches. Coolidge reflected public attitudes toward a debt write-off in a succinct comment: "They hired the money, didn't they? Let them pay." Nor was it acceptable to hold Germany ultimately responsible for the obligations of Allied governments. The United States had elected to forgo any claim to German reparations and wished to be detached from this source of friction. But the American attitude was also shaped by another consideration. In the discussions of the time, the question of the war debts was of interest more as an issue of domestic public finance than as an international transfer problem. During the war years, the national debt had swollen more than twentyfold and a substantial part of this increment was attributable to loans to Allied governments. In consequence, the burden of debt service on the U.S. taxpayer had mushroomed. With the "return to normalcy," interest charges absorbed about 30 percent of the ordinary expenditures of the federal government.[77] Holding Allied governments to their agreements could thus be seen as important to a program of American tax relief.

As Hoover saw matters, this tangled business should be resolved by working out long-term arrangements for settlement with each debtor country, with the terms and timing adjusted to the debtor's circumstances.[78] He insisted throughout that "every nation has some transferrable surplus which can be made use of" and that the "only sane method of approach to the problem was to settle the debts of each nation on the basis of its capacity to pay without disturbing its social and economic fabric."[79] And he was inclined to speak harshly about those who challenged this assessment.[80]

In the international trading environment of the 1920s, was it reasonable to expect these debts, even when adjusted, to be repaid? Keynes had estimated in the early 1920s that the transfer problem was insuperable unless the United States was prepared to accept a reduction in its trade surpluses and to lend abroad on an unprecedented scale. The magnitudes of the required adjustment in the U.S. balance of payments seemed to be altogether unattainable.[81] Nor did the prospects for a healthy equilibrium in the international clearing system seem to be much brighter by 1925, when most of the debtor countries had concluded settlement agreements with the U.S. government. Each of the main debtor countries – Britain, France, and Italy – was in a deficit position in its merchandise trade with the United States, and the sums they were collectively expected to remit in interest and repayments of principal amounted to about a quarter of their combined earnings from visible, merchandise exports to the United States.[82]

In these circumstances, many influential Americans did indeed wonder whether American commercial policies would permit foreigners to earn the dollars needed to service their debts. At least to his own satisfaction, Hoover felt able to put such doubts to rest. In a manner reminiscent of seventeenth- and eighteenth-century mercantilist thought, he held that the international trading community was organized in a triangular network. One leg linked America with Europe, and in these transactions the United States typically ran a substantial trade surplus. The second linked the United States as an importer with territories supplying raw materials (most of which were under European control). In these transactions, the United States could be expected to be in deficit. Europe could thus acquire the dollars it needed by maintaining a favorable balance of trade with countries supplying raw materials to the United States. But Europe also acquired dollars via another route: through invisible, service transactions with the United

States. Hoover maintained that the flow of tourist expenditures and remittances was essentially one-way (from America to Europe).[83] Moreover, he insisted that the dollars Europe acquired from American tourists were themselves sufficient to cover debt service charges. In 1926, for example, he asserted that "our increase in tourist expenditures [since the war] alone takes care of the whole debt service."[84] In fact, however, it was American foreign lending – particularly to Germany – which permitted the system to function as well as it did in the middle 1920s. The U.S. government had initially encouraged these transactions through its support for the Dawes Plan in 1924. This scheme involved the provision of credits to Germany – the bulk of which were supplied from private American resources – on the understanding that the German government would stabilize the mark and commit itself to a program of annual reparations payments (though they could be postponed in the event of major transfer difficulties).[85] As the Department of Commerce assessed the matter, the Dawes Plan was "the first effort to solve the reparations question purely on a commercial and economic basis" and it could be expected to produce stabilization in Europe.[86]

The end of laissez faire in the 1920s?

In 1926 Keynes published an essay entitled "The End of Laissez-faire," in which he argued the case for reforming capitalism by enlarging the agenda of the state. The profit motive, he maintained, could not reliably be counted on to produce socially advantageous results. The pursuit of private interest needed to be guided. It did not follow that the state should assume complete control of economic affairs. Keynes looked instead to the strengthening of semiautonomous bodies within the state, ones that would be alert to their public responsibilities while still retaining an independent decision-making authority. To accelerate progress in this direction, Keynes attached high importance to "the collection and dissemination on a great scale of data relating to the business situation, including the full publicity, by law if necessary, of all business facts which it is useful to know." Such a measure, he observed, "would involve Society in exercising directive intelligence through some appropriate organ of action over many of the inner intricacies of private business, yet it would leave private initiative and enterprise unhindered."[87] In addition, he proposed that a mechanism be created through which "intelligent judgment" could be applied to the community's decisions on saving and investment, particularly with regard to "the scale on which these savings should go abroad in the form of foreign investments, and whether the present organization of the investment market distributes savings along the most nationally productive lines."[88]

Americans of Hoover's persuasion in the 1920s could rightfully claim that they had anticipated most of Keynes's conclusions. They too were eager to expand the agenda of the state. No longer should the functions of government be minimized and restricted essentially to custodial activities (such as provision for law and order, for the nation's security, and for the preservation of the public domain). In their vision, the federal government had an essential function to perform as a catalyst, as a coordinator, as a regulator, and as a stabilizer of economic activity. They believed themselves to be on secure ground in calling for a degree of governmental intervention without peacetime precedent in the American economy. It was on this basis that government had a mandate to collect and distribute economic intelligence, to encourage private producers to organize independent associations, and to instruct both private and public bodies on the way their behavior affected the public interest. They shared the view that the invisible hand could no longer be left entirely to its own devices. It needed guidance from experts sensitive to society's stake in the outcome. It was imperative, however, that this program be executed in a manner that respected American constitutional arrangements delineating the responsibilities of various echelons of government and defining the jurisdictions of economic decision makers in the private and in the public sectors.

Though the Hooverites fell short of realizing their full ambitions in the 1920s, the mechanisms they managed to put in place still represented an arresting experiment in the economics of indirect control. At a time when Stalin was proclaiming a doctrine of "socialism in one country," they saw themselves as developing a new form of capitalism in one country. The initial results seemed to give grounds for general satisfaction. Once the damage of the recession of 1921 had been repaired, most of the nation – apart from sectors (such as agriculture and coal mining) which were afflicted by problems alleged to be structural – had enjoyed an extraordinary prosperity. Wesley Mitchell, writing in February 1929, reviewed the lessons of the experience as follows: ". . . all of the changes making for prosperity . . . can be summed up under a single head – applying fresh intelligence to the day's work. From the use of abstruse researches in pure science to the use of broad economic conceptions and the use of common sense, the method of American progress in 1922–28 has been the old method of taking thought."[89]

CHAPTER 2

Challenges to the new economics of the 1920s

The doctrine developed by the Hooverites in the 1920s was ambitious in its claims that a new economic order could be built in the United States and daring in its insistence that the orthodox "laws" of economics could be repealed through informed manipulation. It is hardly surprising that the various components of this model of a new era should attract critics. Some of the attacks came from the governmental insiders who read the priorities of economic policy quite differently. Other critiques were presented by academicians on the outside. The skeptics, however, did not speak with one voice. While they could ally as disputants to arguments advanced by the advocates of the "new economics," the objectors did so for diverse reasons.

Critiques of the analysis of productive efficiency

In the vision of the Hooverites, it was taken as axiomatic that two types of measures were important to the advancement of efficiency in the production process: (1) governmental support for the collection and distribution of relevant economic data and (2) governmental guidance to producers on best practices to reduce costs and to minimize wasteful product differentiation. Neither of these articles of the new faith won universal endorsement, however.

Within the government, the Department of Justice had put on record its reservations about Hoover's position on the work of trade associations. The rulings of the Supreme Court in 1925 had largely resolved this matter at the official level in Hoover's favor. Doubts about the wisdom of these judgments persisted, nonetheless, among economists in the academic mainstream. Within the conceptual framework of neoclassical economics, the essential precondition of economic efficiency was a market system organized around the principles of genuine competition. This view did not presuppose that the structural conditions required for the ideal functioning of the economy were always reproduced in reality. Nevertheless, the criteria of the model of perfect competition provided norms against which the observable performance of the system could be measured and they could prescribe the appropriate courses of action when departures from ideal conditions occurred. There was thus a case for intervention by government when its authority was used to correct imperfections in markets, for example by checking the price-setting power of monopolists through rigorous enforcement of the anti-trust laws or through public regulation of price making in sectors (such as the utilities) where a competitive structure would be wasteful.

From this perspective, the position of the Department of Commerce as a sponsor of trade associations was suspect. Though no basic objection could be raised against governmental efforts to expedite the flow of statistical information to the public, the practice of encouraging firms to share price and output data seemed to be at odds with the textbook conception of competitive behavior. Why, it was asked, should enforcement of the antitrust laws be relaxed to permit trade associations to engage in such activities? Hoover had argued that this was necessary to ensure that supply and demand were properly coordinated and waste minimized. But, in the view of economists who saw the world through the lenses of neoclassical orthodoxy, these arguments were spurious. A market in which producers competed at arm's length was the natural coordinator and guarantor of efficiency. Official tolerance of producer chumminess in trade associations was an invitation to collusion which threatened the basis of effective competition. Whatever the ultimate outcome of these trends might be, it seemed clear that, at the very least, production decisions were becoming a "collective responsibility" and "less the chance outcome of the independent volition of independent competing producers."[1]

From other quarters, doubts were expressed about the adequacy of Hoover's program to rationalize production by putting pressure on industrialists to adopt the government's recommendations on technical specifications and standards. While some prominent industrialists feared that Hoover's interventions to promote standardization and simplifications were already excessive, the champions of a heterodox body of economic doctrine which grew in prominence in the 1920s insisted that governmental involvement in the operations of manufacturers had not gone far enough. Much of this line of argument was associated with the writings of Thorstein Veblen, who offered a scathing indictment of the existing industrial order.[2] In his scheme of things, massive waste was inherent in an industrial system organized on the basis of the profit motive. Veblen held the creative powers of engineers and researchers to be virtually limitless. But their talents in generating new products and new processes were inevitably frustrated. Business firms would resist innovations if they implied the destruction of existing markets or existing capital values. In their desire to maximize profits, they would also be inclined to underutilize plant capacity already in place in the interests of restricting outputs to keep prices high. These practices amounted to "industrial sabotage." The phenomenon of systematic waste, however, did not end there. It was also built into the behavior of consumers in a social order that bred a leisure class which gained status from frivolous and conspicuous consumption. From this perspective, Hoover's lectures to businesses on waste minimization failed to get to the root of matters. Veblen's proposed solution called for the creation of a "Soviet of Engineers" to direct the allocation of the economy's resources in accordance with technical criteria of efficiency.[3]

Much of the general public was exposed to this line of thinking in the 1920s through the works of popularizers, most notably those of Stuart Chase. In 1925 Chase estimated that, at the minimum, 50 percent of the nation's labor was wasted and that optimal efficiency in resource use could double current levels of production. A satisfactory approach to the problem, he argued, required the creation of "an Industrial General Staff" with powers to compel the adoption of recommended practices.[4] Hoover's efforts to win the compliance of industrialists through persuasion were thus held to fall far short of the action needed.

A similar note was struck by Rexford Guy Tugwell, then an instructor in economics at Columbia, who was later to acquire high public visibility as a member of Franklin D. Roosevelt's "Brains Trust." In the Veblenian spirit, Tugwell attacked both standard academic teaching and the program of the Hooverites. The former, with its assumptions about atomistic competition, was an anachronism; the latter was faulted for its failure to be sufficiently bold. "We tolerate and even foster business organizations which we know to be inefficient, we fail to complete continuous processes and serializations because we hesitate to interfere with the precious principle of privacy in business, we over-develop some phases of production and emasculate others, and we administer our social control on the theory of conflict."[5] The agenda for a genuinely new era required that society be reorganized on the basis of cooperation and public control, rather than on the basis of competition and conflict.

Movement in the direction of greater cooperation in industrial activity, Tugwell noted, was already in evidence. The pooling of information through the vehicle of trade associations was a case in point. But, in his judgment, this type of collaboration could not safely be left entirely in private hands. A greater measure of public intervention was called for. This was held to be entirely appropriate because traditional conceptions of the responsibilities of the owners of private property had largely lost their meaning in the context of the modern corporation.

The trend toward bigness had been accompanied by the divorce of ownership from managerial control. Owners had tended to become absentees and to disengage themselves from the day-to-day operation of business.[6] Tugwell regarded this as a fortunate development, observing that "the separation makes possible a domination by engineering minds which never would have been possible under the older scheme of organization. This seems to be favorable to social ends since engineers will be more interested in smooth operation, always, than in producing profits."[7]

Full realization of the promise of a new era, as Tugwell read the circumstances of American life, required much more aggressive governmental control over industrial activity than the Hooverites were prepared to contemplate. In particular, public authorities should be empowered to allocate capital and to regulate prices. Increasingly, he argued, corporations were relying on internal sources of funds to finance their capital outlays. It was not obvious that accumulation by this mode produced a socially desirable allocation of investment. It did not follow that private ownership of the means of production should be eliminated, but there was a case for governmental controls to guide their use. Similarly, public bodies should be directed to ensure that cost reductions brought by improvements in productivity were in fact passed on to consumers through lower prices. Competition was no longer sufficiently vigorous to generate this result.

This was a call for planning on a grand scale, and the payoff would ultimately be a healthier and more harmonious society. Not only would productivity be enhanced, but, along the way, social frictions would be diminished. Efficient mass production would provide an abundance of goods for all. It would also, Tugwell maintained, create conditions favorable to the emergence of a new morality in consumption that would reduce social differentiation. In a world of mass markets, fed by standardized goods produced in volume with the most efficient techniques, opportunities for ostentation would be considerably restricted. "[A]s we grow used to modern goods," Tugwell wrote, "they will come to seem to us less objects to be flaunted before unfortunate fellow beings and more the common basis of a good life which is to be achieved not in goods but through them. A diversion of an increasing amount of our surplus to education ought also have some effect in shaping a better consumption morality."[8]

These outcomes were unattainable, however, in the absence of a fundamental reorientation in thought. Standard textbook teaching on the beneficent functioning of private markets would have to be rejected. Limitations in the Hooverites' conception of the nature of governmental

intervention would also have to be recognized. Tugwell lamented that
"the epitaph of laissez-faire had been written prematurely." He conceded, however, that the economic record of the 1920s made it difficult
to recruit converts to his position. As he put this point in 1927: "One is
always handicapped in talking about the American standard of living
as being lower than it ought to be, because it is so obviously higher
than it ever was before, or than it is at present in any other part of the
world."[9]

The Hooverites could associate themselves with attacks on orthodox
academic teaching to the extent that they might broaden support for
their campaign for productivity improvement. But Hoover and his associates emphatically rejected the part of this message that called for
direct controls. In their understanding of the new economics, the desired
objectives could be reached through demonstration, education, and persuasion. Indeed, these were the only methods that were acceptable.

Doubts about the high-wage doctrine

To the most ardent champions of "new era" economics, America should
and could rewrite the standard rulebook on the distribution of income.
An economy of high wages promised multiple benefits – among them,
an additional spur to managerial efficiency, an apparent assurance of
abundant consumer purchasing power, and the prospect of harmonious
industrial relations. All of this was expected to contribute to the building of an economy that generated a higher standard of living for all and
of a society in which class frictions were progressively eliminated.

By the mid-1920s there was no question in the minds of the most careful students of labor markets that a striking improvement in real wages
had indeed occurred. Writing in 1925, Alvin Hansen (then at the University of Minnesota) observed that there had been a "phenomenal rise
in real wages since 1919" and that they were 25 to 30 percent greater
than in the prewar years.[10] Statistical studies prepared by Paul H. Douglas of the University of Chicago told much the same story. Using the
decade of 1890 as a base for an index number series on real earnings, his
calculations for all industries indicated a gain from 109 in 1919 to 127
in 1923. He found it particularly striking that real wage improvement
had "continued unabated" in 1921 and 1922, in spite of depressed business conditions and rising unemployment.[11] Douglas attributed some of
the improvement in real earnings of industrial workers to the fall in
the prices of agricultural products during this period and to the effects
of immigration restrictions on the supply side of the labor market. But
he noted also that real wage improvement seemed to have produced

some of the results that had been claimed for it: workers were "not as susceptible to trade-union activity as they were a decade ago," and there was also "a decrease in the opposition of the manual workers to the capitalistic system . . . [and] apparently less interest in socialism than there was a decade ago." [12]

But were the economic consequences of this development unambiguously positive? Hansen expressed doubt on this point early in the decade. As he diagnosed the situation, wages in 1921–22 were already "much higher than the industrial situation warranted" and the consequence was that "an exceptionally large amount of labor went unsold." Moreover, he expected a "contest of high wage versus full employment" to persist.[13] Over the longer term, he anticipated that the secular trend in prices would be downward, a trend with ominous implications when combined with stickiness in money wage rates. As he then put the issue: "the constant struggle against declining prices and a recalcitrant wage level can scarcely fail to result in chronic depression with brief intermittent periods of prosperity whenever a way of escape is offered through temporary price inflation." [14]

By the later years of the decade, there were some disturbing signs that high wages were indeed tending to price labor out of the market. Not all of the facts were in. For sectors on which there were reliable statistics, however, a teaching of orthodox theory seemed to be validated. High wages were costing jobs by pushing employers to substitute capital for labor. In manufacturing, mining, and the railroads, for example, it could be established that employment had shrunk while wages had risen. Sumner Slichter, then at Cornell University, calculated that wages had increased by 5 percent in manufacturing and by nearly as much in railroading between 1923 and 1927; meanwhile, the cost of producer goods had fallen by more than 13 percent. Such price movements obviously made it worthwhile for employers to economize in their use of labor, a process facilitated further by the increased availability of labor-saving machinery. But, as Slichter insisted, "even had no labor-saving devices been invented, recent price movements alone would have caused the displacement of some workers." [15] In the absence of data on the aggregate volume of employment, the extent to which these reductions in jobs had been offset by an expanded demand for labor in other sectors (especially in the services) was uncertain. There were still grounds for worry that the United States might be experiencing a form of secular unemployment as a by-product of a regime of high wages.[16]

For their part, the Hooverites were inclined to believe that the overall growth of the economy had created jobs to compensate for those lost in the sectors where employment was measured. They acknowledged, however, that this conclusion could not be asserted with certainty. Hoover and his colleagues at the Department of Commerce were aware of major gaps in their information about unemployment and its incidence and hoped to see them closed. But this work had not been assigned a high priority in their statistical effort. As late as February 1928, the acting chief of the department's Division of Statistical Research could report that "no information is available concerning most of the lines of wholesale and retail trade of the country and most of the occupations which are ordinarily considered as domestic service." (In this context, "domestic service" was taken to include hotels, restaurants, barbers, hairdressers, and manicurists.) He added that "we believe that the occupations for which no information is available have absorbed a considerable amount of the unallocated addition to the labor supply." [17] (This "unallocated addition" referred to labor released from manufacturing, railroads, and agriculture, as well as to the increment in labor supply brought about by population growth in the 1920s.)

The special case of agriculture in the income distribution

One of the most sustained challenges to the Hooverites' conception of a new era of general prosperity came, not surprisingly, from the farm community. American farmers had demonstrated an impressive capacity to produce. In response to unprecedented foreign demand during the war and in the period of European reconstruction immediately following it, farm outputs had swollen enormously. So also had farm incomes: between 1914 and 1919, net income from farm operations more than doubled. But the early 1920s brought a sharp reversal in fortunes. Foreign demand plummeted, most particularly for staple food grains, and prices collapsed. By 1921 net farm income was only about 37 percent of what it had been in 1919 and less than it had been in 1914. Meanwhile farm indebtedness had more than doubled. Farmers thus entered the decade of the 1920s with a burden of fixed charges made heavier by the fact that prices of the goods they had to sell were falling.[18]

Much of the systematic discussion of the economics of the "farm problem" in the 1920s was initiated within the Department of Agriculture. In 1921 the department created a Bureau of Agricultural Economics and its work was linked with the research of agricultural economists stationed in the land grant colleges in each of the nation's states. As originally conceived, this apparatus was charged to gather and to disseminate data on farm outputs, stocks, and marketings. It could thus be regarded as an information service to farmers analogous to the one provided to business through the statistical program Hoover was launching at the Department of Commerce. In practice, however, the paths of these governmental statistical units diverged. Hoover insisted that the economists in his domain should confine themselves to compiling the numbers; interpreting their significance was a job for others. The economists in the agricultural network enjoyed a greater freedom of maneuver and were organized well enough to fight off Hoover's attempts to clip their wings.

The fruit of the work of the new breed of agricultural economists was a body of doctrine purporting to demonstrate that the model of the Hooverites contained an inherent bias against the welfare of farmers. In the first instance, this claim rested on the proposition that the structural conditions of production in agriculture and in industry were fundamentally different. The farming sector, with large numbers of producers offering standardized commodities, effectively replicated the requirements of the textbook model of perfect competition. Farmers were price takers at the mercy of market forces over which they had no control. The manufacturing sector, on the other hand, could certainly not be so described. Increasingly, producers of industrial goods were in a position to mold the market environment in which they operated by coordinating their production decisions. Indeed the official encouragement given to trade associations lent itself to these practices. This line of argument suggested that it would be reasonable to expect prices of agricultural goods to be more unstable than those of manufactured goods. The existence of this structural asymmetry, it was alleged, automatically placed farmers at a disadvantage.

But, even within the agricultural sector itself, it was argued that the invisible hand of competitive market forces worked perversely. Standard theory would normally lead one to anticipate that conditions of excess supply and falling prices would induce producers to reduce the quantities they offered, if not to abandon unprofitable activities altogether. This mechanism of adjustment, in the judgment of the new breed of agricultural economists, was of doubtful validity. In their view, a substantial block of farmers regarded themselves as effectively "locked in" by the legacy of debt accumulated during war. Saddled as they were with burdensome fixed obligations, farmers would struggle to meet them by increasing production in spite of falling prices. Such behavior might be rational from the perspective of the individual producer. But its aggregative effect would be an increase in supply which would depress prices still further. In the absence of a mechanism to coordinate the production decisions of farmers, continued deterioration of farm prices relative to those of manufactured goods was in prospect.[19] Nor was it likely that the adoption of cost-reducing innovations by farmers would relieve their plight. In light of the structural attributes of agriculture, it was to be expected that this would merely increase supply faster than demand could grow and farm prices would be still further depressed. As Mordecai Ezekiel of the Bureau of Agricultural Economics saw matters in 1926, the "imperfections of our present scheme of social arrangements" seemed calculated to make the returns to farmers "somewhat less" than those available from equal effort in other lines.[20]

If the system was imperfect, how then might it be corrected? Much of the farm lobby in the 1920s rallied around a plea for "tariff equivalence" first issued in 1922 by George Peek and General Hugh Johnson, two veterans of the War Industries Board, who had gone into the agricultural implement business in Illinois.[21] In their line of argument, it was noted that government was less than even-handed in its treatment of the economy's main producing sectors. Industrialists enjoyed tariff protection for which consumers ultimately paid in the form of higher prices. Was it not therefore a matter of simple justice to accord farmers a similar benefit? The Peek–Johnson scheme called for a two-tier price system for the major farm crops. In the domestic market, prices should be set above world prices by a percentage equal to the average tariff rates on manufactured products. Agricultural products that could not be sold at home would then be disposed of abroad at whatever price they could command. The final payout to farmers would be struck as a weighted average of the protected domestic price and the export price. An asymmetry in the structural environment of agriculture and manufacturing would still remain. But this approach to price setting for farm products would at least redress the imbalance in policies toward these two sectors. If this scheme were to be made workable, however, a radical shift in the official approach to tariff making for agricultural products was required. The dual price system implied that tariffs would have to be levied on commodities American farmers exported. Otherwise, American products sold abroad at far less than the U.S. domestic price would be shipped back to the country of origin and undercut the price support that the plan was designed to create.

But not all of the commentators who arrived at a common diagnosis of the ills of agriculture agreed about the appropriate treatment. Rexford Guy Tugwell, for example, endorsed the view that remedial attention to the problems of farmers should be an urgent national priority, but maintained that the Peek–Johnson approach was the wrong way to go about it. "Tariff equivalence" that succeeded in raising domestic prices of farm products would simply compound the problem of agricultural adjustment by signaling farmers to produce still more. The situation called instead for techniques to limit production. Writing in

1928, Tugwell offered a blueprint for a system of production controls with the following elements: "(1) A survey of the amounts necessary to meet normal needs and which will command a profitable price. (2) Notice of limitation of planting, on a basis of ten-year averages, by local (probably county) agents of a Farm Board. (3) Enforcement through denial of the use of railways and warehouses to produce grown on unauthorized acreage."[22] He acknowledged that "the use of governmental machinery for such a purpose is not usual with us." Nevertheless, it seemed to be justified because farmers could not otherwise coordinate their production, whereas "many of the larger industries at the present time are so articulated as to be able to effect a limitation of their production to profitable amounts."[23] There was also a suggestion in some of the writings of Richard T. Ely of the University of Wisconsin that a "national land policy" was needed to limit agricultural expansion and to generate a better balance between supply and demand.[24]

The Hooverites clearly had no sympathy for direct governmental controls over farm production. Nor could they accept the Peek–Johnson remedy, which, when packaged in legislative form, became the Mc-Nary–Haugen Bill. On two occasions, in 1927 and 1928, this bill passed both houses of Congress. It was twice vetoed by President Coolidge, with Hoover leading the cabinet charge against it. Hoover could give his enthusiastic support to the principle that farmers and businessmen alike should be equipped, through the aid of government, with the best available intelligence on market conditions. Such knowledge was crucial to rational decision making by producers in all sectors of the economy. In the case of agriculture, he also endorsed the use of the good offices of government to assist farmers in organizing marketing cooperatives. But the suggestion that the powers of the federal government should be invoked in the overt price fixing implied by McNary–Haugenism was unthinkable.[25] As Coolidge insisted in his veto messages, this intrusion of government in private markets was also unconstitutional. Even if no legal barrier had been anticipated, the McNary–Haugen approach could be held to be misguided for another reason. The international competitive position of American industry would be damaged if foreign rivals could keep their costs down by acquiring U.S. food and raw materials at prices below those Americans would be obliged to pay.

In principle, of course, much of the clamor that government was discriminatory in its treatment of the industrial and the agricultural sectors could have been silenced at a single stroke – that is, by the elimination of tariffs altogether. Most economists of orthodox persuasion would have welcomed such a shift in policy. To the Hooverites, however, an attempt to reduce intersectoral tensions by this means was unacceptable.

A regime of high wages in the United States held a central place in their strategy; the achievement of this goal was not to be jeopardized by exposing American industry to unrestrained competition from underpaid foreigners. Moreover, in rejoinder to the McNary–Haugenities, Hoover and his associates made the claim that farmers were major beneficiaries of American tariff policy in the 1920s. This argument presupposed (and with considerable justification) that foreign demand for America's staple foodstuffs would never again reach its wartime heights. Though cotton and tobacco growers might still be able to find a vent for their domestic surpluses abroad, food producers should expect to look to markets at home for their salvation. Farmers thus had a clear stake in a protective system that buttressed the purchasing power of workers in manufacturing industries. As Hoover saw the issue: "For the American farmer to have the sole market of a full stomach in the United States is better for him than the competitive market for a never full stomach abroad."[26] But farmers, he maintained, also stood to gain from a tariff structure imposing high rates of duty on agricultural products that the United States imported even though the nation had the resources to produce them at home. This use of tariff policy, it was suggested, promised to relieve part of the distress experienced by the growers of staple foods. The reallocative impact of high duties on agricultural imports, Hoover insisted, could be seen vividly in the case of flax. The acreage committed to its production had nearly doubled between 1921 and 1925. "If we had not protected the American flax industry," Hoover wrote, "I have no doubt these extra acres would have been devoted to wheat, to the further demoralization of the wheat farmer. The same can be said with regard to sugar, wool, and other protected agricultural products."[27]

The policy skirmishes of these years left the agricultural interests bloody but unbowed. Their spokesmen remained persuaded that the correctness of their analysis would ultimately be demonstrated, but that the nation might pay a high price in the process of learning that lesson. Prosperity in other sectors of the economy, they maintained, could not permanently coexist with a depressed agriculture. Farm incomes represented an important source of demand for manufactured products: in the years of agricultural prosperity at the close of the war, they had accounted for roughly 40 percent of the national income. In this line of reasoning, it seemed obvious that the subsequent erosion in the purchasing power of farmers imperiled the stability of the macroeconomic system. A variant on this theme argued that depressed farm prices in the 1920s had themselves contributed to an unsound and unsustainable form of prosperity outside agriculture. In the view of George F. Warren, professor of agricultural economics at Cornell, much of the construction boom in the 1920s could be explained by the collapse in food prices. Urban workers thus had more discretionary purchasing power, much of which had been allocated to housing. "Cheap food," he concluded, "normally causes a building boom." But this expansion in urban construction at the expense of farm incomes was abnormal and, in the long run, would prove to be destabilizing.[28]

The Hooverites did not dispute the reality of maladjustment in the agricultural sector. But remedies for its ills, they insisted, were not to be found in schemes for fixing prices or controlling production in which government participated. The long-term solutions should instead be sought in measures to accelerate a reorientation of farm production toward domestic markets and in policies to stimulate the growth of purchasing power and employment opportunities in other sectors of the economy. There was also a lingering suspicion that farm groups were inclined to protest too much. Within the Department of Commerce, for example, doubts were raised in 1926 about the accuracy of the index numbers prepared by the Department of Agriculture on the purchasing power of farmers. The procedures in use, it was suggested, failed to "represent the true farm condition."[29] As one of Hoover's aides insisted in 1926, the purchasing power of farmers was, in fact, substantially higher than was indicated by the Agriculture Department's calculations. He was thus convinced that imperfections in these statistical series "were responsible for a considerable proportion of the agricultural discontent in this country" and that they "simply [provided] ammunition for certain types of agricultural agitators who thrive on showing that the farmer is on the verge of bankruptcy and ruin." The preparation of an accurate measure of farm purchasing power, he maintained, "might be instrumental in changing our whole national psychology with regard to the farmer's economic position."[30]

Critiques of the fiscal strategy for economic stabilization

One of the proudest claims of the advocates of the new economics was that a formula had been discovered to tame the business cycle through the countercyclical phasing of public spending. Despite their lobbying efforts, the bills that would have embodied this principle in federal legislation had not been enacted. Nor were all of Hoover's cabinet colleagues persuaded about the merits of this approach to macroeconomic management. The attitude of Secretary of the Treasury Andrew Mellon, for example, was lukewarm at best. From his perspective, the central priorities of fiscal policy were expenditure containment, debt retirement, and tax reduction.

The argument that the business cycle could be brought under control was also received with considerable skepticism by economists in the academy. In the view of the orthodox, some instability in the system was thought to be inescapable, at least if the virtues of decentralized economic decision making were to be preserved. A dynamic economy implied that the patterns of costs and of demand were constantly subject to change. From time to time, particular sectors or industries would discover that their prices were unsustainable and that readjustments were called for. Some bumpiness in economic activity was thus to be expected. Indeed, it was held to be therapeutic in correcting mistakes in the allocation of the economy's resources.

From this point of view, public intervention in the downswing of the cycle (such as increased spending on public works) was likely to aggravate the economy's basic problems. Artificial attempts to buttress the demand for labor by spending on public account would tend to frustrate the system's inherent mechanisms for realigning costs and prices. In addition, capital outlays by the public sector to combat unemployment would claim resources that could be used more productively by private investors. Moreover, if the root of the unemployment problem was secular rather than cyclical, the damage caused by accelerated public spending would be even greater. As Sumner Slichter cautioned in December 1928: "If unemployment has grown because prices, especially wages, have failed to adjust themselves to shifts in markets or to changes in technique, might not the expansion of public works be exactly the wrong kind of relief? Might it not tend to perpetuate the very price relationships which are causing the trouble?"[31]

Hoover's thinking about fiscal techniques for macroeconomic stabilization was also subjected to criticism by some commentators who were enthusiastic in their support of his objectives. The work of two amateur economists, William Trufant Foster and Waddill Catchings, is a case in point.[32] As they read matters, countercyclical spending on public works was not only desirable; it was imperative. Hoover had not adequately diagnosed the magnitude of the problem, however. A proper understanding of tasks of economic policy, they argued, should begin with a recognition that the economic system contained an inherent bias toward underconsumption. Accordingly, compensatory public spending should be designed with bold strokes.

Throughout the 1920s, Foster and Catchings did much to raise public consciousness on the necessity of aggressive fiscal intervention to counteract deficiencies in private spending. Their collaboration generated a steady flow of publications that appeared in the leading national periodicals, in columns syndicated in the national press, as well as in book form. Though they reached a wide popular audience, they had less success in gaining a serious hearing for their message among professional economists. They overcame part of the indifference of the academy by offering a prize of $5,000 for the best "adverse criticism" of *Profits*, a book they published in 1925. A total of 435 essays were submitted in this competition, which was judged by a distinguished jury composed of two former presidents of the American Economic Association (Wesley Mitchell of Columbia University and Allyn A. Young of Harvard) and Owen D. Young, chairman of the board of the General Electric Company.[33]

The organizing thread of Foster and Catchings' argument was that the system of industrial capitalism was fundamentally unstable because of its inherent tendency to generate insufficient consumer purchasing power. This premise was at odds with the central tenets of both orthodox academic teaching and Hoover's version of a new economics. The question they posed was not arrestingly new. Controversy over a similar point had emerged in debates between Malthus and Ricardo after the Napoleonic Wars concerning the efficacy of Say's law and its claim that "supply creates its own demand." Part of the Marxist tradition had kept the issue alive in the later nineteenth century. In the early twentieth century, J. A. Hobson, an English socialist, had continued to press this theme. Foster and Catchings took it to be their task to translate the underconsumptionist message into an American idiom and to relate it to the observable facts of the American economy of the 1920s.

How, in this view of things, might deficiency in consumer demand be explained? Foster and Catchings traced the root of the difficulty to "the dilemma of thrift." Saving quite obviously implied some withdrawal from the expenditure stream. Unless this withdrawal was offset with another form of spending, some outputs would remain unsold. Neoclassical orthodoxy held that saving would automatically be linked with investment and that incomes not spent on consumer goods would be spent on producer goods. As Foster and Catchings saw matters, confidence that an automatic linkage between saving and investment would ensure adequate total demand was misplaced. They noted, for example, the increasing tendency of industrial firms in the United States to finance their capital requirements from retained earnings. When corporations chose to be their own accumulators, opportunities for individual consumers to put their savings to work were correspondingly reduced. Even if all savings were ultimately to be absorbed in capital spending, it seemed unlikely that this would take place instantaneously. In any particular period, some leakage from the spending stream was likely to occur.

But there was a more fundamental potential difficulty. If, in the short term, saving and investment were to be perfectly synchronized, this achievement was likely to mean that the job of creating sufficient aggregate demand to buy back the economy's output would be more difficult in the future. After all, the purpose of investment was to enlarge the capacity to produce. While today's capital spending might sustain effective demand today, today's capital spending also meant that a larger volume of output would be seeking markets tomorrow. As Foster and Catchings saw matters: "to enable people to buy the output of our present facilities, we have to build new ones; and then, in order that people can buy the output of the new ones, we have to build more new ones."[34] But could private industrialists, motivated by the profit incentive, reasonably be expected to continue expanding their capital commitments at the required rate? Foster and Catchings thought not.[35]

This analysis suggested that the capacity of the system to generate enough total spending to sustain capacity levels of output could not be assured. But what of the claim, offered in the Hooverite version of a new economics, that a regime of high wages would provide adequate purchasing power? Foster and Catchings dismissed this assertion summarily. Businesses, they noted, required profits if they were to continue to produce and, so long as profits were positive, the wage bill alone would never be large enough to absorb the economy's product.[36] Similarly, they rejected the orthodox position that income not spent for consumer goods would end up being spent for investment goods. They acknowledged that much of the savings by members of the public found its way into bank accounts and thus was potentially available to finance further spending. It did not necessarily follow, however, that borrowers would take advantage of the banking system's increased capacity to lend. One could not rule out the possibility that the flow of saving into bank deposits would simply lead to the accumulation of idle balances. In that case, they noted that "such money is no more a stimulus to business than is gold in the bowels of the earth."[37] There was at least a suggestion here of the possibility of a phenomenon later to be described as a "liquidity trap."

Yet another question called for attention. If deficiency in total demand was an inherent property of the economic system, how could the prosperity of the American economy since its recovery from the recession of 1921 be explained? Foster and Catchings maintained that two extraordinary features of the 1920s had temporarily neutralized the system's underconsumptionist features: the widespread use of consumer credit (particularly in financing consumer durable goods) and capital exports on a major scale. Neither of these offsets to saving could offer a lasting solution to the dilemma of thrift. The amount of installment credit for which consumers were eligible was limited; moreover, when consumer debt was retired, demand for current outputs would be reduced. Nor could the country safely rely on continuous lending to foreigners to dispose of its potential surpluses. These loans would ultimately have to be repaid and this would require Americans to allocate more of their spending to the purchase of foreign goods. If effective demand for domestic outputs was to be sustained, Foster and Catchings concluded that "the search for new markets should begin at home."[38]

The solution appeared to be transparently obvious. When additional spending was required to support the economy, it should be provided through the agency of the government. To this end, they joined company with the Hoover forces in calling for the creation of a federal board charged to monitor the state of the economy and to signal when the public works spending tap should be turned on. But, they insisted, the additional spending should ideally be financed through borrowing. The ability of governments to spend to sustain demand in periods of slack should not be constrained by prior provisions of reserves earmarked for this contingency.

Foster and Catchings anticipated that two lines of objection might be raised against their proposals. The first was prompted by fears that their plan might require an increase in the public debt. This concern, in their judgment, was false. The mere announcement of the preparedness of governments to borrow to finance public works when necessary to bolster spending would itself reinforce business confidence and thus minimize the need for deficit financing. In their view, business concerns "naturally want to grow. They do not curtail operations, as a rule, unless they fear a recession of business. So possibly the fact that they know the Government stands ready to increase consumer income promptly, if the need arises, will induce them to increase their own capital expenditures at a sufficient rate to make additional Government expenditures unnecessary."[39] But even if the public debt did increase, this was no calamity. It meant simply that "the people of the United States collectively owe themselves more money. The country does not lose thereby."[40] Moreover, the nation stood to gain from compensatory deficit spending. Not only would the stock of public assets (such as highways and canals) be increased, but the community would also enjoy the benefits of outputs from the private sector which would not have been available if idle capacity had been tolerated. Nor did

Foster and Catchings see merit in the charge that the implementation of their plan would increase governmental control over business. They dismissed this possible objection as follows:

First, the Government provides more accurate and more comprehensive information than at present, and distributes it more promptly and more widely. That means less interference with business. Second, under our Policy, the Government administers its own expenditures with reference to the needs of business, slackening its competition with private concerns for men and materials when competition is keenest, and adding to the income of buyers when buying is falling off. That also means less Government interference with business.[41]

Hoover and his official colleagues were not prepared to follow Foster and Catchings in their diagnosis of inherent underconsumption, nor could the Hooverites concur with the doubts expressed about the effectiveness of high wages in supporting consumer demand. But they could make common cause in campaigning for the coordination of countercyclical spending on public works. With Hoover's blessing, Governor Ralph O. Brewster of Maine, accompanied by Foster as an expert witness, set out the case before the Conference of State Governors meeting in New Orleans in late November 1928. The scheme presented to this gathering called for various units of government to arrange standby credit authorizations in the amount of $3 billion, which could be activated for public works expenditure when a federal board signaled that the indexes of business conditions suggested that a downturn was in prospect.[42] When reporting to Hoover on the reception of the proposal, Brewster indicated that "there was ample evidence of widespread interest . . . and a rather general recognition that it was economically sound. . . . The volume of friendly comment was an indication that the field had been somewhat plowed."[43] In extolling the work of the Governor's Conference to their readers, Foster and Catchings wrote: "The Plan is not philanthropy. It is business, guided by measurements instead of hunches. It is economics for an age of science – economics worthy of the new President."[44]

Doubts about economic stabilization through monetary management

To some, the "age of science" meant that the day was at hand when the "laws" of the business cycle could be repealed through rational management of the money supply. The leading spokesman for this point of view was Irving Fisher. The volume of trade, he had argued, could be stabilized if the purchasing power of the dollar were held constant. And this desirable objective could be reached if the central bankers controlled the money supply to assure general price stability. Hoover was also convinced that the Federal Reserve could and should do its job better, though he did not embrace Fisher's approach to the problem.

The central bankers in the 1920s were true to form in resisting unsolicited counsel on the way they should conduct their affairs. The autonomy and independence of the Federal Reserve System was to be guarded jealously. In their view, American political life was highly susceptible to panaceas peddled by monetary cranks. Experience with the greenbackers and free-silverites in the nineteenth century and, more recently, with proposals advanced by Henry Ford and Thomas Edison to demonetize gold and to adopt a commodity-based currency – schemes that attracted wide attention in the early 1920s – solidified their conviction that the monetary authorities were duty bound to fight off outsiders.

But the central bankers were inclined to take particular exception to the line of argument advanced by Fisher. Most of them had a deep-seated suspicion of any recommendations for intervention based on "quantity theory" reasoning.[45] Central banking, in the judgment of the insiders, was an art and it could not be reduced to a mechanical formula. Nor did they believe that their powers to discipline the general price level were as complete as Fisher had claimed them to be. In the first instance, they had direct authority over but a minority of the nation's banks.[46] In addition, they insisted that trends in the general price level were subject to influences (such as gold movements, bumper harvests, productivity improvements, and technological changes) over which they could exercise no control. The mere suggestion that the paramount goal of the Federal Reserve System should be specified as stabilizing the general price level (as stipulated in the Goldsborough Bill) was at that time held to be malicious. Benjamin Strong, for example, found the proposal disturbing because he feared that the agricultural interests – which had given strong support to this bill – understood it as a directive to the Federal Reserve to "fix up" depressed farm prices.[47]

Nor did Fisher's prescriptions for the management of monetary policy win favor among those academic economists who looked to the gold standard's "rules of the game" as the basis for determining the general price level. In their view of the way the world should operate, a nation's domestic money supply should necessarily be linked to its gold reserves and its price level should fluctuate upward or downward in response to the state of its international balance of payments. Attempts to stabilize the general price level through policy interventions were thus at odds with the international adjustment mechanisms that the gold standard should properly produce. This position was vigorously championed, for example, by Edwin W. Kemmerer of Princeton, who had acquired an international reputation as the "money doctor."[48]

In the view of some commentators, proposals to direct the monetary authorities to regard general price stability as their primary objective were misguided for a further reason. In a gold standard regime, the world price level, over the longer term, should tend to fall unless gold available for monetary uses expanded at a rate that matched or exceeded growth in the world's output of goods and services. There seemed to be no reasonable basis in the 1920s to believe that this would, in fact, be the case. On the contrary, it appeared to be far more likely that aggregate production would increase faster than the supply of monetary gold. It was thus essential for members of the international trading community to allow prices to be flexible downward. If an individual country tried to set its prices at artificially high levels, it could expect to experience rising unemployment or an inflation that would compromise its position in international trade.[49]

Fisher was fully aware that a country could not commit itself to maintaining constant purchasing power for its domestic monetary unit while simultaneously living under gold standard "rules" with fixed international exchange rates. But he had no doubts about the choice that should be made: stability in internal price levels, not stability in external exchange rates, should be the overriding priority.[50] He held it to be the height of irrationality to accept a system in which the ultimate regulator of the world's economic lift would be the amount of a yellow substance extracted from the ground. When the world economy had the capacity to grow at a faster rate than gold could be produced, a regime organized on strict gold standard rules would commit the international community to persistent deflation and to chronic instability. As early as 1923 Fisher argued that Americans had a moral obligation to lead the world toward a different and happier future. It was unacceptable to "take the ground that we must simply drift with the tides of gold and credit." This would "be simply fertilizing the soil of public opinion for a dangerous radicalism."[51] Monetary policy should instead be liberated to stabilize the domestic price level while foreign exchange rates should be allowed to vary. Gold could still play a role as an international reserve. Its value in terms of a nation's domestic monetary unit, however, should fluctuate. In effect Fisher sought to put in place a system of floating exchange rates. And he was convinced that, if the United States took the initiative, other countries would fall into line.[52]

This scheme won few converts among the academic economists or among the central bankers. Nor did Hoover find it persuasive, though there was an ambivalence in his thinking about domestic and international monetary affairs. On the one hand, he believed in stable exchange rates and welcomed the return to gold convertibility by countries making this commitment with sufficient reserves to make it credible. He was also sympathetic to the orthodox notion that the gold standard should provide a discipline against irresponsible fiscal and monetary policies in deficit countries. On the other hand, he was uneasy about an incompatibility between his goals for macroeconomic stabilization in the United States and the disposition of American central bankers to prop up the gold positions of European countries. His concern became acute in 1927 and 1928. In Hoover's judgment, the American monetary authorities should then have been applying the brakes. Instead, the Federal Reserve pursued easy money policies throughout 1927, a course of action that was shaped in large part by its fear that gold losses in a number of European countries (and particularly in Britain) might force them off the gold standard unless interest rates in the United States were lowered. With priority assigned to international objectives, the open market and discount rate policies of the system supported a major expansion in member bank credit at a time when Hoover believed restraint on the domestic economy was called for. In his view, Benjamin Strong, whom Hoover later characterized as a "mental annex to Europe," was the leading villain of the piece.[53] Strong's misguided sense of priorities, in Hoover's opinion, bore a heavy responsibility for the convulsions the American economy was subsequently to experience. Though designed primarily to ease strains on European gold reserves, the strategy of low interest rates also made borrowing to finance stock market transactions more attractive than would otherwise have been the case.

But there was an irony in this tale. The central bankers were certainly genuine in their dedication to the proposition that an ideal world would be one in which the principles of the gold standard were universally adopted. Their practice, however, diverged from their theory. In all but two years in the 1920s, the United States was a net gold importer and by 1929 its gold stock was about one-sixth greater than it had been in 1921.[54] Meanwhile, the price level, which had fallen during the recession period of 1921–22, had thereafter been remarkably stable. This result was at odds with the model of the international adjustment mechanism. The impact of gold movements to the American economy in the 1920s was largely neutralized by open-market operations.

The debates about the strengths and weaknesses of scientific management of monetary policy sharpened a number of the issues that divided the contending parties. They also revealed some inconsistencies in the

positions of major participants. Hoover, for example, never fully explained how the "America first" dimension of his thinking about macroeconomic stabilization at home could be reconciled with his belief that
the principles of the gold standard should guide the reconstruction of
the international monetary order. Nor did the central bankers who
worked from a more international perspective provide a well-articulated
account of why actions on their part should impede the price adjustments that gold movements were supposed to produce under the "rules
of the game." Though the discussions of the 1920s did not resolve these
matters, they did drive home one practical point: that what happened
(or failed to happen) in monetary policy would ultimately be determined by the judgments of the central bankers and not by those of
outsiders.

Questions about the neomercantilist component of Hooverism

The Hooverites were emphatic in their view that America's trade relationships with the rest of the world should be organized to support
rising standards of living in the United States and, more particularly,
that tariff policies should be designed to defend American wage standards. The "cheap foreign labor" argument for protection was regularly
invoked as providing a self-evident demonstration of the merits of this
view. This doctrine won applause from interest groups that stood to
benefit from high duties. But it gave more than a little pause to most
economists, including some who were associated with Hoover during
his Commerce Department years and sympathetic to other parts of his
program.

Frank W. Taussig of Harvard University, then widely recognized as
one of the nation's most thoughtful students of international trade,
characterized the view of the professionals when he wrote: "I know of
no economist, certainly none in England or this country, who would
sanction the pauper-labor argument." He did not question the sincerity
of those who believed "in their hearts that our standard of living and
the very basis of our prosperity rest on the maintenance of a system of
high duties."[55] But economic theory could show that this belief was
just plain wrong. If relative wage rates governed transactions between
countries, how could the United States – with the highest wage standards
in the world – manage to sell anything abroad? It was obvious, however, that American exporters could undersell foreigners when the differential in labor efficiency exceeded the differences in wage rates. Tariffs
might indeed keep American wages artificially high in the less efficient
sectors of the economy. To that extent, it was correct to assert that

protection propped up some domestic wages. Such shelter to the inefficient, however, was an economic error. In an ideal world, resources committed to lines of production in which Americans could not compete head to head with foreigners should be reallocated to sectors in which they could meet the test of competition. In the long run, all trading nations would be better off. This was what the free-trade theory of specialization and exchange was all about.

Achieving that ideal arrangement, however, would require some painful adjustments in industries that had grown accustomed to the tariff as a security blanket. Nor could there be any doubt that interest groups enjoying shelter from international competition would bring to bear all of the political pressure they could mobilize to resist change. Taussig certainly was aware that in the world of reality, as opposed to the world of economic theory, one often had to live with "second-best" solutions. To his way of thinking, there was no strain between his intellectual commitment to the ideals of freer trade and his willingness to serve as chairman of the Tariff Commission when that institution was created in 1916. At the time, the new governmental agency was conceived of as a mechanism for "taking the tariff out of politics." No longer should tariff making be simply the resultant of mutual back scratching by congressional delegations. Instead the terms of debate should be guided by the findings of fact produced by an independent and bipartisan commission. The authority of Congress to make the ultimate judgment on raising or lowering tariff schedules was not to be usurped. The reports of the experts, however, would neutralize the more extreme claims of the advocates of special interests and impose a higher order of rationality on the deliberative process.[56]

This position rested on the belief that protectionist attitudes were deeply engrained in the American body politic and that they were unlikely soon to disappear. Economists could still make a useful contribution to general enlightenment and, when invited, could work with government in support of change in the right direction. It would be utopian, however, to expect that the ideal world of complete freedom of international commerce would be easily within reach. The best that could be hoped for was cumulative progress in reducing trade barriers. Though many of the academicians would have preferred more sweeping solutions, the professionals with the richest sense of the complexities of political economy set more modest short-term goals. Their analyses of trade policy, however, were still markedly different from Hoover's. The economists tended to regard protection as an evil, though perhaps an inescapable one, in an imperfect world. Hoover, on the other hand, attempted to justify it. Nor were many of the academicians comfortable with the nationalistic overtones of the Hoover doctrine. They hoped instead to move the world toward greater internationalism and looked with favor on multilateral conventions to define the conditions of commerce between nations. One component of Hoover's policies toward international commerce – his attack on the foreign raw material "monopolists" – was, however, generally applauded by the economists. Nationalists and internationalists could make common cause in denouncing this departure from free trade.

Altogether, the exchanges of the 1920s raised a plenitude of questions about the theory and practice of the economics of a so-called new era as promoted by Hoover and his associates. Both the desirability and the feasibility of Hoover's program were subject to challenge, but on few points was there consensus among the skeptics. They spoke from a variety of divergent analytic perspectives. Nor could those advancing criticisms agree among themselves about whether Hoover was disposed to intervene too little or too much. The results of the presidential election in November 1928 provided Hoover with greater leverage over those in official circles who did not share his vision of the way the American economy could be made to function. Intellectual ferment among the skeptics on the outside, however, did not diminish in vitality.

CHAPTER 3

The new economics at center stage in 1929

No American president has come into office with a more detailed conception of what he wanted to accomplish in economic policy and of the way to go about it than did Herbert Hoover in 1929. His apprenticeship as secretary of commerce had sharpened his thinking on both strategy and tactics. The White House provided an opportunity to press forward with projects that had not yet fully matured and with some which he had pushed, but without success, as the servant of Presidents Harding and Coolidge. As president, Hoover now had a much freer hand to act, though his sense of liberation was still not complete. In his memoirs, he lamented that the public could not fully appreciate the burden an incoming president must carry when he succeeds a member of his own party. He may wish to shift course, but, as an heir who is expected to pay decent respect to his inheritance, he may be constrained from doing so too abruptly.

Setting the initial agenda for economic policy

It has become standard practice for newly elected Presidents to commission "task forces" to provide expert counsel on the challenges a new administration is likely to confront. For Hoover, a special exercise of this sort on economic policy was unnecessary. He already knew what he wanted to do. A function analogous to the latter-day task force for a president-elect was, however, performed by a study group organized under the auspices of the President's Conference on Unemployment in January 1928. As secretary of commerce, Hoover had then commissioned the preparation of technical monographs by scholars affiliated with the National Bureau of Economic Research and had appointed Wesley Mitchell to direct their work. The findings of the experts were to be submitted to a committee, chaired by Hoover, which would write its own report interpreting the significance of the research. Both phases of this undertaking were completed in February 1929 and were published in May to the accompaniment of considerable fanfare.

This document, titled *Recent Economic Changes in the United States*, was not intended to enlighten a new president on economic issues. He was already well acquainted with them. Its broader purpose was instead to inform the general public and to enlist its support in bringing the promise of the new economics to complete fulfillment. *Recent Economic Changes* was at once a look backward and a look forward. Not surprisingly, a note of self-congratulation was struck on many of its pages. Since recovery from the recession of 1920–21, the economy had been blessed with both growth and overall price stability. From all appearances, the new approach to production had fulfilled or exceeded expectations. Improvements in productivity in most sectors had been impressive and they had been fed by a technological dynamism that had proceeded at an unprecedented pace. The wisdom of the high-wage policy seemed also to have been validated by experience. In the judgment of the committee, the principle of high wages and low costs was not only the "policy of enlightened industrial practice"; its application on such scale was regarded as a "fundamental development" that had properly "attracted the attention of economists all over the world."[1] Indeed, the performance of the American economy had so captured the imagination of foreigners that they were naturally inclined to look to the United States for lessons that could be applied in their own countries. In much the same way that outsiders were to try to understand the Japanese economy in the 1970s and 1980s, they turned to the American model for inspiration in the 1920s.

All of this suggested that the foundations for sustained economic progress had been well laid and that the challenge of the future was to continue to build on them. But there was still work to be done. The contributors to *Recent Economic Changes* drew particular attention to a number of problem areas, each of which had given Hoover concern while he was secretary of commerce. Some of the unfinished business was viewed as a by-product of success in the application of the new economics. Productivity gains associated with the introduction of higher technologies, for example, had produced some disturbing side effects. The volume of employment generated by the manufacturing sector, it was noted, had fallen during the period under review and it had "become evident that unemployment can arise as a result of industrial efficiency as well as of inefficiency." It was thus now important to address the "newer problem of 'technological' unemployment, if we are to forestall uncertainty in the lives of the workers."[2] To improve understanding of this phenomenon, the committee recommended that a high priority be assigned to perfecting the statistical coverage of trends in the labor force.

It also seemed that the economic progress of the middle 1920s had added ambiguities to some old questions concerning the nature of in-

dustrial organization and the implications of the size of firms for productive efficiency and effective competition. According to the best available information, merger activity in the corporate sector had surpassed
all previous records. In manufacturing and mining, 221 mergers were
reported in 1928 (nearly twice the number recorded for 1925). Over the
same period, the number of firms disappearing in these sectors had also
nearly doubled (from 554 in 1925 to 1,038 in 1928). A trend toward increased concentration was unmistakable. The longer term significance
of this development, however, was less easy to appraise. As Willard L.
Thorp, a member of the National Bureau's research team, observed,
the data at hand were "entirely inadequate" to support a fully informed
judgment. On the one hand, he was prepared to allow that "many of
the mergers represent a realignment of industry that should result in
cheaper and more efficient production." On the other, there was some
indication that these potential economies "as often as not [were] more
than offset by real losses in efficiency." Much of the growth in the
market shares of large concerns could be attributed to "greater success
in the field of marketing," rather than to an "ability to produce at a
lower cost." Thorp noted an arresting anomaly: namely, that the Sherman and Clayton Acts tended to "encourage combinations, since the
merged companies can adopt a uniform marketing policy which would
be illegal if undertaken as independents."[3] These matters called for
further investigation.

The shape of those sectors of the economy under the jurisdiction of
public regulatory authorities also required attention. Deficiencies in the
work of the Interstate Commerce Commission were particularly notable.
The Transportation Act of 1920 had charged the commission to prepare
a comprehensive plan for railway consolidation that was expected to
improve operating efficiency and to strengthen the financial position of
the weaker lines. But the commission had failed to come forward with
a grand design and, in the absence of one, had denied approval to proposals for consolidation initiated by the carriers themselves.[4] Improvements in the apparatus regulating the electric industry were also overdue. Better control of interstate power was particularly needed in light
of a striking increase in the number of public utility holding companies that seemed to operate in a regulatory no man's land. From his
office at the Commerce Department, Hoover had called for reforms
along these lines. His judgment was now reinforced by that of the
technical experts.

Though the general message of *Recent Economic Changes* was one
of praise for the accomplishments of the middle 1920s, it was still
recognized that progress had been "spotty." Not all sectors nor all

regions had participated in the general prosperity. Agriculture was at the top of the distress list. The task of bringing farmers "more fully into the stream of successful economic forces" was identified as a "problem of the first order."[5] Their difficulties had also spilled over into a wave of failures among small state-chartered banks in rural areas. The fragility of these institutions suggested that some structural reorganization in banking was called for. In the view of the National Bureau's specialists in financial matters, the number of banks in the agricultural sections of the country was "excessive" and was a source of weakness in the financial system. As they put it: "No community can possibly provide adequate resources, competent officers and experienced directors for one bank for every 750 of its inhabitants, as in North Dakota, or to 1,400 as in Iowa."[6] On the other hand, the central fabric of the financial system seemed to be in solid condition. The committee spoke with assurance about "the popular confidence in the financial structure, especially in the Federal Reserve System, and the power of the System to move available credit to the places where it is needed," a development described "as a great advance."[7] It was noted by the financial experts, however, that the asset position of banks had changed in the recent past: commercial loans had grown only modestly in a period of general expansion, whereas holdings of securities and lending to finance purchases of equities had increased at a rapid rate.[8] Meanwhile, the prices of common stocks had appreciated substantially, a phenomenon further stimulated by the mushrooming of "investment trusts," the ancestors of institutions later to be more commonly designated as "mutual funds." There were occasional hints that all this might not be altogether healthy. The committee alluded to this matter, but guardedly, with the observation that "until recently we have not diverted savings from productive business to speculation."[9]

While the country did not lack unresolved problems when Hoover entered the White House, there still seemed to be a solid basis for confidence about the future. A technique for dealing with troublesome matters had been developed and it had already been given a satisfactory trial run. It was now the task of leadership "to maintain the dynamic equilibrium of recent years." And it could draw on a distinctive American attribute – a trait of mind "receptive to new ideas, ingenious in devices, adaptable."[10] Hoover echoed these themes in his inaugural address with these words: "The larger purpose of our economic thought should be to establish more firmly stability and security of business and employment and thereby remove poverty still further from our borders. ... The questions before our country are problems of progress to higher standards."[11]

Organizing for action on the unfinished business

In Hoover's scheme of things, the various items on the agenda for economic policy called for different types of treatment. Some were ripe for congressional action, others needed more detailed investigation, and still others called for quiet behind-the-scenes diplomacy. Priority on the legislative agenda, however, was assigned to addressing the problems of agriculture. During his campaign for the presidency, Hoover had committed himself to the development of a program for farm relief. The necessity for a policy promising to improve farm incomes was no longer subject to debate. The point at issue was the form it should take. The McNary–Haugen approach of tariff equivalence was clearly not acceptable. Not only would it draw government into fixing the prices of major farm products, it would have the unfortunate consequence of encouraging still greater production of staple crops that were already in oversupply. A defensible approach would have to be free of these objectionable features of the strategy pressed most vigorously by the farm bloc.

The program Hoover recommended to a special session of Congress convened in April 1929 called for the creation of a Federal Farm Board, to be funded by the Treasury, which would be empowered to lend up to $500 million to agricultural cooperatives. This proposal did indeed involve a considerable enlargement of federal involvement in the private economy. Nevertheless, it could be accommodated to Hoover's conception of the legitimate functions of government with little strain. The purpose of the Farm Board was to assist producers in forming institutions they would themselves control. This was analogous to the encouragement government had given to strengthening trade associations in the manufacturing sector of the economy. Government, however, had not provided any financial assistance to trade associations. Special treatment for agriculture could be defended on the ground that farmers were not adequately equipped to build the institutions they needed from their own resources. Government was thus justified in advancing "seed money" for institution building, but its assistance should take the form of loans, not grants.

Once farmer-controlled marketing cooperatives were in place, it would be their function to smooth price fluctuations for the major farm products by stockpiling outputs that might temporarily be in surplus. In Hoover's view, this mechanism should help to stabilize prices by making marketing arrangements more efficient and by minimizing the impact of seasonal ups and downs in production and marketing. This should provide a prop to farm incomes, but without making government a direct party to specific price setting. Moreover, the disciplines of the marketplace would ultimately control the behavior of marketing organizations. They had to worry about their financial integrity and this meant that inventories of commodities in surplus could not be kept off the market indefinitely. The Federal Farm Board was also to be charged to supply technical assistance to help farmers adjust their plantings to market conditions, though the manner in which this task should be performed was not set out in detail,

The Farm Relief Bill that won congressional approval in June 1929 created the new agency sought by Hoover. But the success of this scheme in raising rural incomes depended on another piece of legislative reinforcement. Even though the stockpiling of agricultural products by marketing cooperatives was not supposed to fix prices, it was still expected to keep them higher than they would otherwise have been in seasons of bumper crops. If such intervention generated domestic prices that were above world levels, this result would not be sustainable unless imports were restricted. In particular, it was critical to prevent U.S. farm exports from reentering the home market. Hoover thus recommended revision in the tariff to accomplish this purpose and he linked this request with a proposal to which he had long attached high importance: that the Tariff Commission be reorganized and that it be allowed wider discretion to raise and lower tariff schedules in light of changes in relative costs at home and abroad. Congressional action on tariff legislation was delayed for more than a year, however.

In his first months in office, Hoover was not ready to propose legislation on other matters of outstanding business, though they were not ignored within the executive branch. With his support, the Department of Justice initiated inquiries into the impact of mergers and consolidations. Systematic attention to the problems of banking was deferred until the presentation of his first State of the Union message on December 3, 1929. He then proposed the creation of a commission to investigate the organization of banking institutions, which would consider particularly the desirability of amending the law to afford greater scope to "group" or "chain" banking. The weakness of the smaller country banks, he then noted, stood in "marked contrast" to the "growth in size and stability of the metropolitan banks." He further held it to be disturbing that an increasing number of banks "in great commercial centers" had withdrawn from the Federal Reserve System by relinquishing their national charters in favor of state charters.[12] This occasion was also used to request that Congress extend the authority of the Federal Power Commission to ensure adequate public regulation of interstate generation and distribution of electric power. Such reform, he insisted, should not encroach on the regulatory responsibilities of the individual states. It was intended instead to close a loophole in the regulatory apparatus.[13] At the same time, he recommended amendments in the responsibilities assigned to the Interstate Commerce Commission to expedite consolidations in the railway network.

By the end of his first nine months in office, Hoover had taken steps intended to deal with each of the matters prominently identified in *Recent Economic Changes* as in need of attention. Some of these initiatives grabbed no headlines at the time, though they were later to generate considerable controversy. A case in point was a decision by the president to instruct the Census Bureau to gather data on unemployment in the decennial census scheduled for April 1930. The Committee on Recent Economic Changes had urged that the quality of information on the labor force be upgraded and this seemed to be a useful way to launch such a program.[14]

Concern about the stock market

The matter that most preoccupied Hoover during his presidential honeymoon had scarcely been touched upon in *Recent Economic Changes*. Passing reference had been made to speculation in common stocks during 1928, with an occasional suggestion that this activity was potentially unhealthy. In private, Hoover had made his worries known even before his elevation to the presidency. The reader of *Recent Economic Changes*, however, would hardly be aware of them.

If there were reasons for concern about the behavior of the stock exchanges in 1928, events in early 1929 provided still more of them. In the first months of the year, stock prices again took a sharp leap upward, a trend that was to continue, with only a few interruptions, into the early autumn of the year. Meanwhile, the volume of funds placed at call in "brokers' loans" continued to swell. By September 1929 more than $8.5 billion of bank funds had been placed with brokers affiliated with the New York Stock Exchange (a sum nearly double the amounts so placed at the beginning of 1928).[15] But this did not capture the full sweep of lending to finance the purchase of stocks. By mid-1929 it had become apparent that a number of U.S. corporations had provided additional finance to the "call" money market and that foreign capital had also swollen the flood. The returns seemed attractive – interest rates on loans collateralized by common stock and subject to call were in the range of 15 percent and, at one point, reached 20 percent. The general mood of euphoria was also congenial to accelerated growth in the size and number of investment trusts. During the year 1929, these institu-

tions accounted for more than a quarter of the capital issues of domestic corporations and the sums involved were roughly three times as
great as they had been in 1928.[16]

Hoover viewed these developments with alarm. In his conception of
the way a well-ordered economy should function, there was no place for
speculators. They posed a threat to the stability of the macroeconomic
system. Ultimately, the public would realize that inflated stock prices
were unsustainable. When the inevitable adjustment came, its effects
might disturb normal productive activity. Sound long-term growth was
also being put at risk for another reason. Funds that ought to be chan-
neled into productive capital formation were instead being diverted
into the acquisition of pieces of paper. Meanwhile the banking system
had placed itself in a highly exposed position. Brokers' loans were not
eligible for rediscount with the Federal Reserve Banks. As the share of
commercial bank assets held in this form increased, the access of member banks to "lender of last resort" facilities was correspondingly reduced. But, above all, speculation was immoral. The new economics
was supposed to encourage producers, not plungers.

Hoover was persuaded that much of this speculative orgy stemmed
from mistaken policies of the Federal Reserve in 1927 and 1928. It had
then kept interest rates low, primarily at the urging of European central bankers. When he had then pressed for a change in monetary
policy, he had been brushed off. As president-elect, his views were treated
with greater respect. Meanwhile the guard had changed at the Federal
Reserve. His long-standing adversary at the New York District Bank,
Benjamin Strong, had died in October 1928, and the chairmanship of
the board in Washington had passed from Crissinger, a Harding appointee whom Hoover regarded as incompetent, to Roy A. Young, an
experienced central banker from whom he expected better cooperation.

The central objective of monetary policy in early 1929 – in Hoover's
reading of the situation – should be to choke off finance for stock market
transactions, but in such a way that it would not restrict credit for legitimate business purposes. Ideally, selective credit controls that discriminated against loans to brokers might do this job. The private banking
community had long resisted this proposition and continued to do so.
Nor was the Federal Reserve equipped to impose such a regime. It could,
to be sure, deploy its standard techniques to restrict the general availability of credit. In the circumstances of early 1929, however, the effectiveness of these instruments in suppressing borrowing for stock market
speculation was questionable. The Federal Reserve's holdings of government securities had already been depleted to the point that the sale
of its full portfolio was unlikely to have much impact on the lending

capacity of commercial banks.[17] Nor did the tactic of raising discount rates offer much promise. Hoover concurred with Young's judgment that such a move would not deter those who anticipated quick capital gains on borrowed money, but would merely penalize regular business borrowers.

With Hoover's active support, the Federal Reserve Board in Washington began to apply some pressure in February 1929 when it called on Federal Reserve District Banks to deny rediscounting privileges to members who used these funds to lend to the call market. This was intended to check a practice that many banks had come to find compellingly attractive: to borrow from the Federal Reserve System at $4\frac{1}{2}$ to 5 percent interest and to lend at call at rates of 15 percent or more. For a brief period in late March 1929, this exercise added sufficient strain to the call market to push its interest rates to 20 percent. It was still, however, largely ineffectual. A number of the district banks refused to comply and the board could not compel them to do so. The scheme was further frustrated by the behavior of Charles E. Mitchell, chairman of the National City Bank of New York (who served simultaneously as a director of the New York branch of the Federal Reserve), when he announced that those wishing to borrow to finance the purchase of stocks would be accommodated at his own bank. Following Mitchell's statement, interest rates on call money eased and soon thereafter the volume of credit placed in brokers' loans resumed its expansion.

Though the bankers largely resisted instruction, Hoover hoped to have better luck in educating the general public about the dangers latent in stock market speculation. He profoundly disagreed with a statement President Coolidge issued shortly before leaving the White House to the effect that prosperity was "absolutely sound" and that stocks were "cheap at current prices."[18] Nevertheless, Hoover thought it unseemly to denounce his predecessor so soon after replacing him. He thus proceeded indirectly by instructing Secretary of the Treasury Andrew Mellon to pass on some gratuitous advice to the investing public. Reluctantly, Mellon did so through the following statement released on March 14, 1929: "The present situation in the financial market offers an opportunity for the prudent investor to buy bonds. Bonds are low in price compared to stocks."[19] Few took these words seriously. The *New York Times* reacted editorially with the observation that a statement made "deliberately and officially" by the secretary of the Treasury was a matter of "high importance," but added that "cynical minds may see in this an obscure allusion to the fact that government bonds had not recently been in too great demand and have been selling below par. Thus it may be said that the secretary was speaking one word for the investor and two for the Treasury. In any case, Wall Street characteristically acted upon his opinion that some stocks are too high by sending them still higher yesterday."[20]

In the subsequent months, Hoover also sent messages of warning through other channels. Through private meetings with selected newspaper editors and publishers, he urged the press to offer a counsel of caution to its readers. He pressed officers of the New York Stock Exchange to tighten the rules governing the behavior of its members. He called for the suppression of stock market "tipsters" operating out of so-called bucket shops and urged the governor of New York, Franklin D. Roosevelt, to introduce legislation outlawing such practices and tightening the state government's regulations of the stock exchanges. In addition, he deputized his friend and confidante, Henry M. Robinson, to be a personal emissary to the captains of finance and to tell them to slow things down.[21]

Alternative readings of the stock market's behavior

If Hoover was alarmed by the course of events in financial markets, there were plenty of influential and presumably well-informed voices to assure him and the general public that anxieties were misplaced. Thomas W. Lamont of J. P. Morgan and Company, who had been apprized of the president's worries by Henry M. Robinson, provided a stirring antidote to these fears from a Wall Street perspective.[22] In a lengthy memorandum submitted to Hoover on October 19, 1929, Lamont poured cold water on the notion that a dangerous gambling spirit had come over the American people. He acknowledged that there might be occasional excesses, but the normal functioning of markets would correct them. Over the longer term, the "speculative interest in stocks" could be expected to make a constructive contribution to American economic growth.

Is it not just possible [he asked] that the improved machinery of the Stock Exchanges and the new investment trusts are attracting the savings of small investors all over the country who, induced in the first instance perhaps by merely the hope of a quick speculative profit or by stories of others' winnings, may become in time investors in the best stocks in the best companies? . . . If it should turn out that the speculative interest in stocks and the investment trusts are drawing the savings of the American people into partnership with the great and successful American industries, then the problem of waste of capital through the issue of fraudulent securities (which the state legislatures have futilely sought to solve by blue sky laws) is being solved by making good stocks available to everyone. If that should turn out to be true a greater problem still is being solved. The wide distribution of the ownership of our greater industries among tens or hundreds of thousands of stockholders, should go a long way to solve the problem of social unrest or of conflict or imagined conflict between the corporations and the people.[23]

Nor, in Lamont's judgment, did recent changes in patterns of corporate finance give cause for any fundamental concern. The rising popularity of common stocks had enabled corporations to obtain external financing on very cheap terms. In this environment, the phenomenal growth of brokers' loans was not to be wondered at. It simply meant that "instead of bank funds flowing directly to corporations through commercial loans, they now flow through the route of brokers' loans and new issues of common stock to finance such corporations." Lamont conceded that the "stupendous scale" of the flotation of common stocks issued by investment trusts had been "greatly overdone," but held it wrong to conclude that "this particular development [had] been so excessive as to warrant real concern for its effect upon the general situation in the near future." This institutional arrangement had much to recommend it. As he saw the matter:

If the general body of stockholders of, say, the General Electric Company turn their holdings of General Electric stock over to a dozen different investment trusts and take stock of the investment trusts in exchange (which is what happens in effect), they have in a way elected a dozen trained and experienced agents to represent them in following the affairs of the General Electric Company closely and in making articulate to the management the interest of the general stockholders.[24]

Underlying this position was Lamont's conviction that events on the stock market and recent changes in the structure of American financial institutions were themselves the fruit of prosperity and of public confidence that it would be sustained. "The future appears brilliant," he wrote. "It is this future which the stock market has been discounting." Not only were the economic successes of the 1920s abundantly visible, there were more to come. Growth in scientific research promised shortly to add to the list of new products that would enrich the lives of the American people. And another factor was "coming now into play more strongly each day, and tending towards a steadying influence upon all our economy": namely, "the growing feeling on the part of our American men of affairs that the present Administration intends to pursue policies that are constructive as well as conservative."[25]

But some of those who shared Hoover's point of view on the importance of macroeconomic stabilization − and who welcomed the wider use of the powers of government for this purpose − also parted company with the president's diagnosis of the behavior of the stock market. Foster and Catchings, for example, found fault with the interventions

Hoover had encouraged the Federal Reserve Board to undertake. They took the board sharply to task for interfering with the "long-established practices" of lending on stock exchanged collateral. This method of finance, they maintained, was one of the foundations of American prosperity. It had permitted companies to reduce bank loans and bonded indebtedness by making common stock issues easier to place. This, in turn, had "strengthened the industrial structure of the whole country, for it is sounder business to operate on capital subscribed by the owners of the business than on debts." A venture so capitalized was "in less danger of being forced, even though solvent, into the hands of creditors, and in less danger of having its wholesome growth hampered."[26] This fortunate arrangement was now being placed in jeopardy by the board's attempt to reduce bank lending on stock exchange collateral. This misguided policy, in their analysis, also posed a threat to the health of the social fabric. "Millions of wage earners," they maintained, had been "enabled to buy stocks on installments only because the stocks themselves have in some way been used as collateral for bank loans." With this accommodation restricted, they anticipated that the rich, who, they believed, could borrow without any collateral at all, would acquire even larger shares of the nation's expanding wealth.[27]

Foster and Catchings further drew attention to an inconsistency in the board's behavior. For years, the Federal Reserve System had insisted that it had no desire to interfere in the setting of individual prices. Now, however, it was attempting to control stock prices, apparently on the assumption that they were excessively high. But who could say with certainty what the correct prices of stocks should be? The Federal Reserve appeared to have acted on the basis of opinion rather than on established fact. The result was that the board had "injured business." In July 1929 they did not predict how severe the injury might be. Some of the "depressing effects of arbitrary restrictions of credit supply" would not be visible for several months. Even so, an impact was already observable in declining construction activity (particularly for home building). In addition, they maintained that "a large number of sound, constructive business developments have been postponed solely because, the Reserve System having ceased to function in the established way, these projected enterprises cannot be financed by the sale of stock."[28] Altogether, they concluded that "there is a paralyzing uncertainty among businessmen as to whether the Reserve Board will allow that expansion of bank credit without which such prosperity as we have had in recent years simply cannot last. In short, the Board has created a state of mind which breeds business depression."[29]

If Foster and Catchings had doubts about the sustainability of prosperity in face of restraints on finance for the purchase of stocks, another ardent advocate of macroeconomic stabilization had none. Irving Fisher went on record in September 1929 with the judgment that "stock prices have reached what looks like a permanently high plateau."[30]

CHAPTER 4

Activating the stabilization model in late 1929 and 1930

On September 3, 1929 the Dow–Jones industrial index of common stock prices reached a new all-time high at 381. This was more than double its level in early 1929, and, as it happened, the record established was to stand for the next twenty years. Serious slippage in stock values occurred in early October and the trend was downward throughout most of the month. Even before the panic conditions of "Black Thursday," October 24, and "Black Tuesday," October 29, it appeared that the long-anticipated readjustment had begun. Interpreting its scale and significance was another matter. Interruptions in the upward momentum of the bull market had occurred before, most recently in December 1928 and in March 1929, and had shortly thereafter been reversed. It was not implausible to argue that a similar "technical reaction" was now underway and that the forward momentum would soon be resumed.

After the October erosion had begun (though before Black Thursday, October 24), Hoover observed in private conversation that he had "noted with satisfaction the break and decline in stocks," but that he had been "dubious about doing anything for fear that more harm than good might result."[1] On October 25 (the day after the first major panic on the New York Stock Exchange), Hoover had a different reading of the situation available to him. Reporting on his most recent mission to Wall Street, Henry M. Robinson observed that there were "greater dangers and greater troubles in this situation" than Lamont's analysis indicated and that he was "inclined to think that most of the bankers and industrialists" would agree with him. At the same time, Robinson noted that the "best information" he could obtain suggested that "there is not on the immediate horizon a prospect of any serious failures." This judgment was immediately qualified with the observation that

yesterday's happenings will be followed undoubtedly by a very great number of individual firms and corporation failures, where the funds have been used in the speculative market in a marginal game. There will doubtless be great bitterness against "Wall Street" (so-called) when each individual is explaining to his wife how he lost the family funds or to partners the disappearance of the concern's assets. The blame, of course, must be placed on someone and, as Will Rogers said, "It might be on Hoover's Fedora hat."

Robinson nonetheless remained optimistic that "the public generally will attach no blame to the Administration." On the contrary, it could claim credit for sending warning signals pointing out "what was bound to happen," even though those signals had not been heeded.[2]

Though urged by the financial community in late October and early November to make reassuring statements to "talk up" the stock market, Hoover declined to do so. In a statement authorized for release to the press on October 25, he stated only that "the fundamental business of the country, that is the production and distribution of commodities, is on a sound and prosperous basis."[3] Direct mention of the turbulence on the stock exchanges was scrupulously avoided. He did address this matter on November 5, but in the setting of an off-the-record briefing for the White House press corps. As he then put it, he saw "no particular reasons for making any public statements . . . , either directly or indirectly." In his judgment, the country had gone through a "more or less uncontrollable" period of overspeculation, which ultimately had crashed "due to its own weight." The timing of this collapse, he indicated, was "perhaps a little expedited by the foreign situation." Central banks abroad had raised interest rates in order to repatriate funds that had found their way to New York. At the same time, banks in the interior of the United States were withdrawing money from the call market. Though this created a "difficult situation" in New York, it had also swollen the funds available for lending in the interior, where there was "a tendency for interest rates to fall at once." Moreover, the Federal Reserve Banks in the main financial centers had done their job by lowering discount rates. (In the New York District, the discount rate had been reduced from 6 percent to 5 percent on November 1 and was to be lowered again to 4½ percent on November 15.) Hoover anticipated that the combined effects of the release of funds from speculative activity and the general reduction in interest rates would make more capital available for the bond and mortgage market where there was a substantial pent-up demand for finance. In the recent period of distortion from normal financial flows, many businesses, as well as state and local governments, had postponed capital projects. Conditions were now ripe for them to resume investment spending. Hoover concluded that the country had "gone through a crisis in the stock market, but for the first time in history the crisis has been isolated to the stock market itself. It has not extended into either the production activities of the country or the financial fabric of the country."[4]

By mid-November, however, conditions had deteriorated. The Dow–Jones Industrial Index hit its low point of the year on November 13 at 198, a figure that represented a loss of nearly half of the paper values of early September. The following day, Secretary of Commerce Lamont sounded an ominous note when he advised the president that "the situation is fraught with danger." He reported that there was a "fear of runs on the banks" in the Midwest and that "substantial and conservative business men suggest a statement from you is needed at this time to reassure the people as to the soundness of our banking and business institutions and to prevent an already critical condition from becoming disastrous." While he thought it premature to estimate the final effect of the collapse in the stock market on general business, he maintained that "there can be no doubt that the purchasing power of many of our people has been reduced. Plant operations in some lines will be affected, and unemployment will result." [5]

Demand management, Hoover-style

On November 15, 1929 Hoover broke his public silence. In press conference remarks made available for quotation, he observed: "In market booms we develop overoptimism with a corresponding reverse into overpessimism. They are equally unjustified but the sad thing is that many unfortunate people are drawn into the vortex of these movements with tragic loss of savings and reserves. Any lack of confidence in the economic future or the basic strength of business in the United States is foolish." And he added: "My own experience has been, however, that words are not of any great importance in times of economic disturbance. It is action that counts." [6]

Hoover was now indeed ready to act. The time seemed to have arrived to pull the trigger on the plans for stabilizing downturns in spending which had been worked out in the discussions begun in the early 1920s. As a first step, he asked the heads of all cabinet departments to investigate the possibilities of accelerating their spending on construction projects already authorized and to assess the feasibility of new construction programs for which the appropriations had not yet been obtained. [7]

This step was followed up with telegrams dispatched to governors in each of the nation's states, pointing out that it would "be helpful if road, street, public building and other construction of this type could be speeded up and adjusted in such fashion to further employment." [8] The governors also were asked to initiate a canvass of state, municipal, and county spending programs and to report to Washington on "the volume of expenditure that can be prudently arranged for the next twelve months and for the next six months."[9]

Meanwhile Hoover organized conferences at the White House with leaders of the business community. In the first instance, priority was given to executives in the regulated industries who were responsible for planning much of the nation's infrastructure investment. On November 19, he urged senior officials in the railway industry to maintain and, if possible, to increase their capital spending. A similar call was addressed to the leadership of the major public utilities on November 21. Sessions were also arranged with representatives of agricultural organizations, following which the White House reported that it was the opinion of those assembled that the easing of interest rates then underway would improve the position of farmers and that the savings thus made "would immediately be reflected back into the markets through the purchase of necessary equipment and supplies for the farm." In addition, the contribution of the Federal Farm Board to stabilizing prices was commended.[10]

These actions were clearly in keeping with the strategy that had evolved from the work of the President's Conference on Unemployment of 1921. The initial responses to these extraordinary presidential initiatives were heartwarming. The electric power, natural gas, and telephone industries reported that they intended to spend more for capital improvements in 1930 than they had in 1929. The president of the American Railway Association informed Hoover that his industry was "proceeding with confidence in the future business prosperity of the country," that it was going ahead with a large program of capital expenditures which had already been budgeted, and that a movement to increase such outlays was "being actively and intelligently pressed forward."[11] The early returns from state and local government officials also indicated their willingness to cooperate with the president's program. All in all, the parts of the system which were most readily susceptible to presidential persuasion seemed to be behaving agreeably.

But, in the climate of late 1929, it seemed likely that still more needed to be done. The spending patterns of smaller industries and firms would also have an impact on the aggregative outcome, but it was less easy to mobilize this part of the business community for action. Hoover called on Julius Barnes, chairman of the U.S. Chamber of Comber of Commerce, to take a lead in this effort by urging various trade associations to encourage their members to expand outlays for construction and maintenance work. In early December he asked Barnes "to send out a circular to members of the different industries, stating the necessity for repairs, maintenance, clean up, general betterments and improvements, and that a concerted effort is urgently needed during the three winter months." He also asked that the various industries indicate the amounts they were likely to spend for these purposes in 1930. With such information in hand, along with data gathered separately on the spending projections of railways, utilities, and governments, Hoover believed it would be possible to "form a very quick judgment as to what further measures may be necessary." Quite apart from the value of this information to the administration as it shaped its plans, Hoover pointed out that "such an inquiry would in itself be stimulative, especially if it were phrased as a recommendation to take up the unemployment in their own business and to help out a little with others." Hoover emphasized the importance of this undertaking with the observation that "the news of the general situation continues to grow a little worse. For your confidential information, we are now faced with three million unemployed." [12]

Phase I of the stabilization strategy worked out years earlier was thus launched. Never before had the nation witnessed presidential activism on such a scale during a period of economic disturbance.[13] In pursuing the course he had chosen, Hoover rejected the advice of some senior members of his official family. Secretary of the Treasury Mellon, for example, was outspoken in his opposition to this type of intervention. His counsel at the time was to "liquidate labor, liquidate stocks, liquidate the farmers, liquidate real estate" and to let the market provide its own correctives.[14] Hoover would have no part of it. The new learning accumulated during his service as commerce secretary called for the use of the powers of the federal government to cushion the shocks by stimulating others to spend. Government should not coerce, but it could and should cajole. And it also had a duty to inform. Indeed faith in the efficacy of knowledge as a stabilizer remained alive and well. The Department of Commerce celebrated the 1 hundredth issue of the *Survey of Current Business*, published in December 1929, with the following words: "While it may be too early to say that the utilization of business data has entirely eliminated the business cycle, there is agreement today among business leaders everywhere that the wider use of facts will mitigate in a large degree many of the disastrous effects of the one-time recurrent business cycle." [15]

Stabilization through confidence building

Hoover was well aware that the task of stimulating spending involved more than simply signalling the timing for action. It was also an exercise in applied psychology. As he diagnosed matters in mid-November, the fundamental problem was "a question of fear." [16] Franklin D. Roosevelt was later to offer a similar diagnosis when he proclaimed in his inaugural address on March 4, 1933, that "the only thing we have to fear is fear itself." Hoover's style in 1929 was different. He chose not to talk about this matter publicly, but spoke about it only off the record. As he put it, he wanted "action to speak for itself." [17] Even so, he maintained that the news media could assist in the campaign against fear. In his background briefings with representatives of the press, he invited their cooperation in restoring public confidence. Telling people not to be alarmed would be counterproductive. He suggested instead that reporters confine themselves "merely to the statement of the things that actually happen" and that the "most helpful form of news" was that which reported the activities of the various units of government in spurring public works and of the progress of business groups in "see[ing] that those things take place that have been promised to us." [18]

For its part, the administration did its best to supply the news media with "facts" drawing attention to the positive aspects of the situation. This campaign was spearheaded by the Information Office of the Department of Commerce, which issued weekly announcements indicating that the volume of spending on public works and by utilities promised to be greater in 1930 than it had been in 1929. The going was not always smooth, however. In April tension between the Department of Commerce and the Federal Reserve Board had begun to surface. Whereas the former emphasized the growth in construction contracts for public works and public utilities, the Federal Reserve Board's press statement of April 24, 1930 observed that these increases were "more than offset by a decrease in residential building." In the view of the Commerce Department, this comment was mischievous; one of its information officers characterized the board's press release as a "first class advertisement for an undertaking establishment." [19] When this matter was referred to the White House, Hoover asked Lamont to take it up with Governor Young of the Federal Reserve Board, noting that "it is very discouraging in the face of all we are trying to do." [20]

By May 1930 Hoover was ready to spread the word personally that his strategy of stabilization was working. As he told the U.S. Chamber of Commerce, the "acceleration of construction programs has been successful beyond our hopes" with the result that "the intensity of the slump has been greatly diminished by the efforts that we have made." Monetary panic and credit stringency had been avoided and "those dangers are behind us." These fortunate consequences could be attributed to a "great economic experiment, possibly one of the greatest of our history." He was "convinced we have now passed the worst and with continued unity of effort we shall rapidly recover."[21] Hoover enlarged on these themes in early October when addressing the American Bankers Association. He insisted that the nation's difficulties had been more severe in the recession of 1922, and yet America had then led the world to recovery. The unprecedented steps taken in the past year had "prevented a large measure of unemployment" and had "maintained a higher degree of consumption than would have otherwise been the case."[22] But there was still more to be done. "The income of a large part of our people is not reduced by the depression," he asserted, "but it is affected by the unnecessary fears and pessimism, the result of which is to slacken the consumption of goods and discourage enterprise." He charged the bankers to stimulate the productive use of credit by instilling a "feeling of assurance" among their clients in industry, agriculture, and commerce.[23]

Hoover never ceased to emphasize the importance of public confidence to the success of the fight against depression. In early 1930 he spoke with some assurance that the program he had put in place would help to regenerate it. Later, however, he was to insist that quite different types of measures were needed if the faith of the community in the health of the economy was to be restored.

Bolstering aggregate demand through wage policy

One of the cardinal principles of the new economics of the 1920s was the priority it assigned to an economy of high wages. Hoover was determined that there should be no lapse from this commitment. Indeed, as he saw matters, it took on added importance in circumstances when greater spending was needed. In his meetings with business leaders in November and December 1929, he drove this point home forcefully and he then won the assent of those assembled to resist the temptation to cut wages at a time of slackening employment. But there was a rider to this agreement: that organized labor would forgo demands for pay increases and refrain from use of the strike weapon for the duration of the emergency. In separate conferences with heads of labor organizations, Hoover obtained their endorsement for this program.

This intervention was without precedent and one in which Hoover took pride. In May 1930, for example, he observed that "for the first time in the history of great slumps, we have had no substantial reductions in wages."[24] He was later to be congratulated for his efforts by William Green, president of the American Federation of Labor. By the reckoning of the executive council of the AF of L, only 7 firms per 100 reporting to the Bureau of Labor Statistics had cut wages during the

year 1930, by contrast with wage cutting by 92 of a 100 firms in the recession year of 1921.[25] This was clearly a reversal of employer behavior
from past form.

In Hoover's conception of the "high-wage" economy, there was also
an important place for tariffs to shield Americans from the competition
of underpaid labor abroad. The proposals for revision in the tariff that
he had submitted to the special session of Congress in April 1929 had
not been acted on, however. When the Tariff Bill (labeled as the Smoot–
Hawley Bill) emerged from the congressional pipeline, it was more
sharply protectionist than Hoover had intended. Most of the increases
in duties, he insisted, were "directed to the interest of the farmer,"
though it was also noteworthy that rates had been increased on 890 of
roughly 3,300 items enumerated and reduced on only 235 of them.[26] If
the Smoot–Hawley Bill was not ideal, Hoover still thought it possible
to live with it. One of its provisions gave statutory embodiment to a
reform that had long been close to his heart: it delegated authority to a
restructured Tariff Commission to alter rates upward or downward by
50 percent with the approval of the president. The principle of flexibility, in Hoover's judgment, would make it possible to set tariff rates
by "prompt and scientific adjustment" which would be guided by differences in costs of production at home and abroad. American income
levels would thus be adequately secured and the anomalies generated
by political logrolling could be eliminated.

The place of tax reduction in administration thinking in 1929

Some latter-day Keynesians, most of whom have not been notably sympathetic to other aspects of Hoover's management of a depression economy, have applauded his decision to recommend a tax reduction in December 1929. This step, however, was not regarded at the time as a
response to the downturn in economic activity in the last quarter of the
year. Instead the tax cut was viewed much more as a continuation of
the Treasury's conception of business as usual. Planning for this measure had begun in midsummer 1929, and the events of the autumn had
little bearing on the recommendation Hoover included in his budget
message the following December. He then noted that four such reductions had been made since the fiscal year 1921 and that each had been
associated with higher revenue yields than had originally been projected
with the reduced rates. "Undoubtedly," he observed, "an increase in the
prosperity of business brought forth by tax reduction is partly responsible for this experience."[27] With a budget surplus (even after provision
for statutory debt retirement) apparently securely in hand for the fiscal

year ending June 30, 1930, there seemed to be no reason not to go ahead
with this plan.

As a matter of general principle, it had long been held to be sound
for government to keep its claims on private incomes to the minimum.
In keeping with that principle, tax rates, at least when judged by today's standards, were modest. Federal tax receipts in the year 1929, for
example, absorbed only about 3.7 percent of the gross national product;
by contrast, the federal tax claim amounted to more than 21.3 percent
of the GNP in 1981.[28] Nor was Hoover's proposal for a reduction in
taxes payable on incomes, both personal and corporate, earned in 1929
overwhelming in its magnitude. The estimated sacrifice in the Treasury's receipts was only $160 million (a figure representing less than 4
percent of the tax receipts anticipated under the original schedules and
less than one-sixth of 1 percent of GNP). Put another way, the absolute amount of the proposed tax reduction was only about one-quarter
of the amount allocated to retirement of the federal debt (a transaction
treated in the Treasury's accounts as an "expenditure chargeable against
ordinary receipts.")[29]

While the current state of the economy had no significant impact on
the president's proposal for a tax cut, it did affect thinking about
whether or not the reduced rates should become permanent features of
the tax structure. The Treasury took the position that the tax cuts
should apply only to tax liabilities due in 1930 and that further congressional action would be required to extend them. Its rationale was
that accurate estimation of revenues in the years beyond 1930 confronted "extraordinary difficulties." Undersecretary of the Treasury
Ogden L. Mills advised the president in November 1929 as follows:
"The immediate problem is how to give the taxpayer the benefit of the
surplus which seems reasonably certain in the fiscal year 1930 without
running the risk of incurring a deficit during the fiscal year 1931."
Forward projections of revenues, he maintained, were uncommonly
precarious in existing circumstances. Mills noted that the Treasury in
the preceding two years had enjoyed unusual increases in receipts from
the capital gains tax. It was not clear, however, what effect the "pre-
cipitous decline of security values recently witnessed" would have on
future revenues from this source. Hence, the administration should keep
open its taxing options for the following year.[30] Even so, this approach
to tax policy for 1930 could be applauded as a stimulant to private
spending, if only a modest one. In the fiscal thinking of the day, much
more weight was assigned to accelerating spending on public works as
a spur to the economy.

The initial responses of economists

During the first months of the depression, the reactions of economists to the condition of the economy and to the strategies Hoover had chosen to deploy contained few surprises. Those who had advocated various types of stabilization measures in the discussions of the mid-1920s generally applauded the president's initiatives. The more orthodox, on the other hand, remained skeptical about the effectiveness of Hoover's intervention in moderating the course of the business cycle.

Most of the economists in the first of these camps could readily associate themselves with Wesley Mitchell's observation of December 4, 1929, that "a more significant experiment in the technique of balance could not be devised than the one which is being performed before our very eyes." Mitchell, however, was cautious about forecasting its results. As he put it: "While a business cycle is passing over from a phase of expansion to the phase of contraction, the President of the United States is organizing the economic forces of the country to check the threatened decline at the start, if possible." He anticipated that "further steps toward industrial equilibrium" would be needed in the future, though he did not specify the form they should take.[31]

On the other hand, Foster and Catchings, the arch-champions of countercyclical public works spending, spoke with high confidence in the success of the president's efforts. In their assessment,

the new policy of the chief executive renders the present emergency unlike any other. The concerted action of private and public business, under his leadership, makes it in the interests of each individual to do precisely what is good for business as a whole. . . . Now, for the first time in our history, we have a President who, by technical training, engineering achievement, Cabinet experience, and grasp of economic fundamentals, is qualified for business leadership. And for the first time in our history the heads of our largest business enterprises are prepared to follow such leadership. Long before they were called to Washington, they understood the President's program. That did not happen by chance. For several years, the President and others have been preparing these men for precisely what has just taken place. When the emergency came, it was not necessary for the President to sit down and laboriously explain the why and wherefore of his plan, and wait for several months for his ideas to sink in.[32]

State governors, they noted, had received a similar economic education. As of January 1930 the capital spending commitments in hand from the big spenders in the private and public sectors indicated that their outlays in 1930 would be substantially greater than they had been in 1929. This would give smaller businesses in the tens of thousands "confidence to go ahead with their own enterprises." The activity of small firms, they pointed out, would not lend itself to grand announcements from the White House, but it would nevertheless be significant and its results "will appear, after a while, in the growth of bank credit, payrolls, and consumer buying."[33]

Irving Fisher was no less restrained in his praise of the president's interventions. In consequence, Fisher insisted that "for the immediate future, at least, the outlook is bright."[34] Hoover had correctly perceived that the "panic of 1929 was peculiarly dominated by the psychological factor" and his conferences provided "useful reassurance." Thus, the

threat to business due to the dislocation of purchasing power by reason of transfers of stock holdings will be temporary. Fulfillment of the pledges by the nation's business leaders that industrial programs will be adhered to, that wages will not be reduced, and that the 'tempo' of production on which all our prosperity has been built will be maintained, should suffice to bridge across the business recession that slightly antedated and accompanied the crash.

In addition, Fisher congratulated the Federal Reserve System for the great wisdom it had displayed following the stock market crash by keeping the banks "liquid and strong so as to prevent tight money and bankruptcies."[35]

Much the same note was struck by Professor John Maurice Clark of Columbia University in remarks prepared for the panel on "Public Works and Unemployment" at the December 1929 meeting of the American Economic Association. Hoover's actions were described as "a great experiment in constructive industrial statesmanship of a promising and novel sort." The president was commended for insisting that businesses forgo wage reductions. Should there be a suspicion that the committees of business leaders which Hoover had created were being used "to unify the power of employers to fight for wage reductions, all the good [they] might accomplish would be lost in the resulting aggravation of class hostility."[36] Clark further applauded the initiatives of the White House in urging the private sector to maintain its capital spending. He added the qualification that it might be "too much to hope that these measures alone should be completely successful," but emphasized that "whatever success they attain has the important effect of reducing the burden on public construction, reducing the need for undertaking extraordinary works of any sort."[37] Clark also emphatically dismissed the suggestion that the aggregate impact of expanded capital spending would be offset by reductions in expenditure by consumers. It was "well established by the study of business cycles," he observed, that "the short-run effect of enlarged expenditure in one direction, and correspond[ly] enlarged productive activity, is not necessarily to diminish expenditure and activity elsewhere, but more likely to increase it, the stimulus being diffused in cumulative fashion."[38] Nor was there any contradiction in Hoover's "excellent and statesmanlike" State of the Union message, which called at the same time for the government "to 'fertilize the soil of prosperity' by spending less money and so reducing taxes" and for it also "to rescue prosperity by spending more money, which must some time come out of taxes." Clark subscribed fully to the official line on this point. As he put it: "Economy is the permanent policy; and spending to promote prosperity may, under favorable conditions, turn out not to require spending more over a term of years so much as timing what we do spend so that it will do business the most good. Relief measures may be kept within these limits fairly easily so long as business is basically strong as it is now in this country." Striking the right balance, however, would "require more than ordinary political intelligence." It was fortunate, he concluded that "we have something more at present in the White House."[39]

But not all of the contributors to the strategy of macroeconomic stabilization formulated in the mid-1920s were convinced that the president's program was adequate. In remarks to the American Economic Association in December 1929, F. G. Dickinson of the University of Illinois, for example, addressed the uncertainties. The "earnest pledge of full assistance" given by key business executives to the president, he cautioned, might "not blossom into full fruition." Though he believed that "a considerable number of establishments will assume their responsibility for maintaining the general level of business activity," it seemed likely that "a much larger number will be content to maintain or reduce operations . . . and to let their own building wait until prices reach the bottom." This meant that a heavier weight would fall on the public sector if aggregate spending were to be sustained at acceptable levels. In particular, quick action by state and local governments was necessary. But the kit of tools for this purpose was less complete than it should be. In Dickinson's opinion, a major expansion in road building offered considerable promise. The federal government could usefully expedite it by informing the states that its grants in aid would henceforth be linked to the condition of the economy. With the foreknowledge that this tap would be turned off in periods of high employment, state governments would be stimulated to make greater use of this funding resource when employment was slipping. "Doubtless," Dickinson observed, "a state governor would hesitate to forfeit a federal grant by cutting the appropriation for hard roads during a period of depression." In addition, he returned to a proposal he had made earlier: that federal debt retirement be suspended in periods of slack and the monies thus released from the budget be reallocated to finance road building and other public works.[40]

But deeper skepticism about the effectiveness of Hoover's approach to the first phase of the depression could be found in predictable quarters. Rexford Guy Tugwell, for example, had argued that the economy had already entered a depression before the presidential election of 1928. The candidates, he wrote in May 1928, were "going to have to talk to unemployed people, people, perhaps, who are hungry and who next winter will be cold." A serious problem of unemployment, he maintained, was at hand long before the public at large was aware of it and it was a by-product of failure to apply appropriate social controls to the economic process. In their absence, new investment had been put in place haphazardly and businessmen were frequently mistaken in their anticipations of demand for the products to be offered from newly created capacity. When such mistakes occurred, "overhead costs are increased by failure to operate at capacity, and the profits which could be made by low prices and capacity operation – which would be the policy consumers would choose for industries – are sacrificed to those equally high ones which can be made by the restriction of operations and maintenance of high prices." But this restriction, in turn, both choked off production and cost jobs. "The resulting depression," Tugwell observed in 1928, "seems not to be a serious one; but part-time shutdowns, added to the substitution of machines for men, . . . have created an unemployment situation which is serious." Though he was a year premature in his forecasts, Tugwell had both a diagnosis and a prescription in hand when the crash came. What was needed was public direction of the flow of private investment and controls to compel producers to reduce prices as average costs fell. Competition was no longer sufficiently vigorous to generate the socially desirable outcomes. Compulsion by public authority was thus a *"sine qua non* of prosperity . . . and regular employment."[41]

Economists in the orthodox mainstream could share part of Tugwell's critique of the failure of much of the business community to behave in accordance with the textbook model of perfect competition, though they were not disposed to endorse his proposed remedy. They were inclined instead to hold serious reservations about the wisdom of Hoover's appeal for "no wage reductions." This ran counter to standard teaching on the way the labor market should adjust to a reduction in demand. In the orthodox reading, the attempt to sustain wages would simply swell the ranks of the unemployed and aggravate the difficulties of reaching a satisfactory equilibrium. Hoover was thus faulted for pursuing a policy that could only make the situation worse.

But the academic mainstream spoke most loudly and with the greatest unanimity in its opposition to the tariff legislation of 1930, which was supposedly – in the official view – to provide a bulwark for high wages in America. In the spring of 1930, more than a thousand economists and "teachers of economics," representing 179 colleges and universities from every state of the union (save New Mexico and Wyoming), petitioned in opposition to any measure that would produce a general upward revision in tariff rates. This statement, which was made public on May 4, 1930, urged the Congress to avoid such action and called for a presidential veto in the event Congress did not follow their advice. The case for freer trade was developed along familiar lines of neoclassical argument. Particular attention was directed to an inconsistency in American trade policy in the following language: "There are few more ironical spectacles than that of the American government as it seeks, on the one hand, to promote exports through the activity of the Bureau of Foreign and Domestic Commerce, while on the other hand, by increasing tariffs it makes exportation ever more difficult."[42] This was the first occasion during the depression, though it was not to be the last, on which groups of economists memorialized public officials on controversial points of economic policy.[43]

CHAPTER 5

Preliminary readings of the results of the stabilization strategy

The novel experiment in constructive industrial statesmanship had been set in motion in late 1929 and early 1930 with high hopes that it would cushion the most serious shocks to the economy and accelerate its return to normal levels of activity. As 1930 drew to a close, signs of recovery remained elusive. It could still be argued that the situation would have been much worse if Hoover had not acted as he did. Even so, the immediate prospect was far from bright. Hoover acknowledged as much when he wrote to the secretary of commerce on October 1, 1930, "it seems to me that any hope of industrial recovery between now and winter is rapidly vanishing and that we will need to face a very serious problem of unemployment."[1]

By autumn of 1930 it was pertinent to ask whether new departures in economic policy were called for and, if so, what form they should take. The attempt to find answers to these questions required, in the first instance, a review of the accomplishments and shortcomings of the original strategy in light of the preceding year's experience. Had the stabilization plan failed? Or had it simply not had enough time to work? Was more vigorous intervention in order? Or should the system's alleged natural powers of recuperation be allowed freer scope to assert themselves? Both inside and outside official circles, opinion diverged widely on the course of policy for the next phase of depression.

Evaluating the results of 1930

In his public statements during the first year of depression, Hoover had insisted that his strategy of intervention would make the course of this downturn unlike that of others in the nation's experience. Indeed, some things were genuinely different. A number of Hoover's admonitions had been well heeded. Most of the major employers had held the line on wage rates, and this was a welcome departure from the normal pattern. Similarly, capital spending in those sectors of the economy that Hoover had targeted for direct attention had been encouraging. Not all of the key spenders had delivered fully on the pledges they had given to the president in late 1929 and early 1930, but the general response to his appeals to maintain and expand such outlays was still gratifying. From the evidence available, it seemed certain that investment by the regulated industries and by public authorities was greater in 1930 than it had been in 1929. Though not all of the relevant numbers were in, this conclusion was not fanciful. On the contrary, it has been validated by subsequent measures of the value of construction spending in these sectors. (See Table 5.1.)

Table 5.1. *Value of new construction* (millions of dollars)

	1929	1930	Percentage change
I. Regulated industries in the private sector			
Railroads	592	606	+2.4
Electric light and power	350	377	+7.7
Telephone and telegraph	354	333	−5.9
Gas	185	181	−2.2
Totals for enumerated industries	1,481	1,497	+1.1
II. Public sector			
Federal ownership	155	209	+34.8
State and local ownership	2,331	2,649	+13.6
Total public sector	2,486	2,858	+15.0

Source: Historical Statistics of the United States, Part II, pp. 618–19, 622. It should be noted that federal grants in aid (primarily for highway construction) supported state construction spending by $80 million in 1929 and by $104 million in 1930.

These figures reflect changes in the value of construction at current prices. When these magnitudes are adjusted to reflect the decline in the prices of building materials in 1930, it appears that expansion in real construction spending was of the order of 7 percent in the enumerated regulated industries and approximately 20 percent in the public sector.[2]

This was the bright side of the tale, but there was another side as well. Though spending on public works had expanded more or less as planned, the increment in this category of spending was more than offset by reductions in capital outlays by small businesses and for residential construction. The stabilization model had presupposed that an acceleration of spending on public works, in combination with the pledges given by the executives of the regulated industries to sustain their investment programs, would give smaller firms the confidence they needed to carry on their spending at normal levels. Disappointingly, this expectation had not been fulfilled. Nor had housing markets responded to reductions in interest rates in the way that had been expected. This component of construction spending had shown signs of weakness well before the collapse in the stock market deranged the overall economy. New housing starts had peaked in 1926, a year when they accounted for nearly half of the nation's construction activity, and had declined thereafter. At the time, this phenomenon had been interpreted as a by-product of the diversion of funds into stock market speculation. But the bursting of the speculative bubble had done nothing to revitalize this important sector. On the contrary, outlays for residential construction in 1930 tumbled by nearly $1.6 billion from their 1929 levels (which were already more than one-third below the record established in 1926).[3]

The scorecard for round 1 of the stabilization strategy thus had both pluses and minuses. On the plus side of the ledger, the sectors that Hoover had attempted to influence at first hand had generally behaved well. But the expected spillover effects on other parts of the economy had not been forthcoming. Overall, total construction spending was off by more than $2 billion, a drop of nearly 20 percent from 1929.[4]

The effort to spur construction spending was not, of course, an end in itself. Its ultimate objective was to achieve full employment. On this score, the record was far from satisfactory. Information on the precise dimensions of the problem was cloudy at best. Accurate current data on trends in the labor force were simply not available. The Committee on Recent Economic Changes had lamented this shortcoming in its report in 1929 and the administration had sought to do something about it by gathering information on employment status in the census of April 1930. In official circles, this exercise was hailed as a courageous attempt to gather, for the first time, systematic and accurate information on the volume of unemployment and its incidence. In fact, however, this undertaking contributed more to confusion than to enlightenment.

Preliminary publication of census results in August 1930 indicated that, as of the inquiry date in April, approximately 2.5 million persons were "out of work, able to work, and looking for employment." If that number were accepted as a correct measure of the situation at that time, it would suggest that only about 5 percent of the labor force was then unemployed. But did these findings faithfully depict the reality? Hoover maintained in his State of the Union message in December 1930 that "the number of those wholly out of employment seeking for work was accurately determined by the census last April as about 2,500,000."[5] This way of putting the matter, though defensible on narrow technical grounds, was misleading. The ambiguity arose from the procedure used by the Census Bureau in classifying the unemployed. The jobless were divided into two categories. The first (schedule A) enumerated those who were not working, but able and willing to do so and also actively seeking employment. These definitions excluded many who were also jobless, but did not describe themselves as looking for work because they regarded themselves as on temporary "lay-off" and expected to return to their regular activities when economic conditions improved. Persons in this category were classified separately in schedule B. In its statements on unemployment in 1930, the Hoover administration referred only to the narrow definition of schedule A. Charles S. Persons, the official in charge of the preparation of the census tabulations, resigned in protest over the exclusion of the jobless in schedule B from the unemployment figures and charged the administration with suppressing information that would reveal the gravity of the problem.

Agreement on the facts remained hard to come by. Hoover tried to make some headway on this matter when he appointed an Advisory Committee on Employment Statistics in August 1930.[6] When the committee submitted its report in the following February, the Census Bureau had still not completed a comprehensive tabulation of the returns. On the basis of the data available, the committee's best judgment on the unemployment situation as of April, 1930 was that "the combined total of Classes A and B run from 3,000,000 to 3,350,000 depending on whether deductions are made from Class B of persons estimated to be employed on part time."[7] In an independent study completed in February 1931, Paul Douglas and Aaron Director of the University of Chicago estimated that the minimum number of unemployed at the time of the census in April 1930 was around 3.4 million – greater by more than one-third than the figure released from the White House.[8]

Quibbles about the precise magnitude of unemployment were to continue. So also did attempts to refine the concept of unemployment.[9] Even so, there was no mistaking the essential truth: unemployment was indeed a serious matter and the efforts to contain it had not worked as well as had been hoped.

Canvassing for further policy options

It was at least arguable that the deployment of the stabilization model had cushioned a part of the shock the economy experienced in 1930. By comparison with the contraction of 1921, the performance had not been too bad. Measured in current prices, the fall in GNP between 1929 and 1930 was about half that recorded between 1920 and 1921. Comparisons of the shrinkage in real GNP in these two time periods were less reassuring, though there was not a great deal to choose between them.[10] With considerable justification, Hoover could assert, as he did in October 1930, that the economy was still functioning at about

85 to 90 percent of normal levels. There was still, to be sure, considerable room for improvement. He reaffirmed his faith in the "spirit of
modern science" and the "genius of modern business" to identify the
causes of macroeconomic fluctuations and to bring them under control.[11]

In thinking about next steps, it seemed obvious to ask whether more
could not be done to stimulate spending and employment in those
sectors that had failed to sustain 1929 levels of activity in 1930. A prime
candidate for such attention was the housing industry. Even in the
early months of 1930, reports reaching Hoover indicated that new housing starts were far below those recorded in 1929 (which was already a
slow year for this industry). He was convinced that residential construction offered major opportunities for absorbing slack in the labor
market. The president set out his thoughts on this matter in March
1930 as follows: ". . . we can be sure that improvements in production
and distribution are going to release a very large amount of labor in the
next decade and that we must find employment for it in some new direction. It seems to me that one direction which is always economically and
socially sound is in home building, in which there is a large consumption of labor directly and indirectly through producers' and consumers'
goods. Increasing improvement in housing conditions is of the utmost
social importance."[12] The failure of residential construction to respond
to easier credit conditions in early 1930 was puzzling as well as disappointing. Hoover believed that much of this outcome could be attributed to inadequacies in arrangements for financing residential construction, which he held to be "the most backward segment of our whole
credit system." The heart of the problem, as he diagnosed it, was a
combination of restrictions on the amounts financial intermediaries
were prepared to advance on first mortgages (typically no more than
half of the value of the house) and the extraordinarily high rates of
interest attached to second mortgages. In short, financial intermediaries
had discriminated against potential homebuilders and had been more
disposed to hold bonds and securities, which were both more liquid and
less expensive in administrative time, than to provide mortgage finance.
To break part of this bottleneck, Hoover proposed that the Federal Reserve System consider making first mortgages eligible for rediscount at
the Federal Reserve Banks.[13] This amendment, he noted, had a further
point in its favor. In view of the substantial shrinkage in the volume of
commercial bills (the member bank assets with primary eligibility for
rediscount privileges), a revision that increased the access of banks to
"lender of last resort" facilities would strengthen the financial system.

Hoover's suggestions received a cool reception from the Federal Reserve authorities. The board's response, prepared by A. E. Goldenweiser

of its Division of Research and Statistics, pointed out that the Federal Reserve System had been created as "a system of commercial credit . . . to aid in the financing of current requirements of trade and industry. It is not adapted to making fixed capital advances, and was not intended to do so. It could not safely undertake such long-term credit operations as are necessarily involved in the construction of houses." In addition, Goldenweiser observed, there was no need to assist banks by amending the rules to make mortgage paper available for rediscount. "Our banking system at the present time has $7,500,000,000 of eligible paper, including Government securities, and it is not likely to have use for an amount approaching that total for a great many years to come. This means that, in so far as obtaining Federal Reserve Bank credit is concerned, the channels into the reserve banks are adequate for all present and prospective needs of the country." Moreover, he maintained that improving the terms on which new housing could be financed would offer little promise as a stimulant to the economy. In his opinion, the evidence was "conclusive that a great many of our urban areas at the present time are overbuilt, having more residential and office space than can be absorbed at the present time and at present prices." [14] He allowed that the backward state of financing for home construction, and the high interest costs which went with it, was a disincentive to this type of spending. A case could thus be made for institutional innovations (such as nationally chartered home mortgage banks) which might ultimately reduce the cost of financing homes. This matter, however, was not properly within the jurisdiction of the central bank.

But was it not then possible to devise new techniques to encourage private businesses to increase capital spending? Hoover was intrigued by a proposal for investment tax credits submitted by Paul Shoup, a West Coast railway executive and a personal friend. Shoup suggested that firms be authorized to reduce their corporate income tax obligations if their investment expenditures in 1931 came to one-third or more of their capital outlays in 1929. [15] The Treasury found this approach wanting on several grounds. Not only did it anticipate that there would be insuperable administrative difficulties in validating entitlements, it was further feared that revenue losses would be excessive. In the appraisal offered by Ogden L. Mills, undersecretary of the treasury, there was an even more "fundamental weakness" in the scheme: it would include expenditures that would be made in any event, though the purpose was "to encourage industry to make capital expenditures at this time which without some kind of inducement would be postponed." Mills suggested an alternative approach that would tie tax credits to the certification that the "proposed work would not have been undertaken except for the Government's offer." He recognized that such an arrangement would still have objectionable features: among them, inequities in the treatment of corporations which had already expanded their spending "with the general public in mind," as opposed to those which had earlier "hung back." [16]

If there was little enthusiasm within the governmental establishment for either of these unconventional schemes, could not the accepted tools for macroeconomic stimulus be applied more effectively? Pressure from outside in favor of still more federal spending on public works, for example, was increasing. Hoover insisted that this program was already being pursued as fast as it feasibly could be. Though it should be sustained, there were no big new opportunities for spending that would meet the criterion of long-term social usefulness. Agitation for a more expansive monetary policy, particularly one which would raise the general price level, was also building up. The central bankers, however, continued to insist that it was not within their power to lift prices to a desired level and keep them there. Moreover (as Hoover was advised by his appointee, Eugene Meyer, who became governor of the Federal Reserve Board in September 1930), the system was actively promoting conditions of monetary ease. Discount rates had been sharply reduced and open-market purchases of government securities between the autumn of 1929 and October 1930 had brought its holdings to as high a level as any formerly recorded. Meyer insisted that the commercial banks had abundant lending power, as evidenced "by the fact that these banks, in addition to meeting the requirements of their customers, have been purchasing large amounts of securities on investment account." (He estimated that banks in the leading cities had increased their holdings of securities by more than $1 billion during the past year and that the aggregate volume of securities held by banks had surpassed all previous records.) Altogether, the Federal Reserve was already conducting its affairs to encourage business recovery "in every possible way." [17] Though later analysts have called into question how "easy" monetary policy really was in 1930,[18] there can be no doubt that senior officials at the time genuinely believed this to be the case. By their lights, monetary policy had been conducted correctly and in the interests of stimulating spending.

While no fundamental change of course in fiscal or monetary policy seemed to be warranted, it was still clear that something further needed to be done to alleviate distress among those members of the community "in honest difficulty." Hoover insisted that no American should be allowed to go hungry or cold. At the same time, it ran counter to his conception of well-ordered society for the federal government to be a

distributor of handouts. Care for the needy was properly the responsibility of private organizations and of state and local officials. It was
nevertheless appropriate for the president to use the moral authority
of his office to arouse the conscience of the nation to the cause of aiding
those in need. Accordingly, he appointed Colonel Arthur Woods, formerly police commissioner of New York City, to head an organization
styled the President's Emergency Committee for Employment. This
group was to survey the requirements of the populace for relief and to
coordinate the work of private and public welfare organizations to ensure that essential needs were met. In addition, this committee was invited to encourage employers to develop programs for spreading employment by shortening the work week and to make recommendations on
ways new job opportunities might be created.

In 1930 the Hoover administration took one further step to increase
the number of jobs available to Americans. It involved, however, no
original thinking. Beginning in September, restrictions on immigration
to the United States were tightened. By the following May, Hoover
estimated that these measures would preserve some 175,000 jobs for
American workers over the course of a year.[19]

Appraisals from the economics profession

Hoover's reputation as a scientific manager of the economy who would
be guided by facts and by expert judgments had been tarnished a bit in
1930. His approval of the Smoot–Hawley Tariff Bill had been lamented
by most academic economists who regarded this legislation as a tawdry
concession to special interests. In the eyes of the academicians, the
growing suspicion that his administration had been less than straightforward in its presentation of data on the magnitude of unemployment
further diminished Hoover's stature. Nevertheless, the contours of controversy among the economists shifted little during the first year of the
depression. Those who had earlier been in the forefront of the discussion of "new era" stabilization strategies were inclined to give the administration the benefit of whatever doubting second thoughts they
might have entertained. Hoover, after all, had engaged himself far more
actively than had any of his predecessors in similar circumstances. Even
though his interventions had not been rewarded with the results expected, it was still premature to make final judgments on the success or
failure of the grand experiment in the macroeconomics of indirect
control. The original skeptics, on the other hand, were more than ever
convinced that their doubts about the efficacy of Hoover's form of interventionism were well grounded. Not all of the economists who had

been central participants in the earlier debates put on record their views on the conduct of policy during the first year of depression. Those who did departed little from the positions they had earlier taken.

Among the commentators most sympathetic to an activist presidential posture, the general tone remained sympathetically, if cautiously, supportive. Foster and Catchings, for example, did not speak to the details of Hoover's program, but observed that the persisting ills of the economy were the result of an attempt by the public to save too much and to spend too little. "That," they wrote in November 1930, "is what the people of the United States have been doing all this year. . . . [S]aved money is of no use *to the country as a whole* until it is invested." As they further noted, it was "useless to invest money in more mills, mines and machines than the country can use; and the country already has more than it can use without increased consumer spending."[20] It was thus the shortfall in consumption expenditure that accounted for the failure of much of the private business sector to follow the lead of governments and of the regulated industries by enlarging capital commitments. They returned to this theme three months later with a spirited indictment of the views expressed by leading bankers who had suggested that the pre-depression standard of living had been artificially high and was no longer sustainable. This position, Foster and Catchings maintained, was fallacious and simply compounded the nation's difficulties. As they put it: "[T]he way to go ahead is to plan to go ahead, and not to plan to go backward." Tolerating the proposition that further retrenchment in consumption standards was desirable would mean that still more productive capacity would lie idle. Most of this capacity, they observed, had been created "with the encouragement of the banks" and much of it was owned by them. And what would be the consequences for the banking system itself if excess savings meant that these resources were useless? "Shall we," they asked, "put thirty per cent of [the banking structure] out of business?"[21]

During this period, Wesley Mitchell retained his contacts, with the administration, if somewhat peripherally, as a member of the Research Committee on Social Trends, which Hoover had appointed in December 1929. (This study group was commissioned to produce a sequel to *Recent Economic Changes*; scheduled for delivery in 1932, its research report was intended to be the agenda-setting document for a second Hoover administration.) Mitchell's public comments on the first phase of depression were sparse and guarded. In his capacity as an expert student of business cycles, he preferred to concentrate attention on a fundamental question for empirical investigation: namely, what properties of this depression made its pattern different from other historic moments of business disturbance? That a contraction had occurred was not itself a matter requiring elaborate explanation. A recession at about the time it had happened was, he maintained, inherent in "the general rhythm of business." The puzzle concerned its depth and duration. As of April 1931 he held that the "catastrophic form" which the depression had taken was probably accounted for by the coincidence of a number of random shocks, including the necessary correction of the follies of stock market speculation, depression in agriculture, increased tariff barriers, political unrest, fear.[22] This account of matters seemed to imply that the convergence of a number of unfortunate events, a phenomenon that could not have been foreseen when the original stabilization strategy had been constructed, had swamped the administration's attempts to bolster the economy. But were the unusual features of this depression purely the by-product of a collection of random shocks? Or were the shocks themselves part of a more systematic pattern? For Tugwell, extended inquiry into these questions was redundant. His diagnosis of the structural ailments inherent in an uncoordinated market system provided a sufficient explanation both for the causation of the economic crisis and for the inability of the system to recover within the framework of the ground rules for policy laid down by Hoover. Others, however, began to look for deeper patterns. One of the pioneers in this type of inquiry was Josef Schumpeter, then a visitor from the University of Bonn. In his remarks to the American Economic Association's panel on the business depression at its meeting of December 1930, he proposed that the extraordinary depth of the slump might best be understood in terms of various "waves" in the flow of economic events. The world economic system, it appeared, was in the throes of a simultaneous downswing of the long wave of the Kondratieff cycle (with a typical duration of forty-five to sixty years) and of the shorter wave Juglar cycle (which seemed to recur every six to seven years). Moreover, in the second half of 1930, it had also been caught in the trough of a shorter, forty-month cycle.[23] He added that the depression, though it "would have been due anyhow," was further complicated by such matters as agrarian distress, international debt and reparations payments, and maladjustments in the international monetary system more generally.

As a discussant on Schumpeter's paper, Alvin Hansen spoke with general approval of this diagnosis. He maintained, however, that several other special factors had intensified the gravity of this depression. In Hansen's reading of events, Western Europe had largely completed the task of postwar reconstruction by 1928. Meanwhile, two major capital-absorbing sectors in the United States, the automobile and the residential construction industries, had slowed their rates of growth. It thus appeared that "after some years of relative prosperity the empty vessel of fixed capital in many industries both in Europe and the United States has been filled." The job of keeping the stream flowing was not likely to be a simple one though. With population growth rates apparently declining, much of the spur needed to stimulate a fresh round of capital spending was lacking.[24]

But Hansen was also persuaded that governmental intervention in the market's processes of price and wage-making had compounded the problems of recovery. At least for countries on the gold standard, "economic difficulties are intensified rather than minimized by the development of social control in other directions," he asserted in December 1930. "Rigid wage-rates, inflexible railroad rates, controlled trust and cartel prices make a pronounced fall in the general commodity price level a far more serious matter now than in the old days of all around laissez faire. The tension and strain . . . is increased in the measure that institutional arrangements and governmental regulations prevent or render difficult the readjustments without which a new equilibrium in the entire price system cannot be reached."[25] Hoover's interventions had thus made matters worse, not better.

Sumner Slichter turned attention to another aspect of Hoover's policies and found it wanting. In his judgment, the presuppositions underlying the official approach to "voluntary relief" – which had been widely touted as "the American way" – were fundamentally flawed. As Slichter saw matters in December 1930, the sums available for distribution from this campaign were too meager and too tardy. The findings of an official of the Association for Improving the Condition of the Poor, he noted, indicated that many of the men recently placed in emergency jobs (such as maintenance of public parks) had already been idle for six to nine months and that many of them had drained their resources to the point that their ability to pay for shelter was in question. Moreover, much of what was officially counted as "voluntary relief" had taken the form of shortening the work week in order to spread the number of jobs. This meant, in effect, that "the most generous contributions seem to come from the less well-to-do rather than the more wealthy." Employees who cut back their work week from six days to five, he pointed out, were sacrificing one-sixth of their income. "How many millionaires, or men receiving $5,000 or $10,000 a year," Slichter asked, "are contributing one-sixth of their incomes to unemployment relief?" Moreover, the expectation that state and local governments could deal effectively with hardship cases was erroneous. Cities such as Detroit (where an ambitious relief program had been mounted) were obliged to restrict eligibility to residents of at least a year. A person who had given his best effort to job search by traveling was thus left in the cold. This implied, in turn, that behavior in "the American way" was penalized. The country would not get to the root of the problem until a system of unemployment compensation – financed directly by employers – was instituted. Meanwhile, the real beneficiaries of the voluntary relief program were "the great industries of America. They are extracting a percentage of the meager pay of tens of thousands of their employees, obtaining myriads of contributions from churches, charitable organizations, the Salvation Army, city employees, commission merchants, hotels, coal dealers, and thousands of business and professional men in order to pay their labor overhead."[26]

The first phase of experience with Hoover-style depression fighting thus drew mixed reviews from economists. Not surprisingly, their responses diverged. There were, however, no startling departures from past form.

CHAPTER 6

The unraveling of the first official model in 1931

The year 1931 was to mark a turning point in the way the Hoover administration thought about the problems of the economy and about the forms of intervention it was prepared to use in addressing them. Even though there had been slippages and disappointments in the programs pursued in 1930, there were still some grounds for satisfaction. The cooperation of the big capital spenders, of the large employers, and of the monetary authorities had, on the whole, been gratifying. It thus appeared that the worst damage had been contained. On balance, there seemed to be no reason to depart substantially from the course of policy already charted. Accordingly, the president called again for a continuation in 1931 of the same efforts to accelerate capital outlays and to sustain wages. And he asked for still further appropriations for federal spending on public works projects that could be set in motion without delay. This implied that the Treasury would have to increase its borrowings to cover the deficit anticipated for fiscal year 1931. In his budget message to the Congress, Hoover observed that he did not regard this as a matter of great concern, though he believed it prudent to contain the magnitude of the deficit by suspending the modest tax concession that had been awarded in the preceding year.[1]

By the early spring of 1931, there were also some heartening signs that the worst of the crisis had passed. The Federal Reserve Board's index of industrial production registered some upward ticks and there were even some indications that confidence in the stock market was reviving. The impression that the economy was poised for improvement was further reinforced by studies on the course of past business cycles presented to the White House by the Department of Commerce. If earlier patterns were used as a guide, it appeared that the lower turning point of the cycle was within sight.[2]

All in all, it appeared to be sound to stick with the original game plan. And, in the view of the administration, there were more than adequate grounds for resisting suggestions that a more ambitious spending program should be undertaken. Matters seemed to be working themselves out, with the aid of the medicine in the dosages already prescribed. It was still important to push federal spending on public works during the first six months of the year. But, as Hoover assessed the situation, extraordinary spending beyond that point was "outside the emergency period, as we contemplate it."[3] There was yet another reason for the president's determination to stay on course. The elections of November 1930 had produced a significant shift in the balance of political power. The House of Representatives was now controlled by a Democratic majority, and the Senate, though nominally organized by the Republicans, was increasingly unresponsive to White House leadership. With proposals for "massive" appropriations for public works increasingly in circulation and with signs that congressional opinion was likely to be receptive to them, Hoover's determination to resist wasteful raids on the Treasury was stiffened.

Presuppositions and realities

Hoover's belief that recovery was likely to be on track in the spring of 1931 presumably rested on the assumption that the forces that had been called upon to cushion the first signs of downturn would remain in play in equal (if not greater) strength in 1931. In particular, the capital outlays of governments at all levels, as well as those of the railroads and utilities, were expected to be larger than they had been in 1930. Hoover did not make an on-the-record statement on this point. His views on the matter were instead transmitted through his friends at the American Engineering Council. When L. W. Wallace, executive secretary of this organization, met with him in early January, the president suggested that the council could "render a service by pointing out the fallacy" of efforts (such as those of the Emergency Committee for Federal Public Works) to promote a special bond issue of $1 billion to finance additional construction.[4] The council promptly obliged with a statement adopted at its annual meeting in Washington on January 16, copies of which were released to the press and dispatched to members of Congress. Special action along these lines was unnecessary, the statement argued, because the planned construction of states and municipalities in 1931 was expected to exceed the levels recorded in 1930 by nearly 60 percent. In addition, the construction programs "already announced" by utilities, railroads, and "other corporations" for 1931 suggested that the volume of this work would be nearly double the amount undertaken a year earlier. Additional expenditure on the part of the federal government, apart from the accelerated capital spending program already in place, was thus not needed. Nor for that matter would it be feasible. As the American Engineering Council put the issue: "Existing governmental organizations, although greatly expanded, are inadequate to spend efficiently an additional billion dollars within the next two years."[5]

In this vision of things to come, events were well under control and no supplementary federal expenditures were called for. But, even in the existing state of knowledge, were these expectations well founded? Surely, Hoover must have suspected that optimism was misplaced as far as one of the big capital spenders in the private sector – the railroads – was concerned. His first press conference of the new year was devoted exclusively to an off-the-record background analysis of the condition of this industry. With declines in traffic and in revenues, a number of lines had fallen into substantial difficulties to the point that default on their bonded indebtedness was in prospect. The moral of this tale, as he read it, was that the Interstate Commerce Commission should proceed vigorously to press for consolidations in order to enable the stronger lines to buttress the weaker ones. It was now urgent to press forward with the :ationalization of this industry, which (as he reminded the press) was the nation's largest single one, and to cut through the obstacles that had delayed needed reforms for more than a decade.[6]

How solidly grounded was the expectation that state and local governments could improve on their 1930 performance as capital spenders in 1931? The rosier prognostications developed within administration circles began from the assumption that a substantial backlog of worthwhile projects was available to this component of the public sector and that the limitations constraining the federal government's legitimate capacity to spend much further on public works did not apply to state and local authorities. The extent to which this backlog would be tapped was, in turn, held to depend primarily on the terms and availability of credit. No particular difficulty was anticipated on that score. The monetary authorities were thought likely to continue to be cooperative in their policies on interest rates. Even though the federal government would be making some claims on financial markets to finance its deficit for the fiscal year 1931, the magnitudes involved were not expected to affect adversely the climate in which state and municipal bonds could be floated. It was also hoped that a newly created organization, the Federal Employment Stabilization Board, could assist state and local governments in planning the next steps in their capital expenditures. In signing the legislation which created this board in February 1931, Hoover noted that it gave "tangible form" to the type of organizational work developed in the preceding fourteen months and that it gave reality to a ten-year-old dream.[7]

There was a fundamental flaw in these expectations, though, and Hoover appeared to be unmindful of it. The willingness of the subordinate units of government to cooperate with the president's program was not the relevant issue. What mattered most at this stage was their ability to do so – and it had been seriously compromised by the events of 1930. Just as federal tax receipts had shrunk with the downturn of the economy, so also had the revenues of state and municipal governments been diminished. Meanwhile, claims on their resources had been swollen by the need to provide relief funds to assist the most distressed of their citizens. Hoover had always insisted that the federal government should have no part in this activity. The full burden of public assistance to the needy thus fell entirely on the mayors and governors. The sums that they could make available for relief were far from impressively generous. Nor, for that matter, did they have any incentive to make them overly so if that meant that new claimants were attracted from outside. Nevertheless, this additional strain on their budgets reduced their capacity to finance job-creating construction and maintenance work from current revenues and also diminished their ability to float bonds for new capital spending.

Throughout most of 1931, senior officials in the Hoover administration appeared to have been largely unaware of these complications. They were clearly at odds with the assumptions on which the official model of countercyclical public spending had originally been built. Only later did the reports of the Federal Employment Stabilization Board begin to catch up with what was happening. One of its statistical compilations, prepared in October 1932, told the grim story. Construction spending by state, county, and city governments declined by roughly 20 percent in 1931 from the levels achieved in 1930. Meanwhile, construction spending by the railroads and public utilities had fallen by 28 percent. Even though things had not worked out as planned, the tone of this document suggested that the federal government was not at fault. Its concluding observation was as follows: "Had the states, counties and cities been able and willing to expand their construction programs in the same proportion as did the Federal government, the total of all construction work in the United States would have remained at the 1929 level during 1930, 1931 and 1932."[8]

In principle, there was a way to get around this problem. Even if one accepted Hoover's view that the central government was approaching a limit on new construction projects on which it could usefully and appropriately spend, it still might be able to assist capital spending elsewhere in the public sector. If states and municipalities were long on projects, but short on funds, could not the federal government, with its superior borrowing ability, act as a financial intermediary? This was the question posed by a number of congressional supporters of emergency federal borrowing for public works. But Hoover opposed these suggestions. Even if he had been gifted with an insight into the difficulties that were to follow, it is doubtful that he would have endorsed this approach in early 1931. The federal government distinctly should not assume responsibilities that properly belonged elsewhere. This was a persistent theme in his public utterances. In private conversation, he could be even more candid. In remarks in an off-the-record interview with columnist Raymond Clapper in March 1931, for example, he deplored "the decadence of state and local government," adding that "our one hope is in preserving the Federal government as a sound, upright thing as an example to the country." Should the federal government fail in this task, "everything is gone."[9] Similarly, Hoover remained unmovable in his principled opposition to federal "encroachment" on what he took to be the proper domain of private business. On this basis, he vetoed a Senate resolution calling for the conversion of government-owned facilities at Muscle Shoals, Alabama (which had been put in place for the manufacture of explosives in World War I) into what would later become the Tennessee Valley Authority. This proposal was objectionable primarily because it would place the federal government in direct competition with private citizens in the production of power and fertilizers. This type of case, Hoover insisted, could be readily distinguished from others, such as the Colorado River Dam project, in which the production of electric power was a secondary by-product of the performance of other functions that only federal authority could discharge on interstate waterways, most notably flood control and reclamation. The use of federal funds for the development of the economic potential of the Tennessee Valley was not, however, a legitimate form of public works spending.[10]

Fiscal stimulus without design in 1931

One of the central tenets of Hoover's philosophy of the proper relationship between the central government and the citizenry was that the funds of the U.S. Treasury should never be used for handouts. Such a course would invite disaster. Not only would it tend to erode individual self-reliance, it would also pollute the electoral process. This posture, Hoover consistently maintained, was not hardhearted. Those in need should be assisted by private charities and by state and local governments which, in any event, were better equipped to appraise the merits of their claims.

It is doubtful that Hoover fully comprehended the degree of hardship generated in the first years of the depression. He had worked valiantly to mobilize private charities to relieve the distress of the unemployed and this effort, in combination with the contribution of those units of government closest to the people, seemed to be doing the job that was needed. Walter S. Gifford, chairman of the American Telephone and Telegraph Corporation, who took over the directorship of the President's Organization on Unemployment Relief in mid-1931, summed up the official view as follows: "Widespread acceptance of responsibility, community by community, county by county, and State by State, has not only worked for providing relief funds but likewise for their discriminating and effective expenditure." And he added that federal appropriations for this purpose might well mean that "the unemployed who are in need would be worse off instead of better off." This argument rested on the judgment that any commitment of federal monies for relief would be more than offset by reductions in subscriptions to private charities and by reduced appropriations by state and local governments.[11]

Despite growing distress, direct transfer payments by the federal government remained objectionable in principle, not just to Hoover and his associates, but also to a substantial bloc of public opinion. There was, however, a way to transfer federal monies into pockets of individual citizens which could be cloaked with greater legitimacy. In 1925 the Congress, overriding a veto by President Coolidge, had created a scheme for rewarding veterans of World War I. Strictly speaking, this arrangement was constructed as an endowment insurance policy scheduled to mature in 1945. To make advance provision for the ultimate payout, the Treasury had set aside sums averaging about $112 million per year in a trust fund held in government securities. The target was to accumulate a reserve that, with accumulated interest, would amount to about $3.4 billion in 1945. (This sum was referred to as the "face value" of certificates to which ex-servicemen were entitled.) With an arrangement of this sort already in place, it readily occurred to some that the federal government might usefully contribute to the relief of distress by enabling veterans to borrow against funds to which their legal claim had already been established. The Veterans' Bonus Bill of 1931 was designed precisely for that purpose. Its terms specified that some 3.5 million ex-servicemen would be permitted to borrow immediately up to 50 percent of the 1945 face value of their entitlements. This invited a major claim on the resources of the Treasury in 1931. Even though more than $700 million had already been accumulated in the reserve account, still more would have to be found. In addition, government securities held in the trust fund would have to be liquidated to cover the potential claims.

Although Hoover opposed this bill, Congress, including some members who otherwise shared Hoover's views on the unacceptability of federal handouts, voted to override his veto. This use of federal monies, it could be argued, was respectable. While it was not a reward for current services, it was at least a recognition of service in the past. In addition, it was technically not a grant, but a loan. Further, much of the required finance was presumably already in hand. Why then, at a time when the economy was acutely in need of additional spending, should not these funds be put to work? The lobbying of veterans groups was more potent than economic arguments in mobilizing the necessary congressional majorities to enact the Bonus Bill. It was still convenient, however, to have arguments to rationalize this type of transfer payment as something other than the "breach of fundamental principle" which Hoover claimed it to be.

The result of this congressional action was an injection of approximately $1.2 billion into the potential expenditure stream during the calendar year 1931. This amounted to about 3 percent of aggregate personal income for the year. In addition, as subsequent scholarship has pointed out, it meant that the net impact of fiscal policy was stimulative. In only two years during the decade of the 1930s was this significantly the case: in 1931 (thanks to the bonus payout) and in 1936 (when the second half of the veterans' bonus was distributed, despite President Roosevelt's veto of this legislation).[12] At the time, Hoover and his associates disputed claims that the bonus distribution might provide the treatment the economy needed. When Senator Arthur Vandenberg (Republican of Michigan) had suggested that this might be the case in late 1930, Secretary of the Treasury Mellon replied: "[I]t is clear that the retirement of the outstanding certificates would result in an addition of a very large sum to the volume of funds currently available for commodity purchases, and would probably have the direct effect of stimulating buying and thus moving goods into consumption. This would unquestionably have a stimulating effect on business, but it would be temporary stimulation of an artificial character and could hardly be expected to have such lasting qualities as would bring about a permanent recovery."[13] But Mellon further argued that the borrowing required to finance this operation (including the necessity to find buyers for government bonds which had been acquired by the trust fund) would divert finance from capital markets that could be better used to support business expansion. Hoover was even more emphatic in rejecting the suggestion that the bonus payout would stimulate business. In the words of his veto message: "We can not further the restoration of prosperity by borrowing from some of our people, pledging the credit of all of the people, to loan to some of our people who are not in need of the money."[14] This assertion presumably reflected his conviction that the bulk of the veteran population was not suffering hardship and that, to the extent that this measure was thought of as a disguised form of relief, it was highly inefficient. Relief funds should be allocated on the basis of need, not on the basis of some prior status of national service. According to estimates supplied to him by the administrator of Veterans Affairs, only 6 percent of the veteran population was on relief in early 1931.[15] As the administration later came to recognize, this calculation understated the difficulties of this segment of society. Far more veterans exercised the loan privileges available to them than the White House had anticipated. A follow-up survey reporting on conditions as of September 1931 estimated that about 640,000 veterans were unemployed. On the basis of the most commonly cited figures for the size of the surviving population of World War I veterans, this would suggest that unemployment in this group was in excess of 18 percent.[16]

The macroeconomic numbers suggest that this departure in fiscal policy, forced though it was on an administration unsympathetic to it, still should have had an expansionary effect on total demand. But this congressional action in overriding a presidential veto had another side effect. Henceforth, Hoover was all the more determined to resist raids on the Treasury by "irresponsible" congressional spenders.

Symptoms of disarray in the banking system

Men of the new era had long held that the weaker elements in the nation's banking system were vulnerable and that some consolidation and reorganization was overdue. In the normal course of events, it was expected that the frail links in the system – primarily the small state-chartered banks in rural areas – would be thinned out and that this process was not all bad. It would, of course, be desirable if it could be accomplished in a manner that protected depositors. The preferred mechanism was the merger of smaller banks with stronger institutions possessing the advantages of greater diversification in their assets and in their deposit base. But structural reform along these lines was not a matter to be undertaken without thorough deliberation. The American tradition of unit banking placed a high value on decentralized financial institutions that would be responsive to the needs of local communities.

The course of events in 1930 had heightened the place of this issue on the national agenda. Even so, the year 1931 began without a high sense of urgency about this problem. To be sure, the casualty rate among banks in 1930 was slightly more than double what it had been in

1929.[17] But the incidence of failures was concentrated in the areas where attrition was expected: among small banks operating under state charters.[18] This was regrettable, but, after all, no government could reasonably be expected to protect people from their own mistakes.

In the context of early 1931, the more pressing worry seemed instead to be the performance of banks as lenders. Keeping the flow of credit going was regarded as vital to business recovery. Despite Hoover's appeals to bankers to display courage and to transmit a sense of optimism to their customers, the lending activity of commercial banks in 1930 had declined.[19] This was a reflection of the shrinkage of business demand for credit in a period of declining economic activity. But there was also a suspicion that banks had made the terms on which they were prepared to lend unnecessarily restrictive. Irving Fisher drew Hoover's attention to this possibility in May 1931 when he reported that most banks throughout the country had maintained a traditional lending rate (6 percent in most states) despite the actions of the Federal Reserve in lowering discount rates.[20] Though the central bank had done its part in attempting to generate lower interest rates, the commercial banks had not reciprocated. In Fisher's opinion, more direct action was called for. He proposed that the president ask the central bankers to send telegrams to all banks in the country "urging them to help end this depression promptly by lowering their interest rates on customers' loans." Governors Meyer of the Federal Reserve Board and Harrison of the New York District Bank, he noted, agreed with his position "but seemed to think the average banker would not budge." But, as Fisher observed to Hoover, "neither of them . . . has your experience in securing independent voluntary cooperation from thousands or millions of people."[21]

In the climate of 1931, the perceptions of a monetary theorist about behavior required for the common good and those of individual bankers were unlikely to coincide. Not unnaturally, the latter were preoccupied with the promotion of their own interests – and indeed in their very survival. From their perspective, the dominant fact of the situation was the drying up of demand for loans from creditworthy borrowers. This was the primary explanation for expansion in the volume of excess reserves (a phenomenon the Federal Reserve authorities were inclined to interpret as evidence that monetary conditions were easy and that no additional effort on their part was needed to augment the lending capacity of banks). In the minds of bankers, another matter was taking on increased significance. Even though the number of bank failures had not reached crisis proportions by early 1931, enough evidence had already accumulated to make it prudent for even the strongest banks to take precautions against sudden claims by their depositors by increasing their cash reserves. These circumstances generated yet another departure from standard banking practice. In face of declining opportunities to place commercial loans in normal volume, banks naturally looked elsewhere for earning assets and chose to acquire fixed-interest obligations of governments and major corporations. Such a shift in the composition of their assets, well underway in 1930, was to continue in 1931 when the commercial banks reduced their commercial loans, expanded their investments in government and corporate securities, and increased their holdings of cash.[22]

A fragility was inherent in this pattern. Hoover – though he had frequently differed with the central bankers on the details of their conduct of monetary policy – had, up to this point, consistently maintained that the institution of the Federal Reserve System was a bulwark against recurrence of panic conditions that had occurred at intervals in pre-1913 American economic history. Its resources presumably ensured that any well-managed member bank could weather temporary difficulties by tapping the Federal Reserve's "lender of last resort" facilities. Even in August 1931, Hoover had entertained the idea that weaker banks might best be defended by compelling all nonmembers engaged in interstate commerce to join the Federal Reserve System.[23]

Though most of the dimensions of the crisis that was shortly to unfold were unforeseen, there was by late summer of 1931 some basis for wondering whether or not the safety net of the Federal Reserve's discount window was adequate even to defend banks belonging to the system. According to the original architecture of the Federal Reserve System, commercial bills were the primary assets eligible for rediscount at the Federal Reserve Banks. At times, concern had earlier been expressed about the adequacy of the volume of commercial paper to provide this defense. This had been the case, it will be recalled, in 1927 and 1928 when businesses had reduced their claims on banks for short-term accommodation and had increasingly turned to the use of the retained earnings and to the flotation of equity issues and bonds to finance their operations. The banks, in turn, had responded to this situation by increasing their willingness to lend to brokers. The yields were certainly attractive and, because these loans were presumably redeemable on call, the liquidity position of banks – or at least it had so been argued – was secure. Hoover had deplored this activity at the time, arguing that it contributed to dangerous speculative activity and that it was likely to be a source of future instability. But he had also been concerned about its consequences for the security of banks: brokers' loans, unlike commercial paper, were not eligible for rediscount at the Federal Reserve.

By 1931 member banks again found themselves in a situation in which the volume of discountable commercial paper had shrunk. But corporate bonds they had acquired to bolster their earnings were no more discountable at the Federal Reserve window than brokers' loans had been in an earlier period. Thus, a bank needing reinforcement to its liquidity position would be obliged to sell part of its portfolio. The central bank, however, would not be a party to this transaction, nor would the effective rate of discount be predictable before the fact. Banks with commercial paper to present to the Federal Reserve had the advantage of knowing the costs they would have to absorb. A seller of bonds did not. The effective rate of discount to which he was exposed would be determined by the forces of supply and demand. Circumstances in which banks (along with other bondholders) attempted to dispose of any substantial quantity of their holdings could be expected to depress bond prices. In consequence, all holders of bonds, whether sellers or not, would experience erosion of the capital values of their portfolios.

The possibility that this property of the asset mix of banks might present a formidable problem was only dimly perceived in mid-1931. By late August, however, Hoover at least had some inkling of the issue. In correspondence with Secretary of the Treasury Mellon, he advanced an arresting suggestion. Should not the patterns of corporate finance developed in the boom years now be reversed? In the late 1920s, many industries had organized their borrowing by issuing bonds rather than by turning to banks. Would it not be useful, Hoover asked, "if such concerns would now buy in their bonds" and negotiate commercial credits from the banks? This arrangement, he observed, "would greatly assist the bond market and it would make our currency very much more flexible by increasing the available commercial paper."[24] Though nothing was to come of this idea, the mere fact that it was mooted suggests that some doubts had surfaced about how well the banking system could cope in the event that interest rates rose and bond prices sagged still further.

Storm clouds from abroad

By early 1931 it was abundantly clear to anyone who read the numbers that something was severely amiss in the international system of trade and finance. Certainly the fortunes of the United States in world trade had worsened. Measured in terms of dollar values, both U.S. exports and imports were in the process of falling to less than half of the levels that had been recorded in 1929. Though the burden of shrinking foreign markets was widely distributed, it fell with particular weight on American farmers. Wheat producers, for example (who, as recently as 1926, had exported more than a quarter of their total production) found foreign buyers for only about one-ninth of a larger aggregate output in 1931, despite a sharp drop in wheat prices. Meanwhile the sales of exporters of finished manufactured goods in 1931 were only 40 percent of what they had been in 1929.

What was responsible for this distressing turn of events? An explanation favored by Hoover's critics was that the Smoot–Hawley Tariff Act of 1930 had severely compromised the ability of foreigners to earn dollars to buy American goods. Hoover had no patience with this argument. He continued to maintain – as he had from his earliest pronouncements on tariff policy – that foreigners stood to gain from American protective measures which sustained U.S. incomes at higher levels than otherwise would have been possible. Findings reported to him by the Department of Commerce in April 1931 indicated that U.S. imports had fallen proportionately less than had those of other countries, a result that could be read as evidence that American policy had been more successful in sustaining demand (in part, presumably, because of a strengthened tariff) than had been the case in other countries.[25]

But the ability of foreigners to buy American goods was influenced, of course, by more than the amount of foreign exchange they were permitted to earn through the sale of their products in the U.S. market. In the 1920s, much of the flow of dollars to the rest of the world had been fed by American lending abroad and, to a lesser extent, by the spending of tourists. The essay on international economic developments prepared by James Harvey Rogers for inclusion in the study on *Recent Economic Changes* had underscored particularly the importance of American capital exports to the international clearing process. He had concluded in 1929 that U.S. capital outflow was the single most significant factor permitting the United States to run a favorable balance in its merchandise trading accounts.[26]

When U.S. foreign lending and tourist spending fell to a trickle, as happened shortly after the crash of the stock market in late 1929, something had to give. Foreigners could no longer sustain purchases of U.S. goods, nor could they readily service their debts to the United States. Retaliatory tariff walls were rapidly constructed, some of them put in place in anticipation of the Smoot–Hawley Tariff Act, which had been debated in Congress for more than a year before its enactment. For a time some semblance of "business as usual" could be maintained with respect to the servicing of debts, at least for countries with sufficient gold reserves at hand. The resulting gold inflow into the United States,

given this state of affairs, might have been read as a signal of fundamental strain in the international financial system. Hoover refused to
see it that way. In his view the difficulty lay with foreign governments
whose failure to manage their budgets properly and to instill confidence in their own people had generated capital flight to a safer haven
on American shores.

The festering sores of the international financial system came to a
head in the spring of 1931. Signs of acute trouble began in March with
the collapse of the leading bank in Austria (the Kreditanstalt) and the
infection spread quickly to Germany. In June the director of the Reichs-
bank in Berlin announced that German reparations payments could no
longer be met on schedule. The only way in which default could be
averted was if another round of international credits could be arranged.
Hoover was adamantly opposed to committing any resources of the
U.S. government to such a bailout and was only slightly less unsympathetic to countenancing further extensions of credit by private American financiers. His position at this time was of a piece with the skepticism he had expressed during his years at the Commerce Department
about foreign lending for "nonreproductive" purposes. Subsequent experience had only confirmed his earlier convictions. American savings,
in his view of the way the world should work, should be allocated to
supporting capital spending at home, not dissipated in high risk and
unproductive ventures abroad. His secretary of state, Henry Stimson,
took a different stance. If Germany were allowed to default on its reparations payments, it was predictable, he insisted, that Britain and
France would soon follow suit on the servicing of war debts to the
United States.

Hoover dismissed outright the recommendation of the State Department that the United States participate in a financial salvaging of
Germany and Austria. He was, however, prepared to make what he regarded as a major concession in order to ease the strains on the international monetary system. In June 1931 he proposed a moratorium on
the war debt payments of Allied governments to the United States, subject to the condition that other governments would reciprocate by waiv-
ing temporarily their claims to reparations from Germany. His initiative in this matter was widely applauded, both at home and abroad.
The terms of the proposal, it should be noted, were consistent with
principles to which he had long subscribed: (1) that international debt
servicing should be adjusted to capacities to pay and (2) that there
should be no compromise in the doctrine that the contractual obligations of debtor countries should ultimately be honored. There was to

be no mistaking a moratorium for a write-off. The obligation would remain: only the timing of payments would be adjusted.

In Hoover's eyes, the moratorium was an act of extraordinary magnanimity on the part of the United States. Clearly, the decision to forgo receipts from debtor governments (which had been counted on to finance a substantial portion of the interest payments and statutory debt retirements to which the Treasury was committed) compounded his problems in the management of the federal budget. But, he maintained, some compensating gains to American interests would flow from this action. As he put it in a letter to Senator Arthur Capper (Republican of Kansas):

[A] considerable part of the price difficulties of Kansas wheat farmers is due to the present paralysis of the export market arising from the economic crisis in Central Europe which naturally affects not only them but all countries importing our wheat. The major problem in this connection has been solved by the aid given to Germany in postponement of reparations and to other governments in postponement of debts and I am confident that we will bring about a solution to the remaining difficulties. I know of no greater immediate service to the Kansas farmer and to unemployment generally than the reestablishment of normal economic life in that quarter.[27]

With a few adjustments, Hoover apparently believed that the essential fabric of the international monetary system, including the commitment of the major trading countries to the gold standard, could be preserved. The malaise of the international monetary system, however, was more deep-seated, though few Americans at the time perceived this to be the case. One of the exceptions was James Harvey Rogers of Yale, who argued that the gold standard system was not likely to be sustainable – at least not without imposing intolerable and unnecessary strains on deficit countries or without a fundamental change in American policies on tariffs and foreign lending. Countries could not be expected to participate if they lacked adequate gold reserves and were restricted in their opportunities to augment them. In a world in which two countries, the United States and France, seemed bent on acquiring the bulk of the world's monetary gold, the rules of the game would soon no longer be playable. Rogers regarded the gold standard as "one of the most illuminating anomalies of our so-called civilization" and welcomed its demise.[28]

Rogers's analysis of the contradictions inherent in existing international monetary arrangements (completed in August 1931) was soon to be seen as prophetic. A month later the British government announced that it was suspending gold convertibility and soon thereafter most European governments (apart from France) reached the same decision. Meanwhile, foreign holders of dollars, expecting that the departure of the United States from the gold standard was imminent, hastened to convert their holdings into gold. In orthodox fashion the Federal Reserve responded to this drain on U.S. gold reserves by increasing its discount rates. This was to give an entirely different complexion to the problems of managing domestic economic policy in the United States.

The collapse of official model I

The plan developed in the 1920s for combatting depression had rested on three types of measures to sustain aggregate spending: increased construction outlays by governments, low interest rates which would make borrowing for capital spending attractive to business and to home builders, and high wages which would assure adequacy in consumer purchasing power. In 1931 nothing had gone according to plan. All of the main building blocks of the grand experiment in macroeconomic stabilization crumbled.

By the autumn of the year, it was apparent that presidential exhortation to hold the line on wage rates would no longer receive a respectful hearing. Up to that point, many of the larger employers had continued this practice, even though most smaller firms had been obliged to abandon it. This position, however, was no longer tenable. Led by the steel industry, major corporations shaved their wage scales. Some official face could be saved with the argument that cuts in money wages did not necessarily mean reductions in real wages in view of the drop in prices of consumer goods. This assertion was undoubtedly correct. At the same time, money wage cutting did nothing to increase consumer purchasing power.

The expectation that a regime of low interest rates could be maintained – which would, in turn, provide a climate favorable to capital spending – was also battered by events. The Federal Reserve's commitment to protect the gold reserves had thrown this component of the strategy off course. Changes in the discount rates of the central bank did not necessarily get translated into easier conditions of credit to borrowers when discount rates were lowered. It was, however, predictable that increased discount rates would tighten lending conditions. This could be expected to happen in the best of circumstances. But when asset portfolios of banks were highly sensitive to changes in interest rates, as was the case in 1931, it was all the more certain. Any upward movement in interest rates depressed the value of their bondholdings.

Even more seriously damaged were the original premises of the official model on the utility of countercyclical capital spending, particularly for public works, in stemming major contractions in economic activity. The events of 1931 had demonstrated that the leverage of the federal government over the decisions on construction spending by state and local authorities and by the major industries in the private sector was no longer effective. Could not then the federal government do more to take up the slack by expanding its own spending still further? This course of action was increasingly urged on Hoover by voices from outside the administration and both the clamor and the proposed spending numbers had escalated. Early in 1931 the Emergency Committee for Federal Public Works, the body whose views Hoover had persuaded the American Engineering Council to reject, had urged a special bond issue of $1 billion for this purpose. By September Congressman W. N. White was calling for emergency federal spending of $8.5 billion, the *Engineering News Record* for $7 billion, William Randolph Hearst for $5 billion.[29]

These pleas were resisted with arguments that were stated most forcefully in the report of a committee of the President's Organization on Unemployment Relief which was released to the press in December 1931. A year earlier a similar committee had recommended an extension of federal spending on public works. This position was now emphatically reversed. Some of the reasons were familiar: the list of remaining federal projects that would meet the test of social utility was limited; the time lags involved in planning new worthwhile undertakings meant that they could make no effective contribution to the immediate unemployment situation; federal grants or loans to states and municipalities (even where demonstrably worthwhile projects were available) were "unsound in principle" and "would necessarily weaken the sense of responsibility of the municipalities and states to provide for their own local needs and welfare, and would postpone, if not prevent, the adoption of the localities of wise, long-term construction plans."[30] But this document went well beyond these arguments when it rejected the very idea that such an expenditure of funds "would spread through the channels of trade, stimulating many lines of industry and transportation and start business back on the road to recovery." The notion of a spending multiplier, after all, had been a central theme of the work of the President's Conference on Unemployment in the 1920s and of the strategies propounded by Foster and Catchings with which

Hoover had earlier been identified. Now it was claimed that a large public works construction program "would do little to aid even indirectly" many of the nation's most important industries. The construction industry – and, to a lesser extent, the railroads – might enjoy some benefits, but "unless public expenditures were very large indeed they would not lift the volume of work for even the construction industry back to the levels of recent normal years." [31]

Not only was public works spending now alleged to be ineffective, it was further maintained that it would be harmful to recovery. Bond issues to finance such undertakings could only be floated at premium interest rates, a consequence that would be a "handicap, and probably a serious one, to business recovery." In short, the federal government should not "crowd out" businesses – and state and local governments as well – from financial markets. But the case against borrowing for public construction did not end there. Major issues of government bonds at increasingly high yields "would cause serious declines in the market values of the present outstanding low-yield issues, and thus result in severe losses to holders of such securities. It may well be that one result would be a considerable number of additional bank failures." [32]

Thus was the death knell sounded to one of the major ingredients of macroeconomic thinking of the new era. What was being rejected was not simply the view of advocates of extraordinary spending in 1931, but the views as well of those who had earlier seen public works as a stimulant to economic activity in periods of slump. The designers of the original model of macroeconomic stabilization had not, to be sure, anticipated a depression of the magnitude that was now being experienced. Nor had they expected the construction spending of state and local governments to fall away as it had in 1931. Accordingly, their strategy was silent on the course to pursue if these unthought-of occurrences were to become a reality. The doctrinal statement of the committee reporting to the President's Organization on Unemployment Relief in December 1931, amounted, however, to saying that federal borrowing for public works in these circumstances was mischievous. This was a long distance removed from the teachings of Mallery or Foster and Catchings and from positions which Hoover himself had taken not too many months before.

Realignments on the outside

In 1931 the model that was supposed to control the flow of economic events had instead been swamped by them. But Hoover's difficulties did not end there. Just as the theory of economic policy that had in-

formed his actions had disintegrated, so also did much of his partnership with the business community. In increasing numbers, the practical
men with whom he had been closely associated during the Commerce
Department years and during the first phase of his presidency parted
company with him.

The most widely publicized defection was initiated by Gerard Swope,
president of the General Electric Company and a former official of the
War Industries Board.[33] The "Swope Plan," which was set out in an
address to the National Electrical Manufacturers Association in New
York on September 16, 1931, called for a program to coordinate production and consumption by requiring all industrial or commercial firms
with fifty or more employees and engaging in interstate commerce to
join trade associations. These associations, in turn, would be empowered
to gather and distribute information on business practices and conditions and – not least – to promote stabilization of prices. Much of
this work was already being done by existing trade associations, but,
Swope asserted, "a great deal more valuable work of this character is
possible." The objective was to create conditions that could genuinely
sustain high wages and regularize employment. Industrial groupings,
he argued, should be given a freer hand to produce the necessary coordination, subject to the supervision of a federal regulatory agency.
In this scheme of things, government had another function to perform: it should require firms to adopt practices recommended by trade
associations.[34]

There was plenty of resonance from themes of the 1920s in this proposal, such as the social importance of pooled knowledge, of business
responsibility for high wages and stable employment. When first set
out, these arguments had been used as statements of conditions for
sustaining prosperity and improving efficiency. They were not being
adapted to an environment of depression. Hoover had been sympathetic
to this body of doctrine in its first incarnation, but he rejected its second.
As a courtesy, Swope had sent an advance copy of his text to the president. Hoover's reaction was immediate and unambiguous. In an office
memorandum dictated on September 17, he characterized the proposal
as follows:

This plan provides for the consolidation of all industries into trade associations,
which are legalized by the government and authorized to "stabilize prices."
There is no stabilization of prices without price-fixing, and this feature at once
becomes the organization of gigantic trusts such as have never been dreamed
of in the world. This is the creation of a series of complete monopolies over
the American people. It means the repeal of the entire Sherman and Clayton
Acts, and all other restrictions on combinations and monopoly. In fact, if such

a thing were ever done, it means the decay of American industry from the day this scheme is born, because one cannot stabilize prices without protecting obsolete plants and inferior managements. It is the most gigantic proposal of monopoly ever made in American history.[35]

To prepare the defenses against this monstrosity, Hoover immediately requested the solicitor general to render a technical opinion of this scheme, noting that to his "amateur legal mind" the Swope Plan was "thoroughly unconstitutional." He expected, however, that a large organization would be created to support it and that he would "probably have to meet it in Congress."[36]

A campaign to win converts to this doctrine was indeed not long in forming and it had the energetic support of Henry I. Harriman, a Boston public utility executive who had been newly elected as president of the U.S. Chamber of Commerce. Harriman won the endorsement of the chamber for this position at its convention in December 1931. And he proclaimed it as well from a platform provided by the American Economic Association at its annual meeting. The faith of economists that overproduction could be but a temporary condition, he maintained, was a relic of the nineteenth century when the ever-increasing growth of population meant that demand would shortly catch up with supply. That long-term stabilizer was no longer effective. It was now essential to use other techniques to ensure a proper balance between production and consumption. Producers should be enabled to estimate probable demand and to share the production needed to satisfy it among themselves "on an equitable basis, rather than to continue the present harsh and unremunerative competitive system." Business had to be made profitable to permit it to pay high wages and to finance unemployment benefits. In short: "Cut-throat competition must cease, dividends and interest must be paid, and to do this production must be balanced with consumption."[37] If the right balance were to be struck, the antitrust laws would have to be amended to permit industrial groups to coordinate their activities. But this alone might not be enough. Harriman supported the creation of a "national economic council" charged to study and report on economic trends in the country at large. Such a body, however, should be appointed by and financed by the business community.

Sympathy for more direct forms of planning at the macroeconomic level was shared by others who advanced proposals for the creation of an "industrial general staff" or a "peace industries board." The ranks divided over who should control the planning apparatus. To business leaders, the answer was clear: such bodies should be exclusively within their jurisdiction. To others, a different answer was no less so: depression had demonstrated the incompetence of business to manage its affairs in the public interest and public control was imperative. Tugwell had long since reached that conclusion, but he could reassert it in the context of late 1931. "It would never be sufficient," he insisted, "to plan production for an estimated demand if that demand were likely to fail through lack of purchasing power." A much more thorough system of social control, involving controls over profit margins and investment decisions as well as prices, would be needed to achieve the desired balance between production and consumption. Traditional incentives – "hope of money-making and fear of money loss" – would have to be displaced and a "kind of civil-service loyalty and fervor will need to grow gradually into acceptance." [38]

J. M. Clark of Columbia University, who only two years earlier had complimented Hoover on his handling of the first phase of the depression, also recommended new mechanisms for long-range planning and agreed that they should not be entrusted to business groups. Organizations controlled by businessmen could be counted on to restrict output. As Clark and his associates saw matters: "The true objective of planning is not stabilization at any static level, but regularized growth. It is the full utilization of our powers of production, which are continually growing, in order that our consumption may grow correspondingly. To this end the purchasing power of the masses must be maintained and must expand." To accomplish these objectives, a national economic board of seven to nine members should be created. Members should be appointed by the president (with the advice and consent of the Senate) for terms of five to seven years and they should be "men of the highest caliber [capable of] acting in the interest of the whole country and not representing any particular economic interests." Once constituted, the board should conduct comprehensive surveys of the state of the economy and, though it would not have either executive or legislative authority on its own, it should "have the general power to recommend any legislation or any national policy which may contribute to the general end of improving our economic system." [39]

None of these messages could have brought cheer to the White House. For that matter, very little that happened in 1931 did. Despite all the clouds, there was little sign of any silver linings. In a frantic search for good news, the White House apparently believed that it had found some in data prepared by the Office of the Surgeon General. On the basis of information supplied by seven states, the infant mortality rate, which was described as "a rather sensitive index of health conditions," appeared to be lower than it had been in 1928. This finding was cited as evidence that the population had been adequately protected against severe suffering, despite the disappointing performance of the economy.[40] No account was taken of the fact that birthrates had also fallen during these years, nor was there even a hint that families electing to have children in 1931 might, on average, have had higher incomes and better access to health care than was available to those producing children in 1928. From an administration that proclaimed a faith in facts, the sloppiness with which inferences were drawn from such data is disheartening. 1931 was also a year in which Babe Ruth's earnings as a New York Yankee exceeded the salary of the president of the United States. Though some citizens saw an incongruity between the rewards for sport and for statecraft, Ruth pointed out that he had had a better year.

CHAPTER 7

Shifting course in late 1931 and early 1932

Hoover had lost control of the agenda in mid-1931. Events, both at home and abroad, over which he could exercise no effective control had washed away the foundations of the original model of economic stabilization. But if the old model was no longer serviceable, what was to replace it? The pressures of day-to-day crisis fighting afforded little opportunity for reflection to develop a new body of doctrine. Though he had become the captive of events, Hoover was still determined to master them if he could. Certainly he remained persuaded that presidential guidance was crucial in the battle against depression. His long-standing doubts about the compatibility of the pursuit of private self-interest with the larger social good had been reinforced by his experience in the first two years at the White House. On its own, the private sector of the economy could not be relied upon to solve the economy's problems.

A new approach to the management of economic policy began to take shape in October 1931. Unlike the earlier doctrine of macroeconomic stabilization, it was not part of a preconceived grand design. Instead it emerged piecemeal, largely in response to immediate pressures of the moment. As its various components were put in place, it began to take on an internal coherence. Top priority on the new agenda was solidification of the banking system. Securing this base at home was the essential first step. Later, with American leadership, the international monetary system should be rebuilt. These measures were indispensable to recovery, but they alone could not assure it. That could not happen until aggregate spending was restored. But the larger goal was beyond reach unless the public believed in the integrity of the financial system. There could be no mistaking that it did not in the late summer of 1931. Reports reaching Hoover suggested that the hoarding of cash withdrawn from bank accounts had reached alarming proportions.[1] Such loss of faith in the banks not only aggrevated their problems; it was also an obstacle to the recovery of spending. Potential spending was also frustrated by the fact that sizable sums were frozen in banks that had already suspended their operations. As of early September, Hoover estimated that $1.5 billion of depositors' money – or roughly 3 percent of all bank deposits – was immobilized in this way.[2]

From a later vantage point, one might well ask why part of this difficulty could not have been addressed by creating a mechanism through which the federal government could guarantee the safety of bank deposits. Proposals to accomplish this were available and had received some attention in Congress. Their reception in the banking community, however, had generally been hostile. Though bankers themselves stood to be major beneficiaries, few of them welcomed the prospect of adding to their costs by paying the insurance premiums that would be required. Particularly vigorous in opposition were the larger metropolitan bankers, most of whom saw such arrangements as devices to make them bear the burden of the mistakes of less competent members of their fraternity. The view was also widely held that constitutional constraints on the limits of federal intervention ruled out such notions from the start. Certainly Hoover shared that conviction. If at all possible, he was determined to fight depression without doing violence to the established division of responsibilities between the central government and the several states.[3]

Bolstering the financial system: step I

The forces that exposed the weaknesses of the banking system in 1931 had been building up for some time, but they were intensified by the British government's suspension of gold convertibility in late September. Once this bastion of international monetary orthodoxy had fallen, the credibility of the U.S. government's commitment to gold became suspect. In October the drains from the U.S. gold reserves exceeded all previous monthly records. Neither Hoover nor the managers of the Federal Reserve System entertained any doubts about the paramount importance of maintaining the convertibility of the dollar for gold at the established exchange rate. As they saw matters, a lapse from this commitment would destroy all hope of an orderly reconstruction of the system of international trade and finance. As Hoover remarked at the time, "we now were the Verdun of world stability."[4] Faltering on this point, as the administration saw matters, would also intensify the forces of deflation in the United States. With many debt obligations legally denominated for payment in terms of gold, a reduction in the gold content of the dollar would increase the real burden of debt and generate another distressing round of liquidations.[5]

The Federal Reserve acted to protect the gold reserves in the manner the standard rule book prescribed. Between early October and mid-November 1931, the discount rate of the Federal Reserve Bank of New York was more than doubled – from $1\frac{1}{2}$ percent to $3\frac{1}{2}$ percent. Though this was the orthodox way to deal with a gold hemorrhage, it was hardly a formula for a monetary policy to promote borrowing needed to spur recovery. But there were other consequences as well. One of the immediate effects of this upward pressure on the pattern of interest rates was an erosion in the portfolio values of banks and other holders of fixed income assets. This, of course, was not the only factor then working to depress bond values. After two years of depression, the ability of some of the major issuers of long-term corporate bonds to earn enough to service their fixed interest obligations was increasingly in question. These difficulties were compounded by the growth in the public's fears for the security of bank deposits. If depositors wanted cash, banks – if they were to survive – needed to raise it. For many, liquidating portions of their bond portfolio was the only option readily available. Distress sales of bonds, however, depressed their prices still further.[6]

Hoover perceived this state of affairs to be a threat to the entire credit system. In an attempt to avert it, he employed a tactic he had used on many earlier occasions: that of convening leaders of a business group, proposing a program of action to them, and requesting their cooperation. But, in two respects, his session with major bankers called to Washington on October 4, 1931 was different. This gathering was regarded as confidential and it was held, not at the White House on a working day, but in the private apartment of Secretary of the Treasury Mellon on a Sunday evening. Hoover assured those present that he well understood why banks should seek to make themselves more liquid by selling securities. But this behavior meant that banks which succeeded in converting bonds into cash were making "their weaker brethren" less liquid. This process could not be continued without risking further disastrous blood-letting in the banking industry. The Federal Reserve, he noted, could not effectively address the problem at hand for two reasons: (1) because the most serious difficulties were being experienced by small banks that were not members of the system and (2) because the amount of eligible paper, primarily commercial bills, held by weaker banks within the system was insufficient to satisfy their liquidity needs through the channels of the Federal Reserve. Before 1913 it had been normal practice, he noted, for metropolitan banks to aid their out-of-town correspondents when they were in distress. This sense of shared responsibility had subsequently weakened. In this respect, the creation of the central banking network had contributed to an unfortunate state of mind: "that it was to the Federal Reserve System rather than to the banks in the central reserve cities that all banks should look." It was now urgent for the major bankers to reaffirm the obligations they had earlier accepted. Accordingly, he proposed that the metropolitan banks form a consortium that "would furnish rediscount facilities to banks throughout the country on the basis of sound assets not legally eligible for rediscount at the Federal Reserve Bank." This public service by banks in the principal financial centers, he maintained, involved no hazards. Not only was their liquidity position already strong; they also had the "ability to get exceptionally large accommodations from the Federal Reserve Banks."[7]

This approach had all the markings of the vintage Hoover style. Presidential exhortation should guide private groups to act in the public interest. Moreover, the resources required in such a public service operation should be supplied within the private sector, not by the federal government. The response of the assembled bankers to this proposition, however, was less than enthusiastic. Few of them had been noted for their sympathies for the plight of the "weaker brethren" who, in their view, had little claim to survival unless they could straighten out the part of the mess they had produced through their own managerial shortcomings. No less important, the metropolitan bankers had enough problems of their own without taking on responsibility for a body of loans of doubtful quality. And they were inclined to ask a different question. If a major public interest was at stake in all this, why should not public resources, rather than private ones, be committed to the rescue operation?

Hoover believed that he had gathered enough support for his proposals to announce them publicly on October 7, 1931. The White House statement of that date noted that the president had requested the banking community to form a new institution, shortly to be identified as the National Credit Corporation, with at least $500 million at its disposal. These funds would be available for rediscounting assets of commercial banks which were "not now eligible for rediscount at the Federal Reserve Banks." The president would also request congressional action to broaden the eligibility provisions of the Federal Reserve Act and would, "if necessity requires," submit proposals for the "creation of a finance corporation similar in character and purpose to the War Finance Corporation, with available funds sufficient for any legitimate call in the support of credit."[8] The latter commitment was to be of singular significance. The bankers invited to take the lead in the formation of the National Credit Corporation had insisted on such a fallback as a condition for going along with other parts of the program. From Hoover's point of view, this amounted to bending the usual rules on the place of government in the nation's business. Though the prospect of more direct intervention was not pleasing, flexibility on this point could be rationalized as a temporary expedient in times of emergency. Extraordinary interventions by government were certainly justifiable in times of war. As Hoover now saw matters, the crisis the nation confronted was no less grave than the one it had met in 1917. This was reflected in the tone of his public statements during the last eighteen months of his tenure of office. The "battle" against depression was likened to a military campaign "conducted on many fronts." The strength of the nation had to be "mobilized" and it was implied that citizens had a patriotic duty to respond to calls from the commander-in-chief for action.

Signs that the National Credit Corporation might not be able to achieve all that had been hoped from it were not long delayed. On the day of Hoover's public announcement of the new program, George L. Harrison of the Federal Reserve District Bank of New York drew the president's attention to a shortcoming in the scheme. Much of the weakness of the banking system, as he diagnosed it, was a difficulty of solvency, not of liquidity. The National Credit Corporation could address part of the latter problem by rediscounting assets of solvent banks in need of ready cash. But it could not deal effectively with the critical threat of bank insolvency arising from the "drastic writeoff in bond portfolios." The magnitude of the problem was too large and the resources of the corporation were too small. Other measures would be needed if bond markets were to be improved; in particular, he emphasized the crucial importance of "fundamental improvement in the earning powers of the obligers of the bonds" (especially of the railroads).[9]

If there was a question about the ability of the National Credit Corporation to meet the problems of bank restoration successfully, there was also a question about the desire of some of its major subscribers to see it flourish. Only reluctantly had many of them agreed to participate. As far as their private interests were concerned, little could be gained – though much might be lost – by absorbing someone else's marginal loans. Now that the president had committed himself to the use of federal monies for this purpose as a last resort, there was no strong incentive to delay the day when that necessity arose. In his letter to Hoover on October 7, 1931, Harrison noted that there had been "quite general and enthusiastic support throughout New York" for the "revival of some such institution as the War Finance Corporation."[10]

Bolstering the financial system: step II

By early December 1931 it was clear that the step Hoover had preferred not to take would no longer be avoidable. The National Credit Corporation simply had not done the job. The corporation by that time had placed only $10 million in loans and bank failures had continued. The banks most in need of help had lacked access to the rediscount facilities of the National Credit Corporation, either because they were unable to satisfy the stringent collateral requirements or because they could not afford the membership subscription that was required for participation. Meanwhile the ardor of the larger banks for this project, which had not been abundant in the first instance, was dampened further when their hope that collateral taken on by the NCC would be made eligible for rediscount at the Federal Reserve seemed unlikely to be realized quickly, if at all.[11]

Hoover's hand was thus forced. In his State of the Union message on December 8, 1931, he proposed the creation of a new public body to be designated as the Reconstruction Finance Corporation. Its central purpose was to provide a vehicle through which resources of the federal government could be directed to support the beleaguered financial system. The RFC was to be specifically empowered to lend against adequate collateral presented by the full range of financial intermediaries: commercial banks, savings banks, trust companies, savings and loan associations, insurance companies. This arrangement was expected to provide safeguards that neither the Federal Reserve system nor the National Credit Corporation had been able to supply. But protection for the financial network also required that the lending facilities of the RFC should be available to the railroads. Railway bonds figured prominently in the portfolios of financial institutions and their values had seriously deteriorated.[12] George L. Harrison, governor of the Federal Reserve Bank of New York, drew the attention of a congressional committee to the importance of help for the railroads when he noted that "railway bonds which in the past have been prime investments for investors throughout the world, form about one-fifth of the total bonds outstanding."[13] Action to strengthen the position of railroads was thus imperative if a still more widespread round of financial disasters was to be averted.[14]

Though the railway industry was obviously a special case, Hoover also sought authority for the RFC to make loans to finance the working capital requirements of private industries, subject to two conditions: (1) that they were solvent, going concerns with orders for their outputs in hand and (2) that they had been unable to obtain credit through normal banking channels. This would involve moving government still further into territory where it was normally thought not to belong. Hoover insisted that he had no intention of putting government into the banking business on a permanent basis. All of this was designed to address conditions of an emergency in which it was vital to restore public confidence in financial institutions and to insure that no employment would be sacrificed because of bottlenecks in the supply of credit. Accordingly, RFC was to have a limited lifetime: it was expected that it would suspend lending operations after two years, though they could be extended for one additional year by Executive Order if the need arose. In December 1931 Hoover spoke as if the latter contingency was highly unlikely. The very existence of RFC as a "bulwark" could be expected so to strengthen confidence that "it may not be necessary to use such an instrumentality very extensively." [15]

There was something remarkable as well in another feature of the administration's architecture of the RFC. The corporation was to be launched with an initial subscription by the Treasury to its capital stock in the amount of $500 million. In addition, RFC would be empowered to issue debt instruments in its own name, though with the guarantee of the Treasury, in sums up to $1.5 billion. The Treasury's initial endowment to the capital stock of the corporation would appear as an ordinary expenditure of government in the federal budget for the fiscal year 1932. Borrowings negotiated by the RFC, albeit ultimately obligations of the U.S. government, would be excluded from the Treasury's budgetary accounts. This procedure was unusual in light of the federal accounting conventions in use at the time. The segregation of RFC borrowing from direct Treasury borrowing, however, was a point to which the administration assigned high importance. When defending this approach before a senate committee, Undersecretary of the Treasury Ogden L. Mills spoke as follows: "I would much rather see this corporation issue its own debentures than to confuse it with our public-debt operations. In the matter of accounting and presenting an accurate picture, I think the accounts of this institution should not be merged with the public-debt accounts of the United States Government. . . . [S]upposing we [i.e., the Treasury] were obliged to furnish a billion dollars, the public debt would go up a billion dollars. I think it would give you a distorted picture of the public debt, because presumably all of those funds would have been loaned on good collateral, and it therefore would be an entirely different form of public debt than the one which is outstanding today and which represents, generally speaking, the war costs and current deficits." [16] But Mills also noted that this procedure would not be symmetrical with the budgetary treatment of the transactions of the Federal Farm Board. Its loans were also collateralized: indeed it held as security "vast amounts of wheat and cotton." But every dollar the Treasury advanced to the board had been charged as current expenditure in the federal budget and, when its crop loans were ultimately liquidated, the proceeds would be recorded by the Treasury as current revenue. [17]

The Reconstruction Finance Corporation began life on January 22, 1931. With the Congress dominated by the president's opponents, enactment of such precedent-shattering legislation within a span of six weeks was no mean feat. Even so, Hoover was annoyed by the delay: he had hoped to have the RFC open for business at the beginning of the year.[18] Nor was the substance of the bill that emerged from Congress totally to Hoover's taste. Congress had given RFC the powers he sought for it in two areas: lending to financial institutions and to railroads. But it had added a claimant to RFC's resources: the corporation would be obliged to earmark $200 million to be placed at the disposal of the secretary of agriculture to finance crop loans. This amendment was acceptable to the White House, though Hoover preferred to have farm relief handled differently. The administration suffered a defeat, however, on a point that Hoover held to be important to his program to strengthen employment. RFC was not entitled to lend to creditworthy industries where work was there to be done but which was frustrated by lack of finance for working capital.

Though the RFC was the centerpiece of the new strategy, Hoover had included another institutional innovation in his legislative recommendations of December 1931: the creation of a Home Loan Discount Bank. A scheme that would ease the flow of credit for residential construction had long been close to his heart. He had been brushed off in spring 1930 when he had attempted to persuade the Federal Reserve to take steps to permit mortgage loans to be acceptable at its discount window. By late 1931 he was ready to bypass the Federal Reserve by establishing a new facility to take on this function. Again the resources of the Treasury would be on tap to get it started. With home building depressed by one-half to two-thirds below normal levels, he saw this mechanism as a key to revitalizing the construction industry and spurring gains in employment. Congress, however, did not share his sense of urgency. The birth of the Home Loan Discount Bank was delayed until July 22, 1932.

Financial reconstruction and the reformulation of fiscal policy

During the first two years of depression, Hoover had not been particularly exercised about deficits in the federal budget. Reductions in tax receipts, he recognized, were inevitable when a falling national income shrank the revenue base. Meanwhile some increases in spending, particularly on accelerated programs for public works, were desirable, even though they widened the deficit further. Some of the funding needed for this type of employment-creating activity could be found by reallocating funds from less essential governmental spending categories. Nevertheless, total outlays were still expected to increase and they did. In his budget message of December 1930, for example, Hoover observed that he did not look with great concern on the moderate deficit then in prospect for the fiscal year ending June 30, 1931 and that he would probably find it necessary to increase it by asking Congress to provide supplementary spending authorizations "in order to increase employment and provide for the drought situation." As he then put the matter: "When we recollect that our Budget has yielded large surpluses for the last 11 years, which have enabled us to retire the public debt, in addition to retirements required by law, to the extent of nearly $3,500,000,000, we can confidently look forward to the restoration of such surpluses with the general recovery of the economic situation, and thus the absorption of any temporary borrowing that may be necessary."[19] Nor in early September 1931 was the president particularly troubled by deficit spending, even though the red ink in the Treasury statements for fiscal year 1931 had recorded much larger numbers than had been anticipated. Part of this result was attributable to the special effort to accelerate federal spending on construction and maintenance to levels about three times above the normal outlays. This "burden" on the federal budget was "the product of the depression and the contribution of the Federal Government to that situation." But the "burden" to the budget carried compensating social benefits with it. The number of men employed, directly and indirectly, in federal construction and maintenance work had been expanded to about 760,000 from 180,000 in January 1930. This effort, he indicated, would have to be continued through fiscal year 1932. Whether it would be necessary in the following year would depend on the state of the economy: an economic upturn would permit economies in that item of expenditure. Deficits meant that the country was consuming some of the "fat" from "'the previous excess redemption of the debt." This situation, he noted, did "not necessarily imply that we can go on living indefinitely on our fat until it is exhausted." Nevertheless, he concluded that "the primary problem and the only problem in governmental fiscal questions is the maintenance of the social obligations of the Government to a population that are in difficulties."[20] Fiscal responsibility, to be sure, was always desirable. But there was no fetishism about annually balanced budgets as an objective of policy in their own right.

The climate of November and December 1931 – when budget plans for fiscal year 1933 were being drafted – was vastly different from the one of only a few months earlier. Not only were there no signs of an upturn that would improve governmental receipts; it seemed instead to be prudent to be prepared for even less welcome economic news. More-over, one revenue source that had been built into the original calcu-lations of receipts in fiscal year 1932 had been written off by the mora-torium on Allied debt payments. The Treasury would still have to absorb all the service charges on the federal debt, but it would not be aided by the usual contribution of some $180 million from foreign gov-ernments. Meanwhile, there was a possibility that Congress might push the spending side of the budget out of control. Certainly there was a continuing threat that the next session might mandate the payout of the remaining half of the veterans' bonus in 1932.[21] But there was no doubt at all about one addition to the outlay side of the budget: the Treasury's subscription of $500 million to the capital stock of the RFC was to be treated as an "ordinary expenditure" of government. All things considered, a balance in the federal budget for the fiscal year end-ing June 30, 1932 was out of the question, even on the assumption that the spenders in Congress could be kept on a tight leash.

But the factor exercising the greatest influence on the administra-tion's thinking about fiscal strategy in late 1931 derived from the per-ceived necessity to adopt measures to preserve the nation's financial sys-tem. Maintaining – and, if possible, increasing bond prices – was held to be crucial to this effort. This was the rationale underlying the National Credit Corporation, the Reconstruction Finance Corporation, and the special measures to improve the debt-servicing capacity of rail-roads. The borrowing claims the federal government made on financial markets were also thought likely to have a significant impact on the course of bond prices and interest rates. There was thus a direct link between the bond-support strategy of financial reconstruction and the management of fiscal policy. From this perspective, it was counterpro-ductive for the federal government to behave in a way that put upward pressure on interest rates (and downward pressure on bond values). Within the administration, it was taken to be self-evident that new debt issues by the Treasury – if offered in any significant volume – could only be placed at higher interest rates.

From a later vantage point, a question about the Hoover administra-tion's approach to this problem immediately springs to mind. Why, it may be asked, could not the job of supporting bond prices have been assigned to the central bank? This technique was used successfully in the placing of massive volumes of government debt at low interest rates during the Second World War. In the circumstances of late 1931, this option was not available to the Hoover administration. Not only was the Federal Reserve System technically independent of the executive branch and determined to protect its autonomy, the legal requirements

on the Federal Reserve System itself then precluded it from active support of Treasury debt management.[22] It still might have been possible
for the Federal Reserve to conduct open-market operations more aggressively and thus to augment the capacity of banks to purchase Treasury issues. But, in the framework of thought dominating policy at the
central bank, this approach would run counter to its efforts to defend
the gold stock. In any event, the banks were perceived as having excess
reserves that were already extraordinary and the target of policy was to
activate them through lending to the private sector, not to the federal
government.

In light of these considerations, the success or failure of the program
of financial rehabilitation (and of the bond-support program that went
with it) seemed to hinge fundamentally on the fiscal operations of the
federal government. This set the context for Hoover's recommendation
in his budget message of December 1931 for major tax increases and
stringent economies in federal spending. The announced aim was "to
balance the Budget for the next fiscal year [1933] except to the extent
of the amount required for statutory debt retirements."[23] To achieve it,
tax measures to enhance revenues by some $920 million would be re-
quired. This implied that the federal tax claims would be about 35
percent greater than they would have been under existing tax law.[24]
Though Hoover maintained that tax increases should be regarded as
emergency measures of two years' duration only, these were not trivial
magnitudes in an already severely depressed economy.

This decision indeed marked a significant departure from positions
the administration had earlier been identified with. On the face of it,
tax increases ran totally counter to the doctrine that more spending was
needed to recharge the economic machine. Hoover now seemed to be
turning his back to those arguments. The new message was that government should retrench its own spending and reduce the potential spending power of the citizenry as well.

A reversion to orthodoxy?

Much of the language used by Hoover and his senior associates in their
public pronouncements about fiscal policy at this time had a ring of
doctrinaire orthodoxy. They extolled the old-fashioned virtues of the
responsible public housekeeping and its importance to public confidence in the stability of government and the soundness of public credit.
Behind the scenes, however, they thought of the fiscal program proposed
in late 1931 as something rather different.

In the first instance, their appeals for a balanced budget did not call for a balance in the form that had been accepted for a decade as the proper official definition. Since the inauguration of the statutory debt retirement program in 1921, the accounting conventions of the Treasury had charged sums allocated to reducing the national debt as current expenditures. In keeping with these procedures, a "balanced budget" was achieved only when the receipts of the federal government exceeded current expenditures by the amount specified for debt redemption. The plan advanced by Hoover for the fiscal year 1933, on the other hand, redefined "balance" to mean that there should be no net increase in the national debt. Even though debt retirement (as stipulated by law) would continue as scheduled, these disbursements would no longer be counted as expenditures in the final reckoning of the state of the budget. This semantic maneuver was not widely publicized, though a qualification along these lines was regularly attached as a rider to administration statements on its fiscal policy.

In practical terms, this conceptual adjustment meant that the government could still borrow and satisfy the new criterion of "balance." Its claims on capital markets, however, would be constrained to the amounts needed to refinance existing debt. In short, Treasury operations in retiring and reissuing debt should be neutral in their impact. This redefinition, in turn, was consistent with the view that governmental financing should not depress bond prices. But it also meant that Hoover had more scope to spend, while maintaining the appearance of a balanced budget, than would otherwise have been available. Allocations to the sinking fund scheduled for fiscal year 1933, which were now to be excluded from the expenditure column, came to about $486 million or roughly 12 percent of the total spending anticipated in his budget proposals.

Another conceptual innovation promised to offer still further room for maneuver. One of the features of the administration's scheme for the Reconstruction Finance Corporation was a provision enabling the corporation to borrow up to $1.5 billion in its own name. These obligations were to be guaranteed by the Treasury but would not appear in its accounts. In principle, the federal government could thus be a party to a form of deficit financing, but in a way that would not jeopardize the appearance of a balanced budget.

This prospective venture into "off-budget" financing was also a marked departure from established practice and it invited questions about just how efficient it might be. It was taken as truth that capital markets would absorb RFC debt issues only if their yields were higher than those available on Treasury offerings. If the government cared deeply about minimizing the cost of funds to the RFC, should it not then plan to let the Treasury do the borrowing directly and turn the proceeds over to the corporation? (Technically, the legislation creating the RFC authorized the Treasury to acquire RFC obligations if it elected to do so, but it was widely expected that they would be instead offered for public subscription.) An approach that might keep the cost of funds to a minimum was, however, dominated by another consideration: the importance assigned to keeping RFC debt issues outside the regular budget in fiscal year 1933.[25] Direct Treasury borrowing to support RFC's financing requirements would conflict with the objective of presenting at least the appearance of a "balanced budget," as now redefined, in fiscal year 1933. It was thus crucial to maintain a sharp distinction between Treasury debt and Treasury-guaranteed debt. So long as this distinction could be maintained, tools were at hand to practice some disguised deficit financing in ways that could be reconciled with the stated goal of achieving a budget nominally in balance and avoiding enlargement of the federal (as opposed to the federally guaranteed) debt.

The new style of fiscal thinking further implied that guidelines for accelerated federal spending on public works would have to be restated. It was no longer sufficient that federal projects satisfy the test of social usefulness; they were now entertainable only if they could be paid for from current revenues. Borrowing for this purpose was ruled out because of its alleged threat to the bond-support strategy. This did not necessarily mean that federal spending for construction would be curtailed: Hoover still hoped to be able to find more monies for this purpose by reallocating funds from other categories of government expenditure. Even so, the "nominal" budget constraint placed obvious limits on how far this could be carried. A change in Hoover's approach was apparent in the language of his directives to subordinates. In January 1932 he informed his secretary of commerce that forward planning of public works should proceed "in terms of finance rather than in terms of projects."[26] Earlier thinking had been organized around the attempt to identify worthwhile projects that could be ranked on the basis of the speed with which they could be activated and the numbers of jobs they were likely to create.

Much of the popular image of Hoover as a "stand-patter" and as a conservative ideologue stems from the posture he adopted in late 1931. His calls for a balanced budget and his rejection of federal borrowing for public works certainly nourished that imagery. These positions could readily be reduced to slogans reminiscent of the Harding and Coolidge administrations.

At many important points of detail, economic policy had indeed been transformed from what it had been in 1929 and 1930. From Hoover's perspective, this was not a retreat from activism to the orthodoxy of an earlier age. His appetite for intervention in the management of the economy had not changed. But the immediate priorities for action were now different. Circumstances, which were both unprecedented and un-anticipated, called for new conceptual formulations and new tactics. Various pieces of the original macroeconomic model had been refitted, and in some cases artfully redefined, and they no longer looked the same. Meanwhile, Hoover was extending governmental involvement in the private sector in a manner that earlier would have been dismissed as unthinkable.

Stimulating spending to lift the economy from depression remained the ultimate goal. But an intermediate objective, rehabilitation of the financial system, would have to be secured first. Only when trust in financial institutions had been restored would the spending needed for full recovery be forthcoming. This was the organizing thread of the approach to policy adopted in late 1931 and early 1932. As events were shortly to demonstrate, some of the presuppositions of that approach were fundamentally flawed. Within its own terms, however, it had an intellectual consistency.

CHAPTER 8

Renewing the offensive in February and March 1932

Once the Reconstruction Finance Corporation was open for business, Hoover believed that a secure foundation had been placed beneath the nation's financial structure. It was now time for measures to reactivate lending and spending.

But a technical detail required attention before the full potential of a new drive for recovery could be realized. Since his session with New York bankers to form the National Credit Corporation in October 1931, Hoover had pressed, but without success, for revisions in the Federal Reserve Act to widen the definitions of assets eligible for rediscount at the Federal Reserve Banks. Revision in the rules governing the conduct of the central banking system took on fresh urgency in February 1932. The law required that its issues of currency – Federal Reserve notes – be fully collateralized, with at least 40 percent of the backing in the form of gold and the remainder in short-term commercial paper. The Federal Reserve, however, now faced a crisis in living within these rules while, at the same time, carrying out its charge to supply Federal Reserve notes on demand. The number of notes requiring backing had been swollen by the increasing preference of the public to hold cash rather than bank deposits. Meanwhile the ability of the system to find the necessary backing had been reduced. The outstanding volume of commercial paper had been shrunk by the drying-up of business demand for credit during two years of depression. And the proportion of the total available to the central banking system had fallen still further when member banks attempted, as a precautionary measure, to hold excess reserves and to avoid rediscounting at the Federal Reserve if at all possible. In light of this state of affairs, the cover requirements for the issue of Federal Reserve notes could be satisfied only by earmarking gold reserves for this purpose. But this use of gold reserves, which was well in excess of the minimum stipulated by law, left precious little margin with which to meet claims from foreigners on the U.S. gold stock.[1] In fact, the volume of "free gold" (gold holdings of the central bank in excess of the sums required to back Federal Reserve notes) had been so diminished by mid-February 1932 that the gold convertibility of the dollar was in jeopardy. A resumption of a gold drain abroad on the scale of the preceding autumn would have obliged the United States to follow the course of the British by departing from the gold standard. Hoover was determined to prevent this at all costs.

Legislation to relieve this threat to the U.S. commitment to the gold standard was hastily pushed through Congress and, on its passage, Hoover congratulated its members for their "fine spirit of patriotic nonpartisanship" in enacting "a national defense measure."[2] In the first instance, the amended law (known as the Glass–Steagall Act of 1932) permitted the Federal Reserve to use government securities as backing for its issues of currency. This meant that the amount of free gold could immediately be increased by about $750 million,[3] a cushion believed to be more than ample to satisfy potential foreign claimants. In addition, the Glass–Steagall Act gave a bit more flexibility to the rediscounting facilities the Federal Reserve could offer its members. Some assets that would not otherwise be eligible would be accepted, though only at higher discount rates, if five members of the Federal Reserve Board were satisfied that such loans were properly secured. The latter provision was to have little practical significance. The former, however, had the effect of liberating the Federal Reserve to conduct a much more expansionary monetary policy. Earlier, opponents of open-market operations to combat depression had argued that such a program would be self-defeating. Purchases of government securities, to be sure, would strengthen the reserve position of member banks; but this, in turn, would be associated with a reduction in rediscounting at the Federal Reserve and a shrinkage in the volume of commercial paper available to the central banking system as collateral for Federal Reserve notes. Further, open-market purchases might stimulate an accelerated gold outflow that would compound the problems of the central bank in fulfilling its statutory obligations to support the currency. These arguments for inaction were no longer valid. In late February 1932 the Federal Reserve launched an aggressive program of open-market operations on a scale without precedent in its history. Over the course of the next six months, its holdings of government securities increased by about $1.1 billion.[4]

The attack on the liquidity trap: February–March 1932

The stage now appeared to be set to get on with the central business – the stimulation of lending and spending. The term "liquidity trap" did not enter Hoover's vocabulary. But he certainly understood the meaning of the concept to which Keynes gave this label in *The General Theory of Employment, Interest and Money* in 1936. Nor did Hoover confuse hoarding with ordinary saving.[5] Hoarding had paralyzed expenditure and had crippled the banking system. It was now imperative to put idle funds back into circulation.

Hoover laid the groundwork for an "anti-hoarding campaign" in early February with an appeal to the citizenry to "enlist" in the war against depression with the same sense of patriotic duty displayed during the war. He estimated that currency being hoarded totalled more than $1.3 billion. "Every dollar hoarded," he observed, "means a destruction of from $5 to $10 of credit." It was thus clear that the behavior of hoarders was "contrary to the common good" and that returning funds to circulation would be "a patriotic service to the country as a whole."[6] Shortly thereafter, he announced the formation of Citizens Reconstruction Organization to be headed by Colonel Frank Knox, publisher of the *Chicago Daily News*.[7] Its mission was to bring home to the man on the street that "hoarded currency means that high-powered dollars are idle and that in turn means idle business, idle men, and depreciated prices."[8]

Knox's national organization set about its work with the aid of a major publicity campaign and within a matter of weeks supporting groups were at work in some 2,395 communities throughout the land.[9] More important, the early reports on results were heartening. Estimates prepared by the Federal Reserve Board indicated that some $112 million of hoarded currency had been returned to circulation during the first three weeks of the campaign.[10] From his headquarters in Chicago, Knox advised the president that "reassuring reports of progress" were coming in "from every quarter," adding that a canvass of banks in parts of the Chicago area where hoarding had been rife indicated "uniformly that deposits are increasing and that a feeling of confidence is supplanting the former feeling of fear."[11]

Spirits in the White House ran higher in these weeks in March 1932 than they had for at least two years. At last, something seemed to be going according to plan. Getting hoarded funds back into the banks, of course, was but the first step. The next one was to get bank credit back in action to support spending. Hoover offered some unsolicited counsel to consumers on how they might help to sustain the momentum. In a public statement on April 1, he observed: "The motor manufacturing companies have all launched their spring models. There is nothing that provides widespread employment more than automobile construction.

Every person contemplating buying a new car this year can make a real contribution to employment by putting in his order now even though he does not take immediate delivery." [12]

Failure of the antihoarding campaign

The enthusiasm surrounding the initial responses to the antihoarding drive was to be short-lived. During the first ten weeks of the propaganda work of the Citizens Reconstruction Organization, some $250 million in currency had been returned to circulation.[13] In mid-April this trend was reversed. A resumption of hoarding, however, was not the only disappointment. Even more disheartening was the mounting evidence that the banks had not seized the opportunities provided by growth in their deposits and by the central bank's program of open-market purchases to expand their lending as they were supposed to. To make matters worse, a gold outflow resumed.

In Hoover's eyes, the behavior of the banks at this point was outrageously antisocial. As he put the issue to Harrison of the Federal Reserve Bank of New York, "I can see a rising tide towards the banks which is going to be perfectly disastrous unless we can secure some better cooperation." To drive the point home, he provided samples of the correspondence he was "being deluged with . . . from all over the country." [14] The chairman of the antihoarding campaign in Kansas, for example, reported that major banks in the state were continuing to call loans and to deny credits to long-standing and well-established customers. This action was forcing more firms to the wall and he was "almost convinced" that it was being taken "in the interest of scavengers who hope to profit from the wreckage." He relayed as well the judgment of "one of the best and most influential" citizens of the state that its major bankers "were nothing less than public enemies, and all should be branded as such." [15]

If the behavior of bankers increasingly aroused his temper, Hoover's displeasure with operators on the New York Stock Exchange was even greater. He had never had a kind word to say for speculators. In the environment of early 1932, he perceived their activities to be particularly reprehensible. He was trying desperately to rebuild confidence in the nation's financial institutions. This effort, however, was being undermined – he insisted – by those who were "selling short" and conducting "bear raids" on the market. As he stated his position to Thomas W. Lamont, his correspondent on stock market trends of October 1929, this activity was immoral: "men are not justified in deliberately making a profit from the losses of other people." It was damaging to the national economy because it "destroy[s] public confidence and induce[s] a slowing down of business and a fall in prices." Moreover, it was unjustified: "prices today of securities do not truly represent the values of American enterprise and property." [16]

Hoover and Lamont were no closer in their analyses of the performance of the stock market in April 1932 than they had been in October 1929. While Hoover held the short-sellers largely responsible for the "pounding of the market," Lamont insisted that this was a "very incidental" factor and one which "cannot accurately be listed as a primary cause." More fundamental forces were at work. Lamont conceded that "quoted values in many cases do not represent real values" of securities. "But what," he asked, "can be called 'real value' if a security has no earnings and pays no dividends? . . . Our investors are so exceedingly hard hit today that they *must* have income. They cannot afford to hold on to stocks that pay them no income. They must sell such stocks, even though far below their book value." [17] In short, the performance of the stock market reflected real economic phenomena, not the machinations of manipulators.

Though the collapse of the antihoarding drive further strained Hoover's relations with the financial community, it also left scars on those who had loyally enlisted in the president's cause. Colonel Frank Knox, who had recruited volunteers to organize local antihoarding committees on the understanding that they would be reimbursed for their out-of-pocket administrative expenses, felt betrayed. Contributions that had been promised, particularly from New York, had not been forthcoming. Meanwhile, his state and local organizers were submitting expense statements and had every right to expect that they would be honored. Knox complained to the White House about the "embarrassment" to which he was being subjected "on account of the anti-hoarding campaign" and that he personally was "already holding the bag on this proposition for over $14,000.00." [18] And there were still more poignant personal stories. A case in point was the grievance registered at the White House in May 1932 by a resident of Chicago who reported that he had followed the advice of the president and Colonel Frank Knox. It was his understanding that the purpose of the Reconstruction Finance Corporation was to prevent the failure of banks. The bank in which he had placed his deposit, however, had just gone under, taking with it all of the earnings of his firm, as well as his lifetime savings. [19]

Despite a promising beginning, the antihoarding campaign ended disastrously. Though the rate of bank failures had been slowed, they had not been eliminated. The resumption of currency withdrawals meant that most of the ground won in the initial phases of the campaign was soon lost.

The anatomy of failure from a White House perspective

Time did not permit an exhaustive postmortem into what had gone wrong in the antihoarding drive. Hoover's instant diagnosis, however, was that he had been let down by the bankers and the financiers. He had set in motion a program to build confidence and to promote recovery. Part of the public had followed him, but key actors in the financial community had not. Whereas he had asked for bullishness, they had responded with bearishness. Hoover remained convinced that the opportunities for putting the country back to work were there and that they would be seized if the financial network functioned properly. If depression had a bright side, it was surely that it generated a backlog of worthwhile spending projects in the private sector. The problem was thus not one of deficiency in the demand for loans. The difficulty instead was obstruction in the supply of finance.

But Hoover also attributed part of the failure of his new approach to confidence building to the behavior of irresponsible partisans in Congress. Massive bond-financed public works expenditures were again being seriously entertained, as were schemes to distribute the remaining portion of the veterans' bonus. All of this, he maintained, had helped to rekindle fears in the public mind. So also had the manifestations of congressional sympathy for the Goldsborough Bill, which would charge the Federal Reserve to conduct monetary policy to reflate commodity prices to their average levels of the 1920s. On May 2 the House of Representatives voted its approval of this legislation. Though the Senate ultimately blocked its passage, the uncertainty generated by the discussion was held to be unsettling, particularly to foreign holders of dollars. Hoover believed that this largely explained the latest run on the U.S. gold stock. But the gold drain had a further consequence. It blunted the impact of the Federal Reserve's open-market purchases as a stimulant to easier credit conditions.[20]

The abortive offensive of the early months of 1932 left another legacy. Hoover's own confidence in his techniques of economic management had been badly bruised. Tactically, the approach to the economics of indirect control developed in the 1920s had presupposed that guidance and persuasion from the White House could generate action for the common good. But recent experience demonstrated that this had not

worked. The president's calls for national service by bankers and financiers, by mayors and governors, by the Congress, and by the public
at large no longer were heeded as he hoped they would be. This was all
the more disturbing in light of the existence of an emergency analogous to war. By implication, there was something a bit sinister about
those who did not answer the president's appeals with patriotic behavior. But perhaps there was a mistake in the earlier judgment that
such exhortation could produce the results that were needed. If that
were the case, more direct techniques of intervention would have to be
considered in further stages of the battle against depression.

CHAPTER 9

The economists and their views on policy for 1932

Hoover had reoriented his campaign against depression in late 1931. The final goal remained the same: revitalization of the economy through the recovery of spending. But new circumstances had dictated a shift in the policy mix. The environment that provoked reassessments in official quarters might also have been expected to inspire new thinking among the economists. Certainly the course of events had diverged substantially from the expectations of both the more orthodox neoclassicists and the champions of stabilization strategies of the new era. Members of the former school had typically held that the economy's natural mechanisms should have produced some evidence of an upturn by early 1932 – but that had not happened. Those of the latter persuasion were also disappointed. Their hopes that the deployment of the first official model would dampen and shorten a downturn had been dashed. None of them, however, had given systematic thought before the fact to the possibility that the institutional fabric of the financial system might reach the state it did in late 1931. The viability of this crucial component of a modern economic system had been accepted as a given when the original prognoses on the course of depression had been offered.

While groping for new intellectual moorings, Hoover himself did not significantly widen the small circle of academic economists with whom he conferred. He was, however, the recipient of a lot of unsolicited advice from members of the academy. The practice of organizing economists to go on record on controversial issues of the moment had built up steam in the late spring of 1930 when more than 1,000 members of the profession petitioned Capitol Hill and the White House in opposition to the Smoot–Hawley Tariff Bill. On a more modest scale, this technique was to continue. In January 1932, for example, a seminar of selected economists convened by the Norman Wait Harris Foundation at the University of Chicago concluded its deliberations by dispatching a telegram to the president. Altogether, twenty-four members of an illustrious group recommended that the Federal Reserve be authorized to use government securities as cover for the note issue, that the central bank pursue open-market operations more aggressively, that the Reconstruction Finance Corporation proceed vigorously to aid the banks, and that the federal government maintain its program of public works at a level not lower than 1930–31.[1]

Hoover had little problem with these recommendations. They were in accord with what he had already done or hoped to have done in the early future. No doubt he would have preferred that the statement on public works be qualified. Like the signers of the telegram, he wanted this category of federal spending to be sustained with magnitudes at least as great as those of the preceding year, but wished to accomplish this without adding to the public debt. Even more to the presidential taste was a statement released to the press on January 16, 1932 by a number of the profession's most respected figures outlining a program characterized as the "least common denominator . . . upon which fairly general agreement appears possible." They called for passage of the RFC Bill, for "proper economy" in governmental budgeting and increased taxation, for a "liberal" Federal Reserve policy, and for a commercial banking policy which encouraged credit expansion.[2] The signers of both these memorials differed fundamentally among themselves on significant points of analysis and prescription. But when they sought common ground, they emerged with positions on domestic macroeconomic policy which were not very different from Hoover's. International economic policy was an altogether different matter: the president was not in accord with the sympathies expressed by these petitioners for reduction or cancellation of intergovernmental debts and for lower tariffs.

As reflections of the state of professional thinking at this stage of the depression, these submissions were far from representative. Some measure of consensus, even among those holding differing views, can always be found when statements on policy recommendations are sufficiently watered down. Such exercises in suppressing fundamental differences have their uses, but they often conceal as much as they reveal. More instructive are the responses of academicians to invitations for comment on specific issues in policy contention. This was a time when the opinions of economists were increasingly sought, both by citizens interested in promoting pet causes and by congressmen who sought support for or instruction on propositions appearing on the legislative agenda.

Fiscal activism in a new key

Calls for spending on public works in amounts greater than the administration had contemplated had been around since the earliest phases of the depression and they accelerated during 1931. The proposal that received the most serious attention was launched by William Randolph Hearst, publisher of a nationwide chain of newspapers. In June 1931 Hearst had called for a $5 billion federal bond issue to support an emergency program of public works. This was far beyond what Hoover had in mind, even before events later in the year led him to revise his earlier position on the place of spending for public works in the strategy for recovery.

To strengthen support for his proposal, Hearst invited M. S. Rukeyser, a financial columnist for the Hearst newspapers and a parttime lecturer in economics at Columbia University, to convene a select group of economists to assess the scheme. The upshot was a report released in early January 1932 endorsing a special bond issue of $5 billion, the proceeds of which should be allocated to additional spending on public works during the subsequent eighteen months. Rukeyser asserted that the report "carries a step forward the contribution which economists can make toward solving our problems. Heretofore the economists have merely advocated the broad principle of accelerating public works in time of depression while retarding them in periods of trade boom." But, he claimed, this report went beyond the general principles by addressing specifically the remedies required in "the existing economic situation." To ensure that the "fruits of this practical economic scholarship [were] available to responsible officers of the Federal Government," copies were distributed to the president and all members of Congress and the full text was reproduced in the *Congressional Record*.[3]

It was no accident that the list of thirty one original signers of this report included names associated with the discussion of public works as a stabilizing agent from the days of the President's Conference on Unemployment in the 1920s and its offshoots in the studies conducted at the National Bureau of Economic Research.[4] The substance of this document did indeed move well beyond the arguments advanced earlier by proponents of the public works strategy. The magnitudes of proposed expenditure were obviously much greater than had formerly been systematically contemplated. In the circumstances of 1932, spending an additional $5 billion on public works would imply that the expenditure side of the federal budget would be nearly doubled. Further, federal borrowing on the scale recommended would produce a deficit amounting to nearly 10 percent of the national income.

This group of economists gave short shrift to the notion that the federal government should be at pains to avoid encroaching on the normal functions of state and local authorities. It was assumed that the subordinate governmental echelons could not conceivably raise the sums needed to support necessary spending. The federal government, how-

ever, could and should do so. Its borrowings could then be rechanneled
to state, county, and municipal governments as grants in aid or as loans.
Aggregate expenditure on public works for the year 1932 of $5.4 billion
was regarded as "entirely practicable," of which $4 billion could use-
fully be spent by the political subdivisions. Projects with social merit
were not lacking. More could be done in road building, flood control,
and water management. But there were lots of other opportunities as
well – for example, airport construction, extension of the national park
system, reforestation, slum removal, the building of hospitals and li-
braries. Nor were the advocates of this approach overly concerned about
the possibility that a crash program of spending in 1932 might mean
that some public monies were allocated inefficiently. Some waste might
be incurred "through haste," they acknowledged, but inaction would
invite still more serious losses in the form of "the tremendous social
waste which results from supporting literally millions of men in enforced idleness" and the irrecoverable sacrifice of the outputs they could
produce. A "courageous program of public works, dramatically introduced and effectively carried through" was thus imperative. In the
words of the report, "such a program may well inject into our depressed
economy the vitality necessary to start us on the road to a real economic
recovery."[5]

The essentials of this approach to recovery were embodied in a bill
introduced by Senator Robert M. LaFollette (Progressive Republican
of Wisconsin) which called for an emergency federal bond issue of $5.5
billion, with $3.75 billion of this sum to be made available to support
spending on public works by state and local governments. Signers of the
"Economists' Plan" were in the vanguard in urging its adoption. In congressional testimony, they emphasized that this proposal was built on
foundations securely laid, with Hoover's active support and assistance,
in the studies of the 1920s. Moreover, the president had acted in the
spirit of this strategy in the first stages of depression fighting and they
commended the federal government for speeding up its own spending.
But the publicity that had surrounded the accelerated program undertaken by the federal government had produced an unfortunate side
effect. As Arthur D. Gayer observed, it was "only during the present
depression that an attempt has been made to speed public works on a
large and comprehensive scale." But its lack of success in warding off a
deepening of depression meant that this technique of policy had "received a black eye in some quarters" and that the public "to some considerable extent [had] lost faith in public works as a relief measure."
This, however, was not the correct conclusion. Even though federal
programs had been vastly enlarged, they had not been sufficient to offset

reductions in capital spending by state and local authorities in 1931. Despite popular impressions to the contrary, the potential of the public works strategy had thus not been put to the test.[6]

To make this case convincingly, it was not sufficient to argue that the public works strategy would do the job if backed by sufficient resources. In the circumstances of early 1932, it was also incumbent on the proponents of this policy to show that it was superior to Hoover's alternative approach. Hoover had backed away from his earlier support for deficit financing for public works primarily on the grounds that an increase in net federal borrowing would push up interest rates – and with consequences for the banks that would frustrate the revitalization of spending. The thirty-one "scientific economists" insisted, however, that this fear was largely groundless. As Gayer put it, "the whole situation [had] been entirely changed by the enactment of the Glass–Steagall bill. The banks must now surely be sufficiently strengthened to rob this argument of any force which it may have possessed in the past." Moreover, he maintained, "the assured prospect of an adequate public works program which would stimulate industrial production and raise commodity prices ought rather to strengthen the prices of all securities, including those held by banks."[7] Rukeyser embellished this argument with the claim that much of the finance needed for the proposed federal bond issue could be mobilized through a campaign in which bonds in small denominations were made widely available to the public. He was convinced that "large amounts of hoarded money would come out of hiding" if the government, as it had done during the war, actively engaged the citizenry in its financing operations. But the way it went about this was important. As he put it: "Instead of saying to John Jones 'You are a hoarder. Buy these anti-hoarding bonds,' it should say, 'You are a fine citizen with some surplus funds. Here is a good investment.' "[8] This handling of deficit financing would be doubly beneficial: not only would it permit Treasury issues to be placed at low interest rates; it would also assure that the effect of fiscal operations on total purchasing power would be unambiguously positive. Government could make sure that these funds were spent; had they remained in idle hoards, they obviously would not be. This view was seconded by Willard L. Thorp, professor of economics at Amherst College.[9]

The advocates of a more aggressive fiscal policy further parted company with Hoover in their appraisals of what might reasonably be expected from other components of Hoover's new program. The Reconstruction Finance Corporation and the open-market purchases of the Federal Reserve System were positive steps. But they alone could not do the necessary job. These measures, as William Trufant Foster saw matters, had been used "to a large extent to save [the banks] rather than to save business." There could be no quarrel about the importance of protecting banks from insolvency. Recovery, however, required that funds at the disposal of banks reenter the spending stream. This was unlikely to happen unless the federal government took the initiative as a borrower and spender on public works.[10] As Foster diagnosed matters: "The fact is that you have a situation where the bank credit which has been available all the time, and every single day of this depression, will not be utilized unless you have a force outside the profit system, which comes in to put it into circulation; and the only agency – whether you like it or not – that can do that is the Federal government." [11] Once the multiplying effects of public works spending had radiated throughout the system, then and only then would a state of confidence return to the private business community. Nor was the fear well-grounded that large-scale borrowing to set these wheels in motion would increase the burden of taxation. As Gayer put this aspect of the case: "If the restoration of business were assisted, tax receipts should greatly increase without the imposition of new or additional taxes. . . . In other words, this course of action should in itself create the values out of which it would be financed." [12]

All of this, Rukeyser maintained, reflected "the best thinking of our ablest contemporary economists." The White House might no longer be receptive to this brand of doctrine. But, he observed, "it augurs well for the future of the country that Congress is in touch with the best scientific thinking on current complex economic problems." [13]

The economists and a more modest proposal for a public works program in 1932

Though the thirty-one original signers of the Economists' Plan for 1932 had clearly moved beyond the thinking of the 1920s on the scale of public works programs in depression, their views were hardly typical of professional thinking at large. More representative was the correspondence generated by Senator Robert F. Wagner (Democrat of New York) who invited the reaction of "a number of the foremost economists of the country and a few businessmen and students of industrial relations" to a bill he had introduced. Its provisions differed significantly from those of the LaFollette Bill. The scale of borrowing contemplated was much lower: a federal bond issue of $1 billion (as opposed to $5.5 billion) was suggested. The projects to be undertaken would be restricted to those which had already been authorized and certified as meeting an established public need. Moreover, financing would be sought only for projects which were exclusively under federal jurisdiction. No transfers from the bond issue would be made to state or local governments. This was a far cry from the dramatic program advocated by the sponsors of the LaFollette Bill. Apart from the stipulation that financing be managed through a new debt issue, the provisions of the Wagner Bill otherwise met Hoover's 1932 tests of acceptability.

Wagner received 112 replies to his invitation for comment of April 20, 1932 from respondents distributed over 28 states and the District of Columbia. The bulk of the correspondence came from academic economists, with a scattering of contributions from business leaders, officials of labor organizations, political scientists, and academic lawyers. There were distinguished and highly respected names among them. Only a few of the signators of the Economists' Plan appeared in Wagner's sample, however. When requesting that the returns from this canvass be printed in the *Congressional Record*, Wagner observed that he found it "highly gratifying" that the views of these economists – whom he characterized as having "a right to be heard on the subject . . . by training and experience" – were "overwhelmingly in favor of the proposal." [14]

Strictly speaking, Wagner's assessment of the returns was correct. But a large number of the "yeas" were qualified. A minority on the favorable side of the ledger (including the few associated with the Economists' Plan) criticized the program for being insufficiently bold. Many more of them, though agreeing that something should be done, cautioned against the risks that unnecessary projects might be funded, adding that care should be taken in the financing to avoid disturbing bond markets or that explicit provision should be made for turning off the public works tap when recovery was in sight. Some were prepared to endorse the general principle, but objected to the notion that only projects previously authorized should be funded. Felix Frankfurter of the Harvard Law School, for example, preferred to see priority assigned to such projects as reforestation, river controls, parks, and adequate penal institutions, noting that further expenditure on highways was unneeded and worsened the problems of the railroads.[15] Richard T. Ely, professor of economics at the University of Wisconsin, suggested the creation of a "peace-time army" as an alternative – one which would be charged to take on such job-creating functions as reforestation, beautification of parks and roadsides, and improvement in the facilities of convalescent homes.[16] Others suggested that funds be allocated to rural electrification or to building improved housing for lower income groups. Frank G. Dickinson of the University of Illinois (one of the designers of countercyclical spending on public works in the 1920s) voiced his approval, but expressed the hope that no minimum-wage clause be included in the bill; the most important objective should be to maximize the number of men the available funds could employ.[17]

The reaction of the profession's "elder statesmen" to Wagner's proposal, however, fell considerably short of being overwhelmingly favorable. Ten economists who had served as presidents of the American Economic Association were among his respondents. Six of them registered their disapproval, while the four who expressed support did so with varying degrees of enthusiasm. In summary form, the views of those lining up in opposition were as follows (the dates of their tenure as AEA presidents are shown in parentheses).

Irving Fisher, Yale University (1918): the proposal for further government expenditure on public works at this time was seen as a "mistake" for two reasons: (1) "the psychology of the country is now in favor of balancing the Budget immediately," and (2) "reflation" was the urgent priority and further appropriations for public works "would take too long to give the immediate relief which is needed."[18]

Henry B. Gardner, Brown University (1919): Though sympathetic to the general principles of spending on public works "under the ordinary conditions of an industrial depression accompanied by great unemployment," he maintained that the essential next step "in the present depression" was to restore confidence in the financial system.[19]

Jacob Hollander, the Johns Hopkins University (1921): Noting that he had given his best thought to the question at hand as a member of the committee studying public works for the President's Organization on Unemployment Relief (which had recommended against further deficit financing for public works), he maintained that all efforts should be concentrated on averting the current "menace to our national solvency and to our credit structure."[20]

Edwin F. Gay, Harvard University (1929): In his judgment, balancing the budget was "imperatively called for" and this required reductions in expenditures. In particular, further extension of the road system – which had been a "major accomplishment" of the past decade – could be deferred "until States and municipalities have also started to economize."[21]

Matthew B. Hammond, Ohio State University (1930): He was "not opposed in principle" to appropriations for "necessary work," provided that provision for this expenditure had been made when conditions were normal. Even so, this procedure was "likely to be more beneficial for short terms of unemployment than as a means of curing such a depression as we are now in." In existing circumstances, further growth in the public debt, even for such a worthy purpose, would be unwise. Not only would the proposed measures "prove very unsettling to business conditions," they might hinder the price adjustments needed before industry could resume its operations.[22]

George E. Barnett, the Johns Hopkins University (1932): The proposal was held to be "inexpedient" on the grounds that a further bond issue would make the financial crisis "more severe."[23]

Four of the past occupants of the presidency of the American Economic Association responded more positively, though not without qualifications, to Wagner's solicitation.

Richard T. Ely, University of Wisconsin (and subsequently Northwestern University) (1900–1): His views, he observed, were "not out of substantial harmony" with Wagner's. They both believed that steps to reduce unemployment were necessary. For his part, however, Ely preferred the creation of a "peace-time army" which would "quicken the process of transfers of labor and capital from old to new fields."[24]

Edwin R. A. Seligman, Columbia University (1901–3): Though he would prefer to see private industry, rather than government, initiate an upward movement in the economy, he saw little prospect that this would happen "even if capital were made entirely costless – that is, if the discount rate were reduced to zero." A program along the lines Wagner had presented was "on the whole the lesser of the evils." Though there might be difficulties in placing a large bond issue "which would undoubtedly depress the market value of existing loans," it was his opinion that the time had come "for some constructive efforts on a really large scale. . . . [W]e must not forget the great dangers of inaction and further drifting."[25]

Frank W. Taussig, Harvard University (1904–5): Wagner was on "sound ground" in supporting "careful and discriminating expenditure on public works" and in financing it through a bond issue. It was possible that this step might "help substantially to give a much-needed boost," though no one could "be sure of just how great an effect will be produced."[26]

Walter F. Willcox, Cornell University (1915): The proposal received his wholehearted support. Its "main advantage" was that "putting the Government into the market to purchase goods and services would tend to check the catastrophic fall in the prices first of goods and then of the securities based on those goods."[27]

The elder statesmen among the academic economists were thus divided in their appraisals of the appropriate course of policy at this stage in the depression. Only a few were prepared to take positions with firm convictions in their rightness. Three years of depression had dealt a shattering blow to the confidence of the business community and had also shaken the self-confidence of many of the profession's leaders.[28] Some, however, were now prepared to associate themselves with new initiatives, not because they could offer a persuasive theoretical rationale for them, but from a belief that some action was imperative, even if it meant departing from the usual rules. The nay sayers among the leaders of the profession, on the other hand, tended to support their positions by invoking arguments similar to those Hoover had used when reshaping policy at the end of 1931.[29]

Polling on monetary questions and the statement of the Chicago position

Once the Glass–Steagall Act of February 1932 had created more space for the Federal Reserve to pursue a stimulative monetary policy, the focus of the public discussion on monetary questions shifted to two other legislative proposals: (1) the Patman Bill, which would finance the immediate payment of the remaining portion of the veterans' bonus through the issue of some $2.4 billion in currency (fiat money that would require no backing); and (2) the Goldsborough Bill, which would direct the Federal Reserve to conduct its affairs to restore the general price level to its average of the mid-1920s. In the confused climate of early 1932, considerable congressional support had been mobilized for these propositions and the economists were again called upon to provide expert testimony on their merits. For its part, the Hoover administration made no secret about its determined opposition to both of these propositions.

When the first installment of the veterans' bonus was legislated in 1931, it had generally been defended as a form of relief which could be legitimized in ways that other handouts from the public purse could not be. This aspect of the argument was still alive when the issue returned to the legislative agenda in 1932. The proponents of the Patman Bill, however, now gave greater prominence to a further argument: namely, that the direct injection of additional currency in amounts up to $2.4 billion would have an immediate impact on purchasing power and that the resulting enlargement of the money supply would tend to raise the general price level.

In mid-April 1932 Congressman Samuel B. Pettengill (Republican of Indiana) solicited the views of a group of the "leading economists of the country" on this proposal, and the responses he received displayed a remarkable unanimity. His sample included a number who had come out on opposite sides when the question of emergency spending for additional public works was under review. Carver of Harvard, Douglas of the University of Chicago, and Goodhue of Dartmouth College had endorsed the ambitious deficit spending called for in the Economists'' Plan. Seligman of Columbia and Knight of Chicago had taken positions quite different from that of Hollander of Johns Hopkins in their appraisals of the much more limited fiscal proposals of the Wagner Bill. But whatever their differences on other issues, they joined with other respondents to Pettengill's polling in rejecting the Patman proposal. This was an inefficient form of relief, as Hoover had long insisted. It was also damaging to suggest that the deficits it entailed should be financed by printing money.

Though most of the academicians responding to Pettengill's request for counsel did so individually and confined their remarks to the details of the specific legislation in question, twelve members of the faculty of economics at the University of Chicago collaborated in the submission of a much lengthier statement. In their collective view, action was indeed needed to raise prices, but "it should take the form of generous federal expenditures, financed without resort to taxes." Fiscal stimulus on the spending side should be sought primarily through a "heavy Federal contribution toward the relief of distress," and through "large appropriations for public and semi-public improvements." Of all of the "available devices" for increasing purchasing power, "generous bonus legislation would be the most objectionable." And, though deficits were healthy in the present state of the economy, they should ideally be financed by selling new Treasury bond issues directly to the Federal Reserve Banks. Printing greenbacks for this purpose, they argued, "must be ruled out unless one is ready to abandon gold immediately." They were prepared to face the possibility of abandoning gold "for a time" if it proved to be a necessary consequence of adequate fiscal stimulation. England's example, they noted, indicated that this could be done without disastrous consequences.[30]

While these arguments were nominally directed to the shortcomings of the Patman Bill, they were also an emphatic rejection of Hoover's economic policy in the spring of 1932. A current danger, they maintained, was that "measures of fiscal inflation may be too meager and too short lived. . . . [W]e should be prepared to administer heavy doses of stimulant if necessary, to continue them until recovery is firmly established." (This suggested another shortcoming in the bonus payout: it would be a once-and-for-all stimulant.) Once recovery was underway, a balanced budget would again be in sight. Federal revenues would increase with a revival in business and expenditures on relief could be retrenched. Temporary inflation induced by deliberate deficits was "the most promising means to restore a balanced Budget." Over the span of the next five years, the adoption of this program should mean that additional tax receipts would produce surpluses in magnitudes adequate to offset the deficits needed in a time of economic emergency. The rejection of key elements in Hoover's approach, such as the importance of expenditure containment and tax increases, the imperative of defending the gold standard, the avoidance of direct federal participation in relief payments, could not have been stated more sharply.

Few of the Chicago economists who took this stance in April 1932 would have subscribed to these positions even two years earlier. Most of the contributors to this document had, after all, been schooled in an analytic tradition which held that occasional downturns in economic activity were inevitable but that they were also self-correcting. It was the job of competitive markets to signal the adjustments in costs and prices that would enable the economic system to resume forward momentum. This automatic mechanism would still work, but, given the way in which the American economy had evolved, it would be painful and slow. "We have developed an economy," they noted, "in which the volume and velocity of credit is exceedingly flexible and sensitive, while wages and pegged prices are highly resistant to downward pressure. . . . As long as wage cutting is evaded by reducing employment, and as long as monopolies, including public utilities, resist pressures for lower prices, deflation may continue indefinitely."[31]

This line of reasoning had its roots in neoclassical orthodoxy and it contained an implicit indictment of the new era's encouragement of high wages and of the activities of trade associations. But the structural legacy of the 1920s could now be read as follows: "This is at once the explanation of our plight and the ground on which governmental action can be justified." A "courageous fiscal policy on the part of the central government" was now the only alternative to a continuation of "acute suffering" and "wastage of productive capacity."[32] The internal logic of this argument could, of course, have been turned in a different direction. Governmental action might instead have been urged to attack the points of "stickiness" impeding the adjustments in wages and prices needed for recovery. But these spokesmen for Chicago economics in 1932 sought a solution through innovation in macroeconomic policy, rather than by appealing for the use of familiar microeconomic prescriptions.

Conflicting interpretations from the heavyweights in monetary theory

Within the speciality of monetary theory, two of the profession's most highly respected thinkers were Irving Fisher of Yale and Edwin W.

Kemmerer of Princeton. Both had been honored with the presidency
of the American Economic Association. Both were eager to make their
views on policy known to the White House, to members of Congress,
and to the wider public. There was also a commonality in the analytic
structure within which they worked: the thought of both was grounded
in the quantity theory of money. Though they converged in opposing
the advance payment of the soldiers' bonus, they otherwise offered quite
divergent readings on the course of policy appropriate in 1932.

From Kemmerer's perspective, the central message conveyed by the
quantity theory of money was that the velocity of monetary circulation
had shrunk drastically during the years since 1929. According to his
calculations, the turnover of bank money (demand deposits) had fallen
to about half of its normal level. The major deflation in the general
price level followed directly from this state of affairs. On these points
of demonstrable fact, he and Fisher concurred. They differed fundamentally, however, on the inferences for policy to be drawn from these
findings.

In Kemmerer's interpretation, little could be accomplished by increasing the money supply, whether by printing money or by pressing
the central bank to enlarge the lending capacity of banks still further.
Currency and credit were already amply available. Attention, instead,
should be focused primarily on creating conditions that would increase
the velocity of circulation. The basic requirement for reaching this objective was the restoration of confidence. The revival of industry, he
argued, chiefly depended on the initiative of the nation's industrial,
commercial, and financial leaders. He characterized America as a young,
large, vigorous, and buoyant country. Normally, its economy grew faster
than that of the rest of the world. The United States could thus be expected to take the lead in lifting the international community out of
depression. But that leadership, he maintained, "will have to come to a
great extent from the people who have been leaders in the past."[33]

Whether or not those latent energies would soon be reactivated depended, in Kemmerer's judgment, on holding firm to established monetary principles and, more particularly, on rejecting schemes which might
further disturb the confidence of the business and financial community.
As far as the fiat money proposals were concerned, he could "imagine
few things . . . that would do more to destroy confidence on the part of
these people, upon whose initiative we must depend to lead us out of
this slough of despond, . . . than to adopt a measure of this kind."[34] Unconventional monetary tinkering would be counterproductive in a further respect: America's commitment to the gold standard would there-

by be placed in jeopardy. As Kemmerer described the likely chain of events:

It would cause a heavy withdrawal of gold from the country by foreigners having liquid credits here, and by other foreigners who would obtain gold through the sale of their security holdings, dumping them on the market even at heavily sacrifice prices. It would temporarily still further reduce the rates of monetary and deposit turnover. All this would spell deflation. Gold would go out of the country; money in the country would be hoarded; people that had it would be afraid to use it, and you would have a temporary period . . . of greater lack of confidence than you now have.[35]

This was certainly not what the country needed. Nor could it look with anything but alarm at the longer term consequences of a departure from the gold standard. Inconvertible paper money inflation would be the ultimate result, with disastrous consequences for future social and economic stability.

Kemmerer conceded that the "shell shock" of 1929 had produced a price level that was now both abnormal and unhealthy. But, he observed, "as soon as we get over this scare, we will swing back much nearer the commodity price level of 1921 to 1929."[36] To get there, the conditions to accelerate the velocity of monetary circulation would have to be nurtured. The open-market policies of the Federal Reserve might help, though he was far from sure on that point.[37] In this reading of the situation, it was the behavior of the V, not of the M, in the equation of exchange that mattered most. And the velocity variable was influenced primarily by psychological factors beyond the control of the central bank. Success in moving the value of velocity in the right direction turned on reaffirmation of the orthodoxies of sound money, the gold standard, and fiscal responsibility. These were the considerations which should guide the conduct of macroeconomic policy. But the United States should also encourage "wise international cooperation" and rally other countries around the banner of the gold standard.[38]

Kemmerer's line of thought, with its emphasis on the importance of rebuilding confidence, was obviously congenial to Hoover in the context of the spring of 1932. Fisher, on the other hand, pressed the Congress and the White House for the adoption of a quite different approach to monetary affairs. Since the early 1920s, he had insisted that business fluctuations were controllable through scientific monetary management directed to the stabilization of the general price level. But the tools to accomplish this had obviously not been effectively used in combatting the post-1929 deflation and the nation had suffered grievously and unnecessarily. By 1932 the right kind of monetary intervention was all the more urgent. The theoretical framework in which he had molded his thought in the 1920s was now extended to perform two jobs simultaneously: (1) it could offer an account of what had gone wrong, and (2) it could point the direction in which the proper types of interventionist strategies could be devised.

Fisher's extension of quantity-theory reasoning to an explanation of depression and its persistence rested on a distinction between two varieties of "disease": the "debt disease" and the "dollar disease." Retrospectively, it could now be seen that the nation had indulged in an unfortunate orgy of borrowing in the late 1920s. In the early stages of the depression, Fisher had not seen it that way. Indeed, he had been among the critics of the central bank's belated efforts (undertaken at Hoover's urging) to restrain borrowing for the purchase of common stocks. From the vantage point of 1932, he recanted that part of his earlier position: "By the debt disease I mean that in 1929 we had accumulated a tremendous overindebtedness. It showed itself first in the collapse in the stock market, because the American public had been speculating to such a tremendous degree, and speculating in the stock market is simply going into debt."[39] Such indebtedness made the system highly vulnerable to any disturbance. As he then put it: "When you have this overindebtedness, and people try to get out of debt by liquidating, . . . it causes distressed selling and the contraction of the currency, and therefore a fall of prices."[40] Deflation, in turn, infected the system with the "dollar disease." Falling prices shrank the revenues of businesses, but expenditures to which they were already committed by contract, particularly for debt service charges, were unchanged. If firms were to stay afloat, they were obliged to cut costs in other ways, notably by laying off workers and reducing the scale of their operations. But the wider significance of the so-called dollar disease was that it increased the real burden of debt, not just for firms, but also for households. This phenomenon generated a further wave of distress selling and still more downward pressure on the price level. Nor – short of universal bankruptcy – were there any mechanisms inherent within the economic system to bring this process to a halt. On the contrary, accelerated deflation was likely to be cumulative.[41]

The remedy was implicit in the diagnosis. "Reflation," by which Fisher meant the restoration of the general price level to its mid-1920s levels, was imperative. Only when debt burdens were relieved could the spending needed for recovery be resumed. The crucial instrument for accomplishing this was a directive to the Federal Reserve to expand the money supply to raise the price level to its altitude of the mid-1920s and thereafter to stabilize it. This was the intent of the Goldsborough Bill, for which Fisher was an impassioned advocate. Fisher applauded the open-market purchases the system had undertaken since February 1932. But this concession to his point of view, he insisted, was not a valid argument against writing specific instructions to the Federal Reserve into the law of the land. If the Goldsborough Bill had been on the statute books earlier, "our Federal Reserve people could not have indulged in this disastrous delay." Nor could the central bankers, on their own, be trusted to stay on course. When lobbying for speedy action by the Senate following the passage of this bill by the House of Representatives, Fisher asserted: "To my mind it is monstrous to entrust to Eugene Meyer's or any other man's or men's unrestrained discretion the fixing of the value of my dollar and yours, and to allow their action, or neglect to act, to increase or decrease public and private debts by fifty or sixty per cent."[42]

While Fisher's approach to monetary policy gave priority to the M, the importance of V was not overlooked. The target was reflation and the value of V had an obvious bearing on the volume of monetary expansion needed to reach it. Fisher proposed that this aspect of monetary reconstruction be dealt with in three ways. In the first place, the law governing the determination of required reserve ratios of member banks should be amended to permit automatic variation in the ratio to compensate for changes in velocity. When velocity was falling, reserve requirements should be reduced, and vice versa.[43] Second, action should be taken to enact a federal program of guarantees of deposits held in member banks. Though he was aware of technical problems in putting an adequate deposit insurance scheme in place, he was convinced that it would go far toward addressing the question of confidence (on which Kemmerer's analysis of the behavior of velocity rested). In Fisher's view, "If you really could convince people that member banks were safe, hoarding would stop overnight and . . . if hoarded money were put back into banks, it would soon go on its way, to be multiplied by 10. There are plenty of people who are willing to borrow at banks."[44] In Fisher's thinking, one of the articles of the "new era" faith – that there was no deficiency in the demand for credit if the conditions of credit supply were right – thus survived.

In mid-July 1932 Fisher added a third ingredient to his program for accelerating the velocity of circulation. This was a proposal for "stamped dollars," which had been brought to his attention by E. S. Barker, branch manager of an oil company in Chippewa Falls, Wisconsin, and Fisher quickly assimilated it. In his formulation of the scheme at that time, the government should print a special issue of dollar bills with space on the reverse side to place a one-cent postage stamp. These bills would circulate as legal tender, provided they were kept current by affixing a one-cent stamp each week. This would have an immediate effect in raising the tempo of monetary velocity. Any holder of such a bill would have a clear incentive to pass it on before being obliged to buy the required stamp. Fisher proposed that this special currency issue be widely distributed, say $100 in notes to every adult identified in the last census. Thus instant purchasing power would be "placed into the hands of every consumer, including the unemployed." This would directly advance the cause of reflation. But the scheme had yet another attractive feature: it would more than pay for itself. At the end of two years, the government would have collected $1.04 from the sale of stamps for each dollar of this special issue. One dollar of the proceeds could then be used to retire the notes, and the surplus could be allocated to a fund to support the unemployed. Thus, two worthwhile objectives could be served at once: the quickening of economic activity through monetary stimulation and automatic provision for relief.[45]

Within the framework of Fisher's brand of monetary interventionism, other issues of the moment could be seen in a different light. For Kemmerer and Hoover, moving the federal finances in the direction of balance was essential to the stiffening of public confidence. Fisher, on the other hand, maintained that the effect of the administration's fiscal program was the reverse: it had not restored confidence, but "spread a new terror in the minds of taxpayers" which had caused more deflation. At the same time, he believed that "it would only confuse the public to contest . . . the policy of balancing the budget." The real significance of the adoption of this policy, he insisted, was that it made the case for reflation all the more urgent. As he put it: "We can't tax a vacuum. . . . If we could reflate first, we would have something to tax later." Nor should prompt action along this line be delayed by fears about its consequences for the U.S. commitment to gold. Fisher had long held that stabilization in the general price level took precedence over constancy in the gold content of the dollar. In the circumstances of deep depression, policies appropriate to initiate recovery should not be immobilized by the mystique of gold. "If, for any reason, the gold standard becomes endangered," he wrote, "we must go off it rather than drown by clinging to it."[46]

The voice of Alvin Hansen as an exponent of neoclassical orthodoxy

Most academic economists in the 1920s had viewed the claims of the economics of the "new era" with considerable skepticism. In their eyes, policies that promoted the coordination of production decisions of businessmen, the maintenance of high wages, or the deployment of public works spending to buffer downturns in income and employment were of very doubtful merit. What they were instead likely to produce was an increased rigidity in the system which would impede its natural adjustment to changes in market conditions. In short, governmental tampering with the delicate mechanisms of the market, whether done directly or indirectly, was likely to produce far more harm than good.

By 1932 some who had subscribed to principles of neoclassical doctrine were prepared to modify their position with respect to the role of government in the promotion of recovery. The rigidities within the system, many of them by-products of misguided intervention in the past, were still lamented. Indeed they were held to be largely responsible for the mess in which the nation found itself and for the failure of the economy to right itself in the normal way. But with the "stickiness" in the mechanisms of wage–price adjustment the inescapable reality – and one that could not be changed quickly without intolerable economic and social strain – they were prepared to support extraordinary governmental intervention to deal with a state of emergency. On this basis, some with well-established credentials as orthodox neoclassicists, with signers of the Economists' Plan for 1932 and of the University of Chicago memorandum among them, could support aggressive and deliberate deficit spending. The validity of the message of the earlier doctrine did not have to be brought into question. The issue instead was its applicability, on practical grounds, in an unprecedented situation.

While some of the more orthodox academicians of the 1920s chose this route, others held more firmly to established positions on the hazards associated with governmental intervention. To students of the history of economic ideas in twentieth-century America, the most fascinating figure in this camp was Alvin H. Hansen. He is now chiefly remembered, and rightly so, as the leading American interpreter of the doctrines of Keynes's *General Theory*. But this stage in his career began in 1938. As late as 1936, he had been unsympathetic to a Keynesian approach to economic theory and policy.[47] In 1932 he was even more negative toward major lapses from laissez faire. Though he joined others in diagnosing the condition of the economy as largely the result of "rigidities" that had been built into the system, he parted company with those who concluded that an emergency compelled accommodation to that situation. The policy of wage maintenance, Hansen argued, had been "inimical to economic recovery."[48] Similarly, the effort to contain a downswing through accelerated spending on public works had been a mistake: this effort, though well-intentioned, tended to delay the needed

readjustments and "work[ed] counter to the forces making for cost reduction."[49] These were restatements of concerns to which he had drawn
attention in the 1920s. By 1932 he had made one concession. Public
works spending, on a limited basis, might have a useful role to play, once
downward adjustments in costs had been "substantially completed."
Nevertheless, this strategy was still not free of ambiguity. On the one
hand, it might "cut short what might otherwise be a long flat bottom of
depression . . . partly by mopping up idle funds and so raising prices,
and partly by restoring business confidence." On the other, "a large
program of public works, financed by bond issues, could easily have the
effect of postponing revival of business by affecting adversely the security flotations of private corporations."[50] Nor could monetary experimentation safely be undertaken. In all probability, unconventional
measures would conflict with the principles of the gold standard. This
method of international monetary organization remained the best hope
for a reconstruction of the international system on terms which would
encourage freer conditions for world trade and investment. The Keynesian style of thinking, from this point of view, amounted to a reversion
to the discredited doctrines of mercantilism and the nationalistic rivalries that went with them.

What then was the way out? In Hansen's reading of matters, a healthy
recovery could not begin until the maladjustments in the structure of
costs and prices, the very maladjustments that had brought the boom to
an end, had been corrected. Government could hasten this process by
encouraging, rather than impeding, wage and price flexibility. And it
could also aid in reducing costs by retraining workers to raise their productivity. He favored generous provision for the needs of the unemployed. They bore the major hardships of the readjustment process and
he held it to be unfortunate that the nation had not put in place a comprehensive system of unemployment insurance. In its absence, adequate
relief payments were imperative. Ideally, their distribution should be
linked with participation in training programs to upgrade the skills of
the jobless. There was thus no lack of unfinished business which properly belonged on the agenda of government. But the priorities of governmental intervention should be defined to assign pride of place to
measures that reduced costs, increased efficiency, and produced prices
that could meet the test of open international competition.

But there was also more than a hint in Hansen's thought in 1932
that the worldwide depression at this time might be fundamentally different from the cyclical disturbances that had recurred in American
economic history. Some longer term structural factors might also help
to account for the extraordinary depth and persistence of this depres-

sion. The boom years of the 1920s, he noted, had been associated with massive investments spurred particularly by a revolution in transportation with the coming of age of the automobile era and by technological advances in the production and distribution of electrical energy. Much of the infrastructure required for this phase of the industrial revolution had now been put in place. Ultimately, research and development would give birth to new products and new processes which would induce a fresh upsurge in capital spending. Unfortunately, no one could predict just when that would happen. A solid recovery could be assured when it did. Meanwhile, unconventional monetary and fiscal stimuli should be viewed suspiciously. They were more likely than not to distort costs and prices. This result, in turn, would postpone the day when the next technological breakthrough would arrive.

Protests against relaxation of the antitrust laws

In the environment of 1932, consensus was certainly lacking among the economists about what the optimum course for macroeconomic policy should be. But a significant block of academic opinion could be mobilized about what should *not* be done in microeconomic policy. In particular, economists whose views on other matters were widely divergent could join forces in attacking proposals brought forward by the business groups for whom the Swopes and Harrimans spoke. Their calls for amendments in the antitrust laws to permit industrial associations to coordinate production decisions and to stabilize prices were now becoming increasingly insistent. By June 1932 pressure was mounting on the major political parties to embrace these schemes in their platforms for the presidential campaign.

Such prescriptions for the ailments of the economy were far from congenial to most of the professionals in the academy. Tugwell and, to a much lesser degree, John Maurice Clark, might be sympathetic to restructuring that encouraged greater coordination and control over the production process. To that extent, they parted company with the bulk of their academic colleagues. Even so, they did not find the formula promoted by business groups to be acceptable. In their view, decision-making authority could not safely be entrusted to businessmen.

In the judgment of Frank A. Fetter of Princeton (American Economic Association president, 1912), members of the economics profession had a social obligation to expose the "absurdity" of the "propaganda for the material modification or repeal of the Sherman Act."[51] Under his chairmanship, a planning group was convened in the late spring of 1932 to draft a statement for submission to the platform committees of the Republican and Democratic conventions. The document that emerged called for the "rejection of the assertion made by those seeking to break down the Sherman Act, that it makes necessary the development of excessive capacity and wasteful over-production" and the rejection as well of "the equally false assertion that this was one of the causes of the present industrial depression." To the contrary, the statement maintained that "the most competent economic opinion, as well in Europe as in this country, can be cited in support of the view that a strong contributing cause of the unparalleled severity of the present depression was the greatly increased extent of monopolistic control of commodity prices which stimulated financial speculation in the security markets."[52] What was needed was more vigorous enforcement of the existing antitrust laws and a strengthening of procompetitive policies.

On short notice, Fetter rallied 127 signators from 43 institutions and 24 states. Their ranks included seven former presidents of the American Economic Association.[53] When reporting on the result of this canvass, Fetter noted that the organizing committee had not polled its full strength. The petition had been hastily circulated to a limited number of economists – in most cases, only one per institution – and they were invited to bring it to the attention of their colleagues. This activity, however, occurred at the end of the academic year. It thus seemed reasonable to assume that many who would have been willing to endorse the principles set out in the statement did not have an opportunity to do so.

The total number of academicians who lent their names to the statement on antitrust law policy was less significant than the identity of those who signed on. A fair number who had not publicly identified themselves as pro or con in the debates over fiscal and monetary policies could readily support this cause. Still more striking, however, was the fact that many who did not see eye to eye on prescriptions for macroeconomic policy could join forces in support of this proposition. The signators included some who had opposed emergency spending on public works (even on the limited scale of the Wagner Bill), such as Hansen and Hammond. Five of the 31 "scientific economists" who supported the Hearst plan for deficit financing on public works on a much grander scale also recorded their opposition to any relaxation in the antitrust laws.[54] Similarly, five of the University of Chicago economists who had called for an aggressive fiscal policy were on the list.[55]

The hasty and selective samplings of professional opinion on antitrust policy by the Fetter committee did not, however, yield endorsements from all quarters. Those whose thoughts had turned to a greater role for government as a planner were not represented.[56] Nor were the names of any of the more prominent agricultural economists to be found among the signers. Faculty members at Yale and Princeton were apparently circularized. The names of the monetary experts at these respective institutions, Fisher and Kemmerer, did not appear among the signators, however.

At a time when professional opinion on economic policy spanned a wide spectrum, it was nevertheless the case that economists in the academy could come closer to agreement on what should not be done in industrial policy than they could on any other issue apart from tariff policy. Hoover may have been able to draw some comfort from this finding. He regarded the Swope–Harriman proposals as monstrous. A very respectable body of academic economists concurred in this judgment.

Challenges and responses

There could be no question that the flow of events in late 1931 and early 1932 generated new challenges to economic thinking. A number of the most thoughtful members of the profession rose to them by endorsing policy experiments that they might normally have viewed with some suspicion. After all, the times were indeed extraordinary. In such circumstances, trying something different, even when the consequences of unconventional interventions could not be forecast with confidence, seemed to be worth doing. The attitudes of some of the advocates of unprecedented deficit financing in peacetime and of a more visible hand of government as a planner can best be understood in this way.

But support for new departures in economic policy during a period of emergency need not imply that economists had lost faith in the models that informed their understandings of the economic process. On the contrary, most members of the profession remained in character with respect to their analytic positions. It is always possible to retain one's belief in the validity of an established set of ideas, even in the face of awkward facts that appear to run counter to it. One of the properties of internally consistent economic models is their enormous survival power. The predictions they generate may be demonstrably inaccurate. But, after the fact, confidence in the essential truth of the theoretical system can be salvaged so long as it can provide reasons to account for the discrepancy between the expectation and the reality.

Within the framework of their initial premises, economists of all persuasions had little difficulty in offering explanations, ex post, for what had happened. Those sympathetic to a laissez-faire approach could maintain that the failure of the system's inherent recuperative powers to reassert themselves was the consequence of excessive governmental meddling and of rigidities in wage and price setting in the private sector. Supporters of the macroeconomic stabilization model offered by the "new economics" of the 1920s could argue that intervention had not been pressed as far or as vigorously as it should have been. Similarly, those who had insisted earlier that the economic system was structurally flawed – so flawed that neither the invisible hand nor a visible one guided by the rules of the Hooverites could address its problems – could see events as confirming the rightness of their convictions.

On the whole, American academic economists tended to read the fourth year of depression through analytic lenses that had been ground in the 1920s. Though an increasing number were prepared to be flexible on points of macroeconomic policy, few were ready to jettison the theories with which they worked. There were, however, some interesting extensions from the original doctrinal positions. One example is Irving Fisher's adaptation of his monetary thought from a formula to repeal the "laws" of the business cycle to an explanation of cumulative deflation; another is the seeds of an idea of secular "stagnation" that began to sprout in Alvin Hansen's attempt to account for the unusual persistence of this depression. For the most part, however, the crisis of the economy was not matched by a sense of crisis about the state of economic theory.

CHAPTER 10

Official model II as shaped in May 1932 and the aftermath

Though debates among the academic economists would continue to rage about the proper interpretation of events and about appropriate courses for economic policy, Hoover could not wait until the professionals resolved their differences before deciding on next steps. By May 1932 it was clear that the attack on the liquidity trap begun in February had failed. Hoarding had begun again, the rate of bank failures – which for a time had been slowed – accelerated, and the gold outflow had resumed.

These setbacks notwithstanding, the experience of the preceding months had still taught some lessons. In the first place, it had exposed the fragility of the banking structure even more clearly, and this seemed to underscore further the importance of a fiscal policy designed to support bond values. Second, it had demonstrated that banks could not be relied upon to stimulate the flow of credit, even when their capacity to do so had been considerably augmented. This finding suggested that other measures would be needed to reactivate lending and spending. Third, the disappointing performance of the economy meant that the administration's hopes that the momentum of recovery would be well underway by the early autumn were unlikely to be fulfilled. In view of that prospect, a rethinking of the federal government's role in the provision of relief appeared to be in order.

Even though the strategy adopted at the beginning of the year had not achieved its objective, Hoover was determined to regain the initiative. He could agree with part of the diagnosis of the situation then offered by Keynes. Writing in May 1932, Keynes observed that "to-day the primary problem is to avoid a far-reaching financial crisis," adding that he believed this point to be better understood in the United States than it was anywhere else. Keynes further maintained that the stimulation of industry was not the "front-rank problem," but one which "must come second in order of time."[1] Hoover would certainly not challenge the importance assigned to financial reconstruction in this assessment. But he was ready to move beyond Keynes on the timing of measures to stimulate industrial activity. Among other things, Hoover faced an electoral timetable which demanded that he produce some evidence of positive results within the next few months. In order to get them, he was willing to make some quite unconventional moves to spur reemployment. They were presented in a manner that maintained continuity with a crucial component of the strategy revisions formulated in the preceding December: that is, it was reasserted that the federal government should not be a net borrower. Nevertheless, official model II as refined in May 1932 contained some novel twists which, though camouflaged, amounted to dramatic departures from some of Hoover's earlier positions.

Reformulation of the functions of the Reconstruction Finance Corporation

In May 1932 the Hoover administration embarked on a full-scale effort to equip government with tools to stimulate capital spending. The vehicle chosen for this purpose was the Reconstruction Finance Corporation, but one with its jurisdiction and resources vastly enlarged. The legislation already in place enabled the corporation to perform useful services in strengthening financial institutions, and these activities were to be continued. The new functions the administration sought for it involved quite different types of lending from the ones it was first set up to handle. Hoover and his senior colleagues now wanted RFC to be empowered to finance capital spending by private industry and by state and local governments for the construction of certain types of public facilities. In its first proposals for RFC in December 1931, the administration had recommended, without success, that the corporation be authorized to supply working capital to going concerns in the private sector which could demonstrate their creditworthiness and their inability to obtain finance through the usual banking channels. What was now urged was something altogether new: that RFC enter the business of investment banking to underwrite spending on fixed capital. Hoover described the purpose of this proposal as follows:

[T]he program contemplates providing the machinery whereby employment may be increased through restoring normal occupations rather than works of artificial character. . . . [T]here are a large number of economically sound and self-supporting projects of a constructive replacement character that would unquestionably be carried forward were it not for the present situation in the capital markets. . . . There is no dearth of capital, and on the other hand there is a real demand for capital for productive purposes that have been held in abeyance.[2]

Adding investment banking to the mission of the RFC meant, how-ever, that the financial resources available to the corporation would need to be augmented. Accordingly, the administration recommended that RFC's entitlement to issue debt obligations in its own name be doubled (from the original provision for $1.5 billion to $3 billion). These issues would still be guaranteed by the Treasury, but they would not appear in the Treasury's budgetary accounts. As Hoover put it: "It is proposed to provide the necessary funds as they are required by the sale of securities of the Reconstruction Finance Corporation. . . . It is not proposed to issue Government bonds."[3]

These distinctions were obviously crucial to presenting the appear-ance of a balanced budget (as the administration had redefined it) for fiscal year 1933. But it did not follow that the impact on the economy of federal financing operations was intended to be neutral. A posture of fiscal neutrality had to be nurtured – partly to remain consistent with the bond-support strategy for protecting financial institutions, partly to reassure those investors whose state of confidence was sensitive to what was reported in the Treasury returns, and partly as a way to rein in congressional mavericks eager to spend freely but on the wrong things. The reality could be different so long as it was kept "off-budget." Not the least of the recommendations for the RFC as the vehicle for in-tervention was that it provided a technique for stimulating spending which would not be reported in the Treasury's accounts. If Congress acted favorably on Hoover's recommendations for extension in the scale and scope of RFC, the agency of federal authority could, in principle, make more than $3 billion available to underwrite additional capital spending.[4] If this funding, in turn, were to be spent promptly on capital projects, the increase in aggregate investment would be of the order of 5 percent of GNP.

Segregating "Treasury debt" from "Treasury-guaranteed debt" was clearly a matter of fundamental importance to the internal consistency of this pattern of thinking. But a sharp line to distinguish these opera-tions was not altogether easy to draw. The ink had scarcely been dry on the act creating the RFC when a firm of government bond brokers in Chicago pressed the Treasury for clarification on two points: (1) Were the obligations of the RFC to be defined technically as "obligations of the United States government," and (2) were RFC obligations redeem-able in gold?[5] The solicitor of the Treasury judged the answer to the first of these questions to be "yes," noting that "although in form a private corporation and liable to be sued as such, [it] is in fact a Gov-ernment Corporation."[6] To the second query, the RFC offered a hedged response in March 1932: "Although the RFC Act provides that the

Corporation may issue debentures, it does not restrict the security to gold. The Corporation, of course, is not considered a part of the U.S. Treasury, and like any other organization, can set its own security. It is not expected that a decision along this line will be made until the Corporation prepares to issue debentures."[7]

Ambiguities on the nature of RFC debt were, in fact, compounded when the corporation began to issue obligations in its own name. When RFC was first discussed, the administration had cultivated the impression that "Reconstruction Finance Corporation bonds" would be made available for purchase by the general public. The text of the final bill authorizing the creation of the corporation included a provision, however, that the Treasury, if it saw fit, could purchase debt obligations created by the RFC. This feature of the bill had been drafted by the Treasury and was regarded as "vitally important."[8] The corporation first activated its borrowing authority on April 26, 1932, when it issued notes for $250 million bearing interest at the rate of 3½ percent and scheduled to mature on October 27, 1932. These obligations were not offered to the public, however, but were instead absorbed completely by the Treasury. For that matter, all of the subsequent issues of RFC obligations during the Hoover presidency were placed in the same way. This method of financing, in turn, required the Treasury to increase its borrowings from the private market. A tight distinction between RFC financing and Treasury financing thus became even more elusive.

Even though the Treasury augmented its borrowings to supply funds to RFC, it was still possible to keep faith with Hoover's claim that no new issues of government bonds would be made for this purpose. Technically, this could be accomplished through the use of Treasury bills and short-dated notes (rather than long-dated bonds). Maintaining that these transactions were fundamentally different from ordinary deficit financing required some additional argument, however. Secretary of the Treasury Mills supplied it when responding to the financial editor of the *New York Evening Post*, who had charged him with misrepresenting the facts in the Treasury's statement about the state of the finances at the close of fiscal year 1932. Specifically, Mills was accused of understating the real magnitude of the deficit in his treatment of the Treasury's borrowing to finance RFC. These transactions, Mills insisted, were properly excluded from the regular accounts. Borrowing, to be sure, had been required for this purpose, but the funds raised had not been used for ordinary spending. Instead they had been used to acquire short-term assets in the form of RFC debt obligations which, in turn, were fully collateralized by sound loans which would ultimately be paid off. If the acquisition of these assets were to be budgeted as an ordinary expense, then at the time of their liquidation or sale by the Treasury the proceeds would have to be recorded as current receipts. This procedure, Mills maintained, would mislead the public by permitting the Treasury at that point to show a surplus that was not genuine.[9]

If this matter was still a bit shadowy, Hoover and his senior associates were at least clear about what they wanted to accomplish. The goal was to put facilities of government to work to spur investment. In principle, there is no reason to suppose that off-budget deficit financing should be any less stimulating to the macroeconomic system than deficits financed "on budget." Indeed Hoover and Mills suggested that the former would be more stimulating per dollar of borrowing than the latter for two reasons: (1) keeping up appearances of a nominal balance in the Treasury accounts should contribute positively to stiffening the confidence of private investors, and (2) capital spending facilitated by the RFC could be set in motion quickly and far faster than outlays of the same size could be spent for an enlarged program of federal public works. If everything fell into place, the off-budget deficit of the federal government might exceed $3 billion – a sum nearly as large as the total "on budget" spending projected for fiscal year 1933.

Equipping RFC to do an investment banker's job was the key ingredient of the new official model. But the administration also proposed another innovation at this time: RFC should be authorized to lend, in amounts not to exceed $300 million, to state governments needing help in supplying relief to the needy. These recommendations called for a major expansion of the domain of federal jurisdiction into territory that had previously been held to be forbidden. The conventional rules about the relationships between the federal government and other governmental units, on the one hand, and federal involvement with the private business sector, on the other, were now being considerably bent.

These departures could have been displayed as part of a bold new program with attention directed to its innovative features. Hoover choose instead to surround them with conservative imagery. The proposed interventions, he maintained, were occasioned by circumstances that were exceptional and were to be limited in duration. Moreover, all of RFC's lending activities would be governed by criteria of "soundness." This meant that its monies would be made available only for "bankable" projects: that is, potential borrowers would have to present adequate security and they would also be obliged to demonstrate that funds would be spent on projects capable of generating sufficient income to service and amortize the debt. Loans for relief purposes were necessarily an exception to this rule. These applications would thus need to be screened with particular care. Hoover insisted that there should be no retreat from the "fundamental policy" that "responsibility for relief to distress belongs to private organizations, local communities, and the States."[10] To ensure that state and local governments remained mindful of their proper duties, federal assistance for relief would take the form of loans, but not grants, and would be available only when the state governor certified that local capacity to address essential needs had been pressed to its limit. In addition, the federal government's financial stake in this activity would be safeguarded through an administrative arrangement that could be invoked in the event state governments defaulted on "relief loans." Should that happen, a state's entitlement to future federal grants in aid for highway construction would be adjusted downward.

The Hoover administration was now prepared to play for high stakes and to use some heterodox methods when doing so. But heterodoxy was garbed in a mantle of orthodoxy. Ironically, the logical necessities involved in making this accommodation were to be partially responsible for the undoing of the new grand design.

The attempt to promote official model II

The task of persuading Congress to move forward with the administration's latest strategy fell primarily to Secretary of the Treasury Ogden L. Mills. His mission was twofold: (1) to sell the desirability of RFC lending for capital projects, particularly to private industries, and (2) to demonstrate that the administration's scheme for stimulating spending was superior to the alternatives being pushed in Congress and to be preferred especially to the large appropriations for bond-financed emergency public works then actively under consideration on Capitol Hill.

In appearances before congressional committees, Mills set out the rationale for additional lending authority for the RFC as follows:

[W]e have had a depression extending over two and a half years that has reached a point lower than any other depression in the history of this country, and in the course of those two and a half years there must have piled up a very large demand, including a very large demand for the replacement of machinery, for reconstruction of all kinds and characters, and certainly in so far as building is concerned, a very real demand in some sections of the country for the building of houses.[11]

Capital spending, he calculated, had fallen to about 25 percent of the levels achieved in 1929. Reviving it should thus be the primary target of a strategy for uplifting business and employment. But, for all practical purposes, the bond market for new corporate issues was paralyzed. It was thus essential to allow RFC to lend "for capital purposes to private industry." To be sure, it was unusual for government to be a party to activities which normally should be handled by investment bankers. Extending the range of RFC in this direction was "necessary if we are to do this job on a large enough scale to be effective." [12] Mills emphasized that the government did not intend to claim more than a temporary place in the investment banking business: "[A]ll we are seeking to do here is prime the motor." [13] When normal economic conditions returned and responsible long-term borrowers could market their debt instruments in the private sector, RFC would stand aside as an underwriter. Nor would government be exposing itself to any significant risks in the meantime. Mills was "morally certain that within five years these bonds [acquired by the RFC] can be sold to the public and the loan paid off," provided that sound judgment was exercised to ensure that the projects so financed were "truly self-sustaining." [14]

This way of looking at matters also provided reasons why RFC's facilities should not be universally available to all potential borrowers who could produce adequate collateral and who could show that the banks had failed to accommodate them. Speaker of the House John N. Garner (Democrat of Texas and subsequently vice-president under Franklin D. Roosevelt) had introduced a bill proposing that the powers of the RFC be broadened to do precisely that. The rationale was straightforward: If greater scope for the RFC was a good thing, why then should not its facilities be made available to the little fellows as well as to potential issuers of large denomination bonds? This proposition was totally unacceptable to the administration. To rebut it, Mills insisted that lending to support capital spending was the paramount objective. While RFC should be allowed to function as an investment banker, it both could not and should not behave as a commercial banker. The former function was essential in view of his diagnosis of the urgent needs of the economy. And it was also manageable: the RFC board could deal responsibly with a limited number of large clients. Retail lending to the general public was an altogether different matter. It would be administratively impossible for RFC "to pass on a loan to, say, John Smith on a second-hand car." [15] Hoover stated his objection even more vividly: enactment of the Garner proposal would make the RFC "the most gigantic banking and pawnbroking business in all history." [16] The Garner proposal was unacceptable for yet another reason. In effect, it would put government into direct competition with commercial banks and this was to be avoided. The original purpose of RFC had been largely intended to strengthen commercial banks so that

they might do their job better. The administration's later recommendations were concerned with a quite different matter: the problem of
mobilizing resources for fixed investment. This was not a field where
commercial banks were supposed to be in any event. Government could
enter it without encroaching on their proper turf.[17]

In light of the administration's eagerness to spur capital spending, it
was natural for others to ask why this job could not better be done by
spending more on public works. This approach, after all, had been a
central theme in official model I. The administration still attached importance to accelerated spending on federal public works, subject to the
constraint that it did not involve Treasury borrowing. On this basis,
it now adamantly opposed the emergency bond issues called for in the
LaFollette and Wagner bills, and in a public works program backed by
Speaker Garner. In rejoinder, Garner reminded his congressional colleagues of positions Hoover had taken earlier on the use of spending
for public works to counter unemployment and particularly of his endorsement of the Foster and Catchings plan for countercyclical spending
when it was presented to the Governors' Conference in late 1928. Garner
maintained that his proposal was but a reaffirmation of a doctrine that
Hoover had earlier held to be sound. In view of that background, he
asked his fellow legislators to consider "how anyone can have the brazen
effrontery to charge Members of Congress with a lack of patriotism,
charge them with being pork-barrel offenders, when they advocate that
same thing in 1932, with the greatest amount of unemployment in the
history of the Nation?"[18]

The administration was obviously vulnerable to charges of inconsistency between its latter-day posture toward public works as a macroeconomic stimulant and the one it had adopted in 1929 and 1930. For
his part, Hoover attached great weight to consistency in economic
policy. The crucial test, however, was the internal coherence of policy
at any given moment and not intertemporal continuity on points of
policy detail. Thus, programs that were right for one set of circumstances should not be slavishly pursued when fundamental economic
conditions changed. From this perspective, the place of spending on
public facilities had to be understood differently in the environment of
1932. This contribution to aggregate spending might still have a useful
role – so long as it could be fitted consistently into the structure of official model II. In the first instance, this meant that such outlays should
not give rise to red ink in the Treasury's budget accounts. This put a
damper on how much further direct federal spending could be pushed
for this purpose. But, in view of the fact that RFC's operations were kept
outside the budget, there was now scope for federal support to con-

struction by state and local governments. RFC lending to the political subdivisions could not only be presented as legitimate; it was also desirable as part of the larger effort to stimulate capital spending. But putting this function within the "off-budget" framework of RFC had a further implication: within its terms of reference, only projects that could demonstrate a capacity to service loans were entertainable.

The logic of official model II thus produced a reconceptualization of public works spending which obliged the administration to move another step away from the doctrine of 1929 and 1930. Hoover now maintained that a distinction had to be drawn between two types of public works: those that were income producing (and thus "self-liquidating") and those that were "non-productive." He placed in the first category "such projects of states, counties and other sub-divisions as waterworks, toll-bridges, toll tunnels, docks and any other such activities which charge for their services and whose earning capacity provides a return upon the investment." On the other hand, nonproductive public works included "public buildings, highways, streets, river and harbor improvement, military and navy construction, etc., which bring no direct income and comparatively little relief to unemployment."[19] There were echoes here of a theme from his Commerce Department days when Hoover had proposed criteria for foreign lending which involved distinguishing "reproductive" from "unproductive" loans. This, however, was the first time this pattern of thought had been systematically imposed on the discussion of expenditures for public works. It was surely no accident that it should be brought into prominence at this moment: it fitted opportunely into the larger scheme of official model II. As Hoover summed up the issue:

The financing of 'income-producing works' by the Reconstruction Finance Corporation is an investment operation, requires no Congressional appropriation, does not unbalance the budget, is not a drain upon the Treasury, does not involve the direct issue of government bonds, does not involve added burdens upon the taxpayer either now or in the future. It is an emergency operation which will liquidate itself with the return of the investor to the money markets.[20]

Meanwhile, the earlier claims about the direct and indirect effects on employment of general spending on public works were abandoned. "Bankability" was now to be the critical test of the desirability of additional capital spending in the public sector. Along the way, the Hoover administration disowned some numbers which it had earlier presented as "facts." In the days when spending on road construction, for example, had been applauded for its job-creating capacity, it had been argued that "at least two persons were employed indirectly by industries supplying and transporting road materials and equipment for every one employed directly."[21] An employment multiplier of this magnitude had been presupposed in Hoover's press conference statement of September 1, 1931 about the amount of direct and indirect employment generated by the administration's program of public works. In May 1932, by contrast, Hoover insisted that the indirect employment spurred by road building was very limited: the employment multiplier was no longer 2.0, but 0.55. And Hoover further maintained that outlays for "unproductive" construction of this type were to be avoided on grounds that the jobs they did provide were only "transitory." "Income-producing works," on the other hand, promised a "follow-up of continued employment."[22]

This was indeed a U turn. Its form and timing, however, were dictated by the new logic of "off-budget" financing to stimulate capital spending. With the aid of such redefinitions, consistency in the intellectual structure of official model II could be retained. But more than the appearance of intellectual consistency was needed before others could be persuaded of the substantive merits of the new strategy. When the administration's initiative of May was finally processed through the congressional machinery in mid-July 1932, the result was a package containing some features that the administration did not want and omitting others to which it had assigned a high priority.

On several points, the Emergency Relief and Construction Act, approved on July 21, 1932, conformed with the president's wishes. The magnitude of the RFC's potential lending authority was enlarged, and by more than he had originally requested. (Hoover had asked that the corporation be empowered to issue its own obligations in amounts up to $3 billion, whereas Congress raised this entitlement to $3.3 billion.) Lending to states for relief purposes was authorized on the scale and in the manner he had requested. Provision was also made to enable RFC to lend to public bodies for "self-liquidating" public works. All of this was welcome and Hoover regarded these features of the legislation as a major step forward.

But a crucial feature of Hoover's scheme was denied him by Congress. The administration had set great store on restructuring RFC to enable it to lend to private industry for capital projects. This proposal had died at the congressional committee level. As a concession, however, the final legislation amended the authority of the Federal Reserve System to permit it to extend direct loans to private industry. From Hoover's point of view, this was a frail and inadequate substitute. If these powers were at the disposal of the RFC, he could exercise some control over them. Once they were assigned to the central bankers, he could not. Even so, there was still scope for spurring some additional capital spending in the private sector through RFC. The legislation enacted in mid-July permitted the corporation to lend to private corporations when they were engaged in constructing income-producing works of a public character. For practical purposes, this meant that private companies would be eligible for the same treatment as state and local governments if they proposed to build such "self-liquidating" projects as bridges, docks, and waterworks. In addition, direct lending to private companies was permissible for low-income housing and slum clearance, provided their charges were regulated by state or municipal law. These provisions fell far short of what Hoover had originally had in mind when the grand design to spur private investment had been shaped. But he could draw some satisfaction from the favorable action of Congress on a proposal he had urged upon it some seven months earlier: the creation of a Home Loan Discount Bank. When signing this legislation, Hoover observed that a survey by the Department of Commerce indicated that "there is today an immediate demand for homes amounting from $300 million to $500 million which could be undertaken at once if financing were available."[23] This new institution was to go to work promptly with the capital required for its start-up subscribed by the RFC.

Though congressional obstruction of the scheme to allow RFC to serve as an investment banker to private industry was the major disappointment, Hoover was also less than comfortable with two other stipulations of the Emergency Relief and Construction Act of 1932. The advocates of accelerated federal public works spending, particularly Wagner and Garner, remained determined to press for this approach to revitalizing the economy, even though Hoover left them in no doubt that he regarded bond issues for this purpose to be unacceptable. In its final shape, the Emergency Relief and Construction Act called for further acceleration in federal construction spending, despite Hoover's objection that such action was incompatible with presenting a federal budget that was nominally in balance. To avert a presidential veto, Congress had provided a loophole. The sums appropriated for supplementary public works would not be spent should the secretary of the Treasury certify that "the amount necessary for such expenditure is not available and cannot be obtained on reasonable terms." More troublesome was provision of the act which required the RFC to report to Congress monthly with details of its lending activities, including the names of borrowers and the amounts they received. The administration had fought vigorously against this "publicity clause." Though its sponsors might reasonably argue that the public had a right to know the disposition of public monies, the administration anticipated that this procedure would be counterproductive. Identifying banks that felt obliged to call on RFC facilities was more likely to weaken public confidence in their financial stability than to strengthen it. Although Hoover gave serious thought to vetoing the bill because of this stipulation, he approved it with the following observation:

The possible destructive effect upon credit institutions by the so-called publicity clause has been neutralized by the declaration of the Senate leaders of all parties that this provision is not to be retroactive and that the required monthly reports of future transactions are of a confidential nature and must be so held by the Clerks of the Senate and House of Representatives unless otherwise ordered by the Congress when in session.[24]

The publicity provision was still objectionable. But with Congress shortly to adjourn until after the election, he believed that this formula could avert the possible damage.

The amendments to RFC's authority produced in mid-July 1932 extended the corporation's mandate in one further direction by authorizing it to lend to Regional Agricultural Credit Corporations which would, in turn, lend to organizations that supplied credit to farmers and stockmen. Hoover had not attached a high priority to this scheme, though he had no difficulty in endorsing it. In particular, more finance for those who would hold stockpiles of agricultural commodities was altogether desirable. If these measures could strengthen the prices of agricultural commodities, the momentum of recovery could be expected to gain further strength.

New tools and their effectiveness (or lack thereof)

Considerable ingenuity had gone into the packaging of official model II. The Hoover administration, however, had not managed to sell it. When congressional disposition of its recommendations was completed, most of the fuel it wanted to "prime the motor" was missing. RFC was not empowered to function as an investment banker for private industry. To be sure, the Federal Reserve Banks had been authorized to provide novel facilities to assist in financing industries. Hoover did not regard this approach to the problem as satisfactory and anticipated difficulties in moving the Federal Reserve to put this machinery to work with dispatch. The act had been law for only two days when Hoover urged that "the Federal Reserve system should at once instruct the Federal Reserve Banks to undertake direct rediscount under authorities provided in the Relief Bill. . . . I deem it necessary to call the attention of the Board to the fact that an emergency of the character denominated in . . . the "Emergency Relief and Construction of 1932" has now arisen." [25] For their part, the central bankers were more conscious of the administrative difficulties the new legislation generated for them. As Meyer pointed out to Hoover, this act "enlarges in a fundamental way the scope of the activities of the Federal Reserve Banks to include a type of business which they were not organized to handle. Naturally, in such circumstances, time is required for the determination of questions of law, policy, and procedure." Among other things, "there were no forms in existence which could be utilized for the purpose of handling applications under this new authority." [26] It thus quickly became apparent that the Federal Reserve was not up to the job Hoover wanted to see done.

But would the boost to private investment which Hoover wanted have been forthcoming if Congress had authorized RFC to supply long-term capital to industry? Hoover's thinking presupposed that there was no lack of demand for funds for productive investment. In the circumstances of 1932, the validity of this assumption was certainly questionable. The president himself might have been led to question it had he given greater attention to reports generated by his subordinates. In May 1932 the Federal Employment Stabilization Board, for example, transmitted findings such as the following from a survey of projected credit needs of major potential capital spenders:

> telephone companies: "in a comparatively strong cash position" and "no new capital is needed;"
> telegraph companies: "no immediate desire for additional credit for capital improvements;"
> electric power companies: "could not use more than $25,000,000 on improvements, in addition to their current programs, even though the terms of credit were made very attractive;"
> electric railroads: "if credit were advanced on very reasonable terms, an amount not exceeding $20,000,000 might be used on desirable but not necessary replacement;"
> gas companies: "money is needed by these companies to repay bank loans and refund security issues more than for improvements;"
> railroads: "not in favor of spending additional amounts on capital improvements at this time." [27]

Material of this sort suggested that confidence in the success of official model II – even if the administration had been given all the policy instruments it wanted – was not well grounded.

If Hoover heard these messages, he certainly did not absorb their implications. To his way of thinking, a latent demand for long-term finance in the private sector was out there. All that was needed to make it effective was a lubricant to the financial markets and improvement in the state of investor confidence. Official model II had been structured to address both of these issues. The appraisal of the situation which went into it may have been out of touch with realities. But Hoover was not alone in working from these premises. Most of the economists in the orthodox mainstream, particularly those who saw budget balancing as confidence building, shared them. Nor did those who saw economic salvation through monetary manipulation (such as Irving Fisher) doubt that there would be any deficiency in aggregate spending if only the money supply were expanded appropriately. A few skeptics could be found in the ranks of the economists who now supported aggressive federal spending financed through deficits. Much of their argument hinged on the notion that in existing circumstances the private sector could not be relied upon to borrow and spend even if credit conditions were made much easier. Hence, the federal government would have to be the spender of last resort. But those expressing these views were in the minority.[28]

If there was a shortcoming in the presuppositions of Hoover's grand design, there was a more immediately obvious one in the part of it that survived congressional scrutiny. The amendments to RFC in July 1932, though more limited than Hoover wished them to be, still gave the federal government more leverage to intervene in the nation's economic life than it had ever before possessed in peacetime. The effective use of that leverage was constrained, however, by the pattern of thinking which had shaped official model II. The case for keeping RFC's activities off-budget depended largely on the argument that its loans represented, not governmental expenditures, but the acquisition of assets which could be disposed of by resale to private financiers at some point in the future. This, in turn, implied that RFC would have to conduct its business in a manner that honored this principle of soundness. Reconciling soundness with speed in spurring capital spending on "self-liquidating projects" under the jurisdiction of state and local governments was another matter.

In the first weeks of operation under its new authority, RFC conveyed the impression that financing of such self-liquidating projects was off to a promising start. Its chairman, Atlee Pomerene, reported in early September 1932 that some 224 applications had already been received which appeared, on first inspection, "to be within the meaning of the Act" and that on an average day the corporation's offices received 150 inquiries about such loans. At the same time, he cautioned that all such loans had to be fully and adequately secured and that project specifications would have to satisfy criteria established by the Corporation's Division of Engineers. He noted also that there was a potential difficulty in providing the funds to private corporations for use in the construction of low-income housing and for the reconstruction of slums. The law required these operations to be regulated by state or municipal governments and, until they had produced the necessary legislation, the RFC would be unable to lend for these purposes.[29]

There was a foreboding here that the RFC could not simultaneously keep faith with its statutory obligation to ensure that its loans were properly safeguarded and also stimulate capital spending in a hurry. But there were questions too about just how liberal RFC should be in its credit terms. It was implicit in the structure of this governmental lending agency that it should complement, but not compete with, private financial institutions. Accordingly, RFC was disposed to make collateral requirements more stringent and interest rates higher than they really needed to be. This was in keeping with the view that it should avoid preempting business that might otherwise be taken on in the private sector. Though this position had a rationale, such an operational policy was not likely to maximize the number of potential borrowers.[30]

In view of the constraints that were built into RFC's operations, it is hardly surprising that the high hopes that this institution would give the economy the thrust it needed were not to be fulfilled. Despite all the trumpeting about stimulating capital spending on so-called self-liquidating projects, no loan commitments for these undertakings were made before September (when three projects were approved). By the end of the year, the RFC board had approved only fifty loans of this type. Outlays of about $147 million for such purposes had been authorized, but less than $16 million of this sum had been advanced by December 31, 1932. Bankable soundness and speed were thus clearly in conflict with each other. Nor was the corporation any less cautious in distributing "relief loans" to states. In this instance, it was compelled to drag its feet: the legal ceiling on the monies that could be allocated for this purpose ($300 million) simply could not be stretched to match the applications placed before it. Rationing the "relief loans" required stringent tests of eligibility with demonstrations that state governments simply could not raise more funds on their own. Despite urgent appeals for help from state governors, the corporation by the end of December 1932 had authorized less than $113 million for relief loans (of which only about $80 million had then been advanced.)[31] Whereas the Hoover

administration had regarded this facility as a pathbreaking manifesta-
tion of federal magnanimity, it came through to others as tightfisted
stinginess.

After all the struggle to create a vehicle to inject a new stimulant into
the economic system, there was very little to show for it. Potentially the
RFC, following the amendments to its mandate in July 1932, had a
total lending authority of $3.8 billion. Loan authorizations approved
by the end of the year, however, were approximately half that sum. Still
more significant, approximately 84 percent of the corporation's lending
during 1932 was directed to bolstering financial institutions and railroads. Direct financing for capital spending was trifling.[32] Even though
RFC's procedures were not well designed to generate a speedy upsurge
in capital outlays, it is still not clear that a less conservative lending
policy, given the state of the economy, would have changed the outcome
significantly. Contrary to the expectations of the administration about
the response to its programs, the demand for finance for capital projects
had continued to shrink. Estimates of the probable volume of construction spending for 1932 prepared by the Federal Employment Stabilization Board should have brought this home. Though the federal
government's mechanisms for facilitating capital spending had been enlarged between May and October, the data available suggested that construction plans had been reduced during this period. In mid-October the
board estimated that construction outlays by state and local governments in 1932 would be 12 percent below the amounts it had projected
in May and that expenditures on construction by railroads and public
utilities would fall short of its earlier estimate by 22 percent.[33]

As early as September Hoover was aware that things were not going
according to plan. He was still determined, however, to play every card
at his disposal to increase aggregate demand. Congress had added one to
the deck, though he had objected to it at the time, by writing a provision
into the Emergency Relief and Construction Bill of July 1932 authorizing supplementary federal spending on public works if funding were
available on reasonable terms. On September 9, 1932 Hoover announced
that the secretary of the Treasury had advised him that there would be
no difficulty in obtaining funds to finance spending from this contingency appropriation. Accordingly, he instructed departments to undertake "at once" previously unbudgeted work on public buildings, on
river and harbor improvements, and flood control projects.[34] There was
no mention here that these additional outlays would have to be counted
as "ordinary expenditures" of the Treasury (and thus undermine budget balancing). Nor, when making this statement, did the president
choose to draw attention to the fact that the categories of additional

spending now enumerated should (in terms of the criterion he had applied in the debates of the preceding May) be classified as "unproductive." These arguments made sense in the context of his advocacy of official model II at that time. But, having failed to move Congress to permit him to put all of the pieces of that strategy into place, he was no longer obliged to live with those definitions. The economy was obviously in need of additional spending. He was ready to use any device still available to him for this purpose.

Rearguard actions in the final phases of the Hoover administration

By November 1932 two things were clear: that all of Hoover's assaults on depression had failed to reach their objectives and that he no longer had the political muscle to mount another one. There were to be no more grand initiatives. For the remainder of his term of office, Hoover was preoccupied with an attempt to salvage a rapidly deteriorating financial system.

The long interregnum between Franklin D. Roosevelt's election to the presidency on November 8, 1932 and his inauguration on March 4, 1933 was to witness the almost total collapse of the American banking system. The defenses that the Hoover administration believed were provided to it by the RFC proved to be inadequate. The continued weakening of the economy, and the further erosion in the capital positions of banks that went with it, was the primary factor responsible for an escalation in bank failures and for a mentality of panic among depositors. Ironically, features of the legislation governing the RFC may have aggravated an already acute situation. Roughly one bank in every four in the nation had been accommodated at the RFC's lending window. But this accommodation had carried a price: to satisfy the RFC of their creditworthiness, many of them had pledged their best and most liquidatable assets to the corporation. This situation, in turn, increased their vulnerability to any subsequent flagging of confidence on the part of their depositors. Nor were the problems of the banks eased by the publication of the names of those who borrowed from the RFC. On the basis of a private understanding with leaders of the Senate, Hoover had believed that this information would not be made public when Congress was not in session. While the corporation would file reports (as required by the "publicity clause" of the Emergency Relief and Construction Act), their contents would be held in confidence. At the insistence of Speaker Garner, however, this material was made public knowledge in August. This turn of events meant that some banks that could benefit from RFC assistance were reluctant to seek it for fear of public exposure of their weakness.[35] Moreover, the mere existence of RFC may (though this is far from certain) have had something to do with the passivity of the Federal Reserve System during the banking crisis of late 1932 and early 1933. The central bank had stopped its program of open-market purchases in July. When the epidemic of bank failures resumed, the Federal Reserve did nothing to increase the reserves of the commercial banks. Its inactivity may, in part, have been attributable to the view of some of the central bankers that measures to ease the strain on banks at this stage were not their job, but that of the RFC.

RFC's inability to contain the crisis was all too painfully evident by mid-February 1933. Within its terms of reference, it simply could not provide the assistance major banks needed if they were to remain open. When a crisis developed in Michigan, its governor seized the initiative by declaring a moratorium on all banking activities in the state. This touched off a chain reaction throughout the country. During the final week of February, withdrawals from banks amounted to $730 million. This brought the increase in "hoarding" (as measured by the Federal Reserve's data on the volume of currency in circulation) to more than $1 billion during the first two months of 1933.[36]

Hoover regarded it as "obvious" that these developments were "a threat to the public interest" and wished "to leave no stone unturned for constructive action during the present crisis."[37] But what stones were left to turn and could he turn them? In the final days of his administration, Hoover was ready to contemplate drastic measures that ran completely counter to his fundamental beliefs about the legitimate domain of federal authority. During the preceding year, he had already placed a federal presence in a number of areas that had formerly been held to be off limits. But the propositions he was willing to take seriously in his last days in the White House went well beyond that. They included federal guarantees of bank deposits, governmental participation in the ownership of private banks (through RFC purchase of their preferred stock), and a presidential proclamation declaring a national bank holiday. All of these measures were distasteful, but, in view of the gravity of the crisis, he was prepared to explore them.

Hoover's activist impulses still had vitality in these last desperate days. He insisted, however, that he could not exercise them unless his actions had the prior endorsement of the president-elect. Roosevelt, on the other hand, refused to make any commitments until the constitutional authority of the presidency became legally his on March 4, 1933. Hoover saw this lack of cooperation as unconscionable. Indeed, he held Roosevelt to be responsible for much of the latest banking crisis because of his failure to go on record in support of "responsible" monetary policies. Hoover came to believe that there was something conspiratorial about the behavior of the president-elect. This impression was fed by a report reaching him that Rexford Guy Tugwell, then a member of Roosevelt's Brains Trust, expected that "the bank situation . . . would undoubtedly collapse in a few days, which would place the responsibility in the lap of President Hoover." On receipt of this information, Hoover wrote: "When I consider this statement of Professor Tugwell's in connection with the recommendations we have made to the incoming administration, I can say emphatically that he breathes with infamous politics devoid of every atom of patriotism. Mr. Tugwell would project millions of people into hideous losses for a Roman holiday." [38]

But Hoover's ire was not directed exclusively toward Roosevelt and his entourage. The central bankers were also guilty of negligence and irresponsibility. He had pleaded with them – as a matter of urgency – for recommendations on measures to stem the tide of bank failures. They had come up with nothing. On March 2 Eugene Meyer advised him that "all sorts of proposals and possibilities for dealing with the general situation with which we are confronted have and are being canvassed and discussed, but so far no additional measures or authority have developed in concrete form which, at the moment, the Board feels it would be justified in urging." And he further noted that the board opposed "any form of Federal guarantee of banking deposits." [39] Late the following day, however, the Federal Reserve Board came forward with something specific: a recommendation that Hoover issue an executive order proclaiming a national banking holiday. It then reported the prospect that gold reserves of the Federal Reserve District Bank in Chicago would be "dangerously depleted" by the end of banking hours on March 4 and "that similar conditions are developing rapidly in other Federal Reserve districts." [40]

All this was now beside the point as far as Hoover was concerned. Roosevelt had again refused to associate himself with a proclamation issued over Hoover's signature and Hoover would not act without a go-ahead from the president-elect. In what was probably his last official memorandum from the White House, Hoover replied as follows to Meyer's recommendation that he declare a bank moratorium: "I received at half past one this morning your letter dated March 3. . . . I am at a loss to understand why such a communication should have been sent to me in the last few hours of this Administration, which I believe the Board must now admit was neither justified nor necessary." [41] Not only was the financial fabric frayed; so also were tempers.

Herbert Hoover left the White House an embittered man. His

strategies to guide the behavior of the economy – strategies that had once appeared so promising – lay in ruins. He had modified and adapted them when circumstances called for changes in approach. And, along the way, he had extended the involvement of the federal government far more deeply into the nation's economic life than had previously been witnessed when the country was not at war. Certainly he understood the importance of stimulating aggregate demand in a depressed economy and the economic policies he pressed for were intended for that purpose. Extraordinary circumstances, he maintained, justified unprecedented measures. But there were still limits beyond which he would not go. No steps should be taken if they were likely to compromise America's commitment to the gold standard, if they threatened to diminish scope for private economic initiative, or if they seemed likely to do lasting harm to the ideals of decentralized public decision making embodied in the principles of federalism.

In partisan rhetoric, Hoover was a much vilified man for most of the next two decades. But the charge that pained him most was also most inaccurate: that he had presided over the greatest depression in the nation's history and had done nothing.

Epilogue: Transition to the New Deal — continuities and discontinuities

As president, Herbert Hoover understood one of the basic insights of a theoretical system later to be identified as Keynesianism: that the behavior of the macroeconomic system is determined by the aggregate volume of spending. Indeed, he grasped this point as well as did anyone of his time – and better than did most of the economists in that period. This was the basis for his initial effort in depression fighting when he called for accelerated construction spending by public authorities and for increased capital outlays by the major private investors. Similarly, his appeals to employers to resist wage cutting was a plank from what later would be regarded as a Keynesian platform.

Nor did he lose sight of the importance of demand management when he made tactical adjustments in his programs in late 1931 and 1932. At first glance, the stance he then took – with his insistence on the importance of a balanced budget and on tax increases to achieve it – seems to be at odds with the objective of stimulating spending in a depressed economy. From Hoover's perspective, such a reading of his actions would be incorrect. The larger goal remained the same. In the circumstances of the time, however, the ultimate objective would be beyond reach unless an instrumental one, solvency in the banking system, could be secured first. The immediate priority was thus to ensure that the institutional preconditions for recovery in spending were in place. Within this framework of thinking, government should manage its fiscal affairs in a manner which would check further erosion in bond values. But this still did not mean that it should aim for a "balanced budget" in the sense in which it earlier had been operationally defined.

The central problem with which Hoover was then confronted was one that Keynes would subsequently label as the "liquidity trap." Hoover did not use that term but was well aware of the reality of the phenomenon it described. The integrating thread of his initiatives in 1932 was a push to unfreeze the channels of lending and spending. In launching it, he shed some of his reluctance to involve the central government directly in the nation's economic life. Government could not be the spender of last resort, but it should be the lender of last resort if

189

its facilities could stimulate aggregate demand. He did not get all the powers he wanted which would permit a governmental agency to perform that function. When Congress denied them to him, he then turned on the spending tap for federal public works to the limit of his authorization. In doing so, there was no hand wringing about the implications of this action for budget balancing.

Hoover's actions – though not his words – suggest that he had an intuitive comprehension of the mechanisms of income determination which was in advance of the thinking of most professional economists. Why then did his management of a depression economy fail so disastrously? A conceptualization that specifies the dimensions of the fundamental problem is a crucial step in the formulation of effective policies. But this alone is not sufficient. Results depend on the successful implementation of programs that the analysis suggests are required. The Achilles heel of the Hoover administration was its inability to follow through with the second step. In part, this shortcoming may be attributed to the political and cultural environment of the times. It was also, in part, a reflection of constraints on action which were self-imposed. The latter were the more important. A leader can try to change society's perceptions of the proper way things should be done. But he can only do so when he himself is prepared to break from the conventional mold. This was something that Hoover was always hesitant to do publicly. Behind the scenes, he could be highly innovative in packaging programs to widen his freedom of maneuver. But there were still limits beyond which this exercise could not be pressed. The end product had to be presentable in a way that kept it within the bounds of Hoover's conception of the legitimate scope of federal authority.

This was the root of a fundamental tension in the mindset of the Hoover administration. The diagnosis of the ills of the economy was reasonably well in hand. But the president's willingness to prescribe remedies was bounded by the premises of his political philosophy. Foremost was the importance he attached to the principles of constitutionalism which defined the division of jurisdictions between various governmental units and limited the scope of federal intervention in the private economy. Walter Lippmann once criticized Hoover for being more inclined to spend his time in the White House talking to business leaders and bankers – whose affairs he could not control – than to concentrate on matters which the chief executive is charged to attend to (such as developing legislative proposals and lobbying for their enactment). Hoover would not have thought this observation to be an indictment of the way he chose to operate from the presidential office, but would instead have regarded it as an accurate description of the manner in which presidential leadership ought to be exercised in a time of economic crisis. He took it to be his duty to enlighten the decision makers throughout society – whether they be businessmen and financiers, labor leaders, governors, and mayors, or ordinary citizens as bank depositors and consumers – on the actions they should take in the public interest. The White House was not to be the "bully pulpit" (as Theodore Roosevelt had once described it) but the site for quiet and undemonstrative persuasion. Though the president should not coerce, he should appeal to the public for economic behavior to advance the common good.

When these appeals went unheeded (as was largely the case during the last two years of his administration), Hoover felt that he had been let down. If the proper method, that of exhortation, failed to generate the healing the economy needed, what alternatives were left? His view of the requirements of constitutionalism precluded the introduction of direct governmental controls over the economy. It also obliged him to oppose vigorously any governmental sanction of controls over the production process administered by private groups. Leaders of both business and farm organizations were increasingly attracted to schemes for "coordinating" supply and demand which had the threat of a big stick behind them. Hoover would have no part of them.

Despite his reluctance in doing so, Hoover did move the federal government a considerable distance into domains that had formerly been held to be reserved for the private sector or for state and local authorities. This was most notably the case in the operations of the Reconstruction Finance Corporation. Political ideology did not blind him to the necessities for innovative interventions that showed promise of stimulating aggregate spending. Though the scope of federal involvement was thus extended, it was still intervention without compulsion. Federal authority could pioneer in institution building, but the way in which these institutions were used depended on the decisions of others. Hoover expected that exhortation would ensure that the opportunities created by new federal funding authority would be seized. Again he was disappointed. In some measure, a residue from his political ideology contributed to that result. A federal presence in financial markets – even in times of emergency – should not be made too attractive for fear that it might produce a lasting distortion from the division of functions that he considered to be normal. The failure of this experiment was not fully apparent until after Hoover's ability to wrest more authority from Congress had ended. But, even had he been given an opportunity to try again to spur total spending, it seems reasonable to conjecture that he would not have proposed direct federal spending in the magnitudes that would have restored full employment. Off-budget financing of loans to the private sector and state and local governments could be accommodated within his scheme of things. This might bend the rules, but it kept the ultimate lines of responsibility clear. Federal preemption of tasks that should be performed by others remained unthinkable.

Hoover also elected to forgo another option which, in principle, might have been available to him in his campaign for economic recovery. America's commitment to gold convertibility at the established exchange rate was something he regarded as an absolute. He took the merits of this arrangement to be so obvious that they were virtually beyond argument. He welcomed monetary policies that might stimulate spending and distrusted the way the central bankers performed their functions. But, even if he had had more powers over monetary policy than the American governmental structure allows to a president, it is clear that he would not have tolerated monetary manipulation which imperilled gold convertibility at its established dollar value.

Hoover's successor in the presidency was far less shackled by these constraints. When Franklin D. Roosevelt took office, the American public was ready to accept – indeed to welcome – much greater weight for federal authority without worrying excessively about its longer term implications for the relationship of the central government to private business or to the political subdivisions in a federal system. The Supreme Court (as its disposition of New Deal legislation in 1935 and 1936 was to demonstrate) was not similarly sympathetic. Nevertheless, the electorate had expressed its willingness to experiment with untried formulas for recovery. Moreover, with the banking system in shambles, commitments to gold convertibility should not be allowed to stand in the way of reconstructing the domestic monetary order.

In shaping economic policies, Roosevelt could begin with a much freer hand. Just how he would choose to play it, however, was far from clear. As a presidential candidate, he had committed himself to the principle of a balanced budget, and at reduced levels of ordinary governmental spending, and had castigated Hoover as a deficit spender who had jeopardized the foundations of the government's credit. At the same time, he had called for "action" and "bold, persistent experimentation" to restore health to the economy. The rhetoric, however, had been short on specifics. Nor, on taking office, did Roosevelt have a clear conception of the precise ingredients of a new "model" for recovery. One of the few certainties in March 1933 was that Roosevelt would approach economic problems in a style quite different from the one adopted by his predecessor. For the most part, Hoover had thought of himself as his own economic adviser. He turned to professionals for assistance in obtaining economic data and for instruction on some points of technical detail. But he had little time for ideas that could not be accommodated to his conception of the way the economy should be made to behave. Roosevelt, on the other hand, had no pretensions as a producer of economic ideas. Instead he regarded himself as a consumer, but one who insisted on his right to consumer sovereignty.

When the economic strategies of the first New Deal began to fall into place, they were built primarily around two strands of doctrine that had been explicitly rejected by the Hoover administration. One component of this mix was inspired by those who had argued in the 1920s that the structural properties of the economic system prevented prices from performing the functions ascribed to them in the standard textbooks and that new mechanisms of economic control – specifically, ones that made government a party to production decisions in the private sector – were called for. This was the fruit of the thinking of the agricultural economists and of the advocates (such as Tugwell) of "coordination and control" in the industrial sector. By 1933 a number of business leaders who had defected from Hoover's camp (such as Harriman and Swope) had come to accept much of the diagnosis offered by the dissenters from the microeconomic orthodoxy of the 1920s. The practical men and the scribblers who attacked laissez faire in the economic journals did not necessarily agree on the methods to be used in correcting the economy's structural defects. But they could unite on two propositions: (1) that competition could be destructive; (2) that visible hands were needed to "balance" supply and demand and to strengthen prices in all sectors of the economy. This line of reasoning found its way into centerpieces of New Deal legislation in the first 100 days. The passage of the Agricultural Adjustment Act brought government directly into price making for staple farm products by permitting the Department of Agriculture to subsidize farmers for restricting outputs. The National Industrial Recovery Act extended this principle. Within its terms, trade associations operating under governmentally approved "codes" would be afforded immunity from prosecution under the antitrust laws. In effect, however, the codes were agreements among members of trade associations not to engage in price competition.

A second doctrinal ingredient of the first New Deal was linked with the thought of the more heterodox monetarists who pressed for a "reflation" of the general price level as the route to recovery. This approach, as Irving Fisher had argued, would reduce debt burdens and increase discretionary purchasing power. This general view was championed by George Warren, professor of agricultural economics at Cornell University, who added that governmental action to increase gold prices (and devalue the dollar) should bring particular benefits to farmers. In his version of the case for monetary experimentation, commodity prices in general were alleged to move in sympathy with gold prices; hence, measures to raise gold prices were necessary as supplements to other interventions to enlarge farm incomes. The influence of this body of doctrine on Roosevelt's views was apparent in his decision in October 1933 to embark on a program to bid up the price of gold through government purchases with the hope that this would simultaneously raise the general price level. Meanwhile, the first New Deal offered little comfort to the advocates of ambitious spending on public works to stimulate the economy. Though Roosevelt was willing to move beyond Hoover by supporting such undertakings as the Tennessee Valley Authority, he still saw monetary policy – not fiscal policy – as the primary instrument of macroeconomic management. Deficits might be inevitable so long as the federal government had to provide funds for the relief of the destitute, but they remained undesirable in principle.

The policy mix of the first New Deal thus was organized primarily around two streams of thought to which the Hoover administration had been totally unsympathetic. Those who had formerly been on the outside were now listened to with respect in the corridors of power. In a time of economic crisis, resort to policies that had not already been given a trial run – and rejection of those which had been tried, but without demonstrable success – had an understandable appeal. From an analytic point of view, however, the intellectual component of Roosevelt's initial attempts to devise a new "official model" was a step backward. Hoover at least had a reasoned grasp of the essentials of an income approach to the macroeconomic process. The architects of the economic strategies of 1933 and 1934, on the other hand, focused instead on prices. The structural interventionists of the Agricultural Adjustment Administration and the National Recovery Administration sought to raise (or, at the minimum, to stabilize) prices in individual sectors, while the monetarists sought to elevate the general level of prices. Hoover had been out of office for five years before the Roosevelt White House fully reoriented its sights toward an income approach to economic strategies.

Though there were striking discontinuities in the transition from the Hoover era to the first New Deal, there were also some arresting continuities. Much of the practical work of the Roosevelt administration in its initial phases was built on foundations laid by its predecessor. The proclamation of a bank holiday (the signing of which was Roosevelt's first official act as president) and the emergency banking legislation that quickly followed it were designed by Hoover's team. The New Deal also drew heavily on the institutional apparatus Hoover had created, and particularly on the RFC. Many of its functions were reassigned and restyled: its operations in financing "self-liquidating" loans to political subdivisions were transferred to the Public Works Administration and its support for relief payments was shifted to the Federal Emergency Relief Administration. RFC's support for banks was continued and was enlarged to enable the corporation to hold their preferred stock (a case for which had been developed by the Hoover administration). In June 1934 RFC was accorded powers for which Hoover had fought two years earlier when it was authorized to lend directly to private industry. Not least, the trade association network (which Hoover had been instrumental in shaping during his service as secretary of commerce) was the device through which the NRA's "code" authorities operated.

Hoover was later to denounce the uses to which the Roosevelt administration put the apparatus he had had a large hand in creating. When doing so, he was not an altogether reliable witness to his own contributions to the shaping of the modern American economy. The volume of his *Memoirs* dealing with the Great Depression is more an expression of his residual bitterness toward Roosevelt than a service to historical truth. As a polemicist, he was at pains to emphasize contrasts between his policies and those he associated with the New Deal. One of his long-standing adversaries, however, has offered a different reading. From the vantage point of the 1940s, Rexford Guy Tugwell observed:

The ideas embodied in the New Deal legislation were a compilation of those which had come to maturity under Hoover's aegis. . . . We all of us owed much to Hoover, [especially] for his enlargements of knowledge, for his encouragement to scholars, for his organization of research. . . . [T]he brains trust got much of its material from the Hoover committees or from the work done under their auspices.[1]

Overall, Tugwell assessed Hoover's contribution to the New Deal as follows: "[I]t is quite plain that all through his public activity and especially throughout his Presidency, regardless of anything he said, there was steady preparation for, even progress toward, the posture assumed by events in 1933. The Hundred Days was the breaking of a dam rather than the conjuring out of nowhere of a river."[2]

Notes

Guide to abbreviations in citations of sources:

HHPL   – Herbert Hoover Presidential Library, West Branch, Iowa
FDRPL – Franklin D. Roosevelt Presidential Library, Hyde Park, N.Y.
NA   – National Archives, Washington, D.C.
PPP   – Public Papers of the Presidents

Prologue: the vision of a new era in the 1920s

1 John Maurice Clark estimated that, at the peak of the war effort in 1918, roughly 25 percent of the national income was committed to war purposes and nearly one-third of the gainfully employed population was engaged in war work (with some 4 million men in uniform and about 9 million civilian workers employed in support activities). Despite these massive reallocations, Clark concluded that "America suffered little in an economic way." His calculations indicated that increased productive effort offset about 40 percent of the claims made by the war on the economy's resources. Though the output of goods for private consumption diminished, this was not the same thing as "decreased consumption." Such shrinkage in private consumption as occurred "was due in considerable part to postponing the renewal of durable [consumer] goods." (John Maurice Clark, "The War's Aftermath in America," *Current History*, 34 [May 1931], p. 170.)

2 Bernard Baruch to President Wilson, November 19, 1918, Commerce Files, HHPL.

3 Irving Fisher, "Economists in Public Service" (Presidential Address to the American Economic Association, December 1918), *American Economic Review Supplement*, 9 (March 1919), p. 7.

4 Ibid., pp. 18, 19, 21.

5 Wesley C. Mitchell "Statistics and Government" (Presidential Address to the Annual Meeting of the American Statistical Association, December 1918), reprinted in *The Backward Art of Spending Money and Other Essays* (New York: McGraw-Hill, 1937), p. 53.

6 Mitchell, "The Prospects of Economics," in *The Trend of Economics*, R. G. Tugwell, ed. (New York: Knopf, 1924), p. 23.

7 With the publication of *The Economic Consequences of the Peace*, Keynes became an international celebrity. This work was a best seller in America

with its first printing (in January 1920) sold out within six weeks. But the notoriety Keynes thus achieved also raised questions in the minds of a number of influential American economists about his scholarly integrity. In his review of the book, Clive Day of Yale University, for example, insisted that it should not be regarded as a contribution to economic literature, but as a political tract. Much of the style was described as "theatrical" and Keynes's treatment of many points of alleged fact was "distorted and misleading." (Clive Day, "Keynes' Economic Consequences of the Peace," *American Economic Review*, 10 [June 1920], pp. 301, 309.) Allyn A. Young of Harvard, on the other hand, concurred with much of Keynes's analysis, but believed that he had treated Wilson unfairly. Young expressed his regret that the book had been used in the United States "as a weapon against the President." He regarded this aspect of the book's impact as unfortunate because "the practical effect of anything that weakens the prestige of the President just now is to strengthen reaction." (Allyn A. Young to Keynes, May 22, 1920, as quoted in *The Collected Writings of John Maynard Keynes*, vol. 17, Elizabeth Johnson, ed. [New York: Cambridge University Press, 1977], p. 49.) In the popular commentaries on this book, there was also a hint that Keynes's motives were not beyond reproach in view of his call for the cancellation of Allied debts to the United States.

8 In 1920 Keynes offered the following appraisal: "Mr. Hoover was the only man who emerged from the ordeal of Paris with an enhanced reputation. His complex personality, with its habitual air of a weary Titan (or, as others might put it of an exhausted prize fighter), his eyes steadily fixed on the true and essential facts of the European situation, imparted into the Councils of Paris, when he took part in them, precisely that atmosphere of reality, knowledge, magnanimity and disinterest which, if they had been found in other quarters, also would have given us the Good Peace." (John Maynard Keynes, *The Economic Consequences of the Peace* [New York: Harcourt, Brace and Howe, 1920], p. 274n.)

9 In a letter written on January 2, 1920, Roosevelt recorded his views as follows: "I had some nice talks with Herbert Hoover before he went West for Christmas. He is certainly a wonder, and I wish we could make him President of the United States. There could not be a better one." (Franklin D. Roosevelt to Hugh Gibson, January 2, 1920, as quoted by Frank Freidel, *Franklin D. Roosevelt*, vol. 2 [Boston: Little, Brown, 1954], p. 57.)

10 Hoover, *The Memoirs of Herbert Hoover: The Cabinet and Presidency*, vol. 2 (New York: Macmillan, 1952), p. 36.

11 This remark is attributed to S. Parker Gilbert, undersecretary of the Treasury in the Harding and Coolidge administrations and later American Agent on the administration of loans to Germany, as cited by Oswald Garrison Villard, *Prophets True and False* (New York: Knopf, 1928), p. 28.

12 *Recent Economic Changes in the United States*, Report of the Committee on Recent Economic Changes of the President's Conference on Unemployment, Herbert Hoover, Chairman (New York: McGraw-Hill, 1929), p. xx.

1. The ingredients of a model of a new economics

1 Hoover, Introduction to *Waste in Industry*, prepared by the Committee on Elimination of Waste in Industry of the Federation of Engineering Societies (New York: McGraw-Hill, 1921), p. ix.

2 Formal invitations to the members of the advisory committee were dispatched on March 16, 1921. See Hoover to Seligman et al., Commerce Papers, HHPL.

3 Hoover to President Harding, June 9, 1921, Commerce Papers, HHPL.

4 Hoover to Attorney-General Daugherty, December 11, 1923, Commerce Papers, HHPL.

5 As reported by M. B. Lane, "The Statistical Work of the Federal Government in Relation to Price Stabilization," *The Annals*, 139 (September 1928), p. 65.

6 Baruch to Hoover, April 27, 1921, Commerce Papers, HHPL.

7 This was the view of W. E. Lamb, solicitor of the Department of Commerce, and Hoover concurred with it. Though Lamb insisted in 1921 that "there should be some governmental agency to which the commercial interests of the country could go for the determination of the legality of proposed plans of consolidation and cooperation," he was not persuaded that the Federal Trade Commission was the ideal site for such authority. (Lamb to Hoover, August 30, 1921, Commerce Papers, HHPL.)

8 Daugherty to Hoover, December 19, 1923, Commerce Papers, HHPL.

9 Hoover to Daugherty, December 11, 1923 Commerce Papers, HHPL. As a reflection of the attitude of trade associations, his assessment was certainly correct. Hoover had frequently been counseled by their representatives that supplying information to government for transmission to the public was not a motivating consideration. As one of them put the matter: "The inspiration of the industrial association is self-interest. The members maintain it and pay the bills because they think they are going to derive some advantage from it." (Walter Renton Ingalls to Hoover, March 9, 1922, Commerce Papers, HHPL. Ingalls was then a prominent figure in the statistical work of the copper, lead, and zinc industries.)

10 Address of the Secretary of Commerce to the Trade Association Conference, April 12, 1922, Commerce Papers, HHPL.

11 Ibid.

12 Hoover to Daugherty, December 11, 1923, Commerce Papers, HHPL.

13 Press Conference Statement by Secretary Hoover, June 4, 1925, Commerce Papers, HHPL. Hoover's comments in this context referred to "the competitive industries" (by which he meant the unregulated ones). In the regulated sector, he was actively engaged in promoting consolidations to lower costs.

14 In October 1921 Edwin F. Gay, in his capacity as president of the National Bureau of Economic Research, reported to Hoover that the bureau was soon to publish Wesley Mitchell's study of *Income in the United States*

and wished to continue this line of work. Its attempts to secure financial support had been hampered by objections from potential sponsors who maintained that the preparation of national income data should be undertaken by the government. Hoover replied: "The kind of work being done by the National Bureau of Economic Research cannot be adequately undertaken by the Government. It involves, in the first instance, interpretive questions which can only be arrived at in the manner that your Bureau handles them. In any event, . . . I do not believe there is any possibility that Congress would for a moment entertain the necessary appropriations to make such studies." (Hoover to Gay, October 20, 1921, Commerce Papers, HHPL.)

15 *Accomplishments of the Department of Commerce, 1921–28*, "Statement of the Division of Simplified Practice," Commerce Papers, HHPL. In 1928 the Division reported that "a recent tabulation covering 82 of the effective Simplified Practice Recommendations shows that acceptances have been received from 815 associations and 7,731 individual firms, corporations, etc."

16 According to an estimate published in 1929, the manufacturing sector contributed $17.8 billion to a national income of $85.7 billion in 1926 (the latest year for which data were then available). See Morris A. Copeland, "The National Income and Its Distribution," in *Recent Economic Changes in the United States*, p. 775.

17 This estimate was made in 1925 by E. E. Hunt, Hoover's general troubleshooter at the Department of Commerce, as reported by Ellis W. Hawley, "Herbert Hoover, the Commerce Secretariat, and the Vision of an 'Associative State,' 1921–1928," *Journal of American History*, 61 (June 1974), p. 125.

18 A conversation in 1964 between Walter Heller, then chairman of the President's Council of Economic Advisers, and Thomas Balogh, then economic adviser to the prime minister heading a Labour government in Britain, is worth recounting in this connection. In an informal exchange the question was posed: "Who is the greatest American of the 20th century?" To the surprise of his American listener, Balogh replied: "Herbert Hoover." When pressed to defend his choice, he noted Hoover's achievement in standardizing electric fittings and its importance for American economic progress. By the mid-1960s Britain had not yet accomplished this feat.

19 Their paths had crossed, however, in wartime Washington. For a brief period, Veblen had held a position (from which he was fired) in Hoover's War Food Administration.

20 George K. Burgess to Hoover, February 9, 1925, Commerce Papers, HHPL.

21 *Accomplishments of the Department of Commerce, 1921–28*, "Statement of the Division of Simplified Practice," Commerce Papers, HHPL.

22 Hoover, Introduction to *The Stabilization of Business*, Lionel D. Edie, ed. (New York: Macmillan, 1923), p. v.

23 There was considerable overlap between the membership of this committee and the Advisory Committee on Economic Statistics, which Hoover had ap-

pointed the preceding March. Holdovers included Mitchell, Seligman, Young, Willcox, Doten, Gay, and Rossiter. Other members of the Economic Advisory Committee to the President's Conference on Unemployment were George Barnett (The Johns Hopkins University), David R. Dewey (Massachusetts Institute of Technology), Samuel McCune Lindsay (Columbia University), Leo Wolman (New School for Social Research), Clyde L. King (University of Pennsylvania), John B. Andrews (Executive Secretary of the American Association for Labor Legislation), E. S. Bradford (a statistician), Bailey B. Burritt (Executive Secretary of the Association for Improving the Condition of the Poor), Samuel A. Lewisohn (a New York banker), Otto T. Mallery (a member of the Pennsylvania State Industrial Board), and Sanford E. Thompson (a Boston industrial engineer).

24 "Advance Summary of the Report of the Economic Advisory Committee to the President's Unemployment Conference," September 22, 1921, Commerce Papers, HHPL.

25 Otto T. Mallery, "A National Policy – Public Works to Stabilize Employment," *The Annals*, 81 (January 1919), p. 56.

26 Ibid., p. 57. In a presentation before the Senate Committee on Education and Labor nearly a decade later, he used a different metaphor: "[A] relatively small amount of new orders, such as a public works program can reasonably offer, will do much to sustain the structure, for new orders multiply themselves with surprising rapidity. The American dollar in circulation is a speed devil. It may jump quickly out of your pocket, but the next fellow is also competing for the record. The dollar, like Paddy's flea, is never where it was. Look for the public works dollar where it was – in public works – and it is not there, having jumped into a corner of the storekeeper's pocket. It jumps so fast that you cannot trace it, but like the flea, it leaves its mark. The steel worker feels it and the ice-cream man, an expert thermometer of prosperity. The teddy-bear maker and the garment worker feel it. It wakes the alarm-clock maker and speeds up the scooter specialist. It creates jobs as apparently unrelated to public works as Spitzbergen is to Africa." (Otto T. Mallery, Statement submitted to Hearings before the Committee on Education and Labor, Senate, December 18, 1928, p. 200.)

27 *Historical Statistics of the United States*, Part 2 (Washington, D.C.: U.S. Government Printing Office 1975), p. 622.

28 *Report of the President's Conference on Unemployment*, October 1921, p. 160.

29 It is interesting to note that the President's Conference on Unemployment had no clear idea of the magnitude of the problem it was charged to consider. The final report of the Conference observed that there were, "variously estimated from three and one-half to five and one-half millions unemployed." (Ibid., p. 19.)

30 F. G. Dickinson, "Public Construction and Cyclical Unemployment," Supplement to *The Annals*, 139 (September 1928), p. 203.

31 Ibid., p. 200.

32 In February 1928 Mallery could also report to Hoover that he had formed

an Economic Advisory Committee that included Irving Fisher, Wesley Mitchell, and H. G. Moulton (of the Brookings Institute of Economics) among its members. (Mallery to Hoover, February 7, 1928, Commerce Papers, HHPL.)

33 Otto T. Mallery, Statement submitted to Hearings before the Committee on Education and Labor, Senate, December 18, 1928, p. 203.

34 Mallery, "The Long Range Planning of Public Works," *Business Cycles and Unemployment: Report and Recommendations of the President's Conference on Unemployment* (New York: McGraw-Hill, 1923), p. 241.

35 Hoover to Harding, January 17, 1922, Commerce Papers, HHPL.

36 *New York Times*, March 19, 1923, p. 19 (as quoted by E. J. Howenstine, Jr., "Public Works Policy in the Twenties," *Social Research*, 13 [December 1946], p. 488.)

37 Irving Fisher, for example, applauded this action. "While we students have been discussing how to do it [stabilization]," he observed, "Mr. Hoover, Franklin Roosevelt, and the bankers have been doing it." (As quoted by Joseph Dorfman, *The Economic Mind and American Civilization*, vol. 4, [New York: Viking Press, 1959], p. 50n.)

38 Governor Brewster had absorbed the teachings of William Trufant Foster and Waddill Catchings, the energetic advocates of a doctrine holding that prosperity was threatened by deficiencies in aggregate demand. At Brewster's invitation, Foster attended the Conference of Governors as an expert consultant. A fuller discussion of the position of Foster and Catchings will be presented in Chapter 2.

39 Though the amendments to the Federal Reserve Act passed by the Congress in 1935 addressed this diffusion of authority by strengthening the position of the board in Washington, a special place continues to be accorded to the head of the New York branch of the system.

40 This relationship was first pointed out in print in *The Federal Reserve Bulletin*, 9 (February 1923), pp. 542–43.

41 In addition to his dedication to monetary stabilization, he was an ardent propagandist for world government, disarmament, and prohibition. For a fascinating account of his life, see Irving Norton Fisher, *My Father: Irving Fisher* (New York: Comet Press Books, 1956).

42 Irving Fisher, "Our Unstable Dollar and the So-Called Business Cycle," *Journal of the American Statistical Association*, 20 (June 1925), p. 179.

43 Fisher's "equation of exchange" was formulated as follows: $MV + M'V' = PT$ (with M representing the stock of currency and coin and M' standing for the volume of demand deposits; the V's designated the respective velocities of circulation for each of the components of the money supply; P represented the average price and T expressed the number of monetized transactions.)

44 Fisher, *The Money Illusion* (New York: Adelphi, 1928), p. 127.

45 Ibid., p. 126.

46 Ibid., p. 133.

47 This type of monetarism, 1920s style, should be distinguished from the version associated with the work of Milton Friedman, which has come into high prominence in the 1970s and 1980s. Though both of these strands of monetarism regard the money supply as the key variable, they differ in their prescriptions for ideal monetary policy and in their analyses of the velocity of circulation. In contrast to Friedman, Fisher argued that the central bank should not commit itself to predetermined or preannounced rates of growth in the money supply. On the contrary, it should have latitude to vary the money supply as needed to maintain stability in the general price level. Nor did Fisher presuppose that the velocity of circulation would tend to be stable. The spending patterns of the community might indeed change, but when they did so, compensatory variations in the money supply should be made to offset them. He was confident, however, that an official commitment to the goal of maintaining a dollar of constant purchasing power would itself tend to stabilize velocity.

48 Fisher, Hearings before the Committee on Banking and Currency, House of Representatives, March 24, 1926, p. 56.

49 Ibid., p. 57.

50 *The Memoirs of Herbert Hoover: The Great Depression, 1929–1941*, vol. 3 (New York: Macmillan, 1952), pp. 6–11.

51 Hoover wrote of this confrontation with pride. "I stirred up my friends in the engineering societies, and on November 1, 1922 they issued a report which endorsed the eight hour day. I wrote an introduction to this report, eulogizing its conclusions, and got the President to sign it. We kept the pot boiling in the press." (*The Memoirs of Herbert Hoover: The Cabinet and the Presidency, 1920–1933*, vol. 2, p. 104.) Reluctantly, the recalcitrant firms yielded in July 1923.

52 Hoover to Samuel Gompers, October 23, 1920, Pre-Commerce Papers, HHPL.

53 For a statement of his position, see Henry Ford (in collaboration with Samuel Crowther), *My Life and Work* (Garden City, N.Y.: Garden City Publishing Company, 1922), especially ch. 8.

54 Edward A. Filene, "The American Wage and Efficiency," *American Economic Review*, 13 (September 1923), pp. 411–15. Filene, it may be noted, was the founding patron of the Twentieth Century Fund, which was created to support research in the social sciences.

55 In his public statements and reports, Hoover often alluded to prohibition as one of the important factors contributing to growth in labor productivity in the 1920s. But he and his associates at the Department of Commerce learned that ambiguities were useful in phrasing such statements. The department received numerous inquiries from church groups and temperance organizations for data that would document prohibition's contribution to economic improvement. The department was not prepared to perform this statistical exercise.

56 For example, Hoover defended the subsidies to merchant shipping as fol-

lows: '[F]undamentally we have imposed American wages and standards of living upon our ships by law, and we wish to maintain these standards not alone in ships but also in our shipyards, and in the making of supplies used by our ships and the employees in their management. We will not have a merchant marine unless we at least give compensation to American owners for some part of these enforced higher costs." In the allocation of the subsidy, however, he urged that priority be given to the movement of cargo and that "construction of racing trans-Atlantic hotels" should be de-emphasized. (Hoover to Harding, February 2, 1923, Commerce Papers, HHPL.)

57 Hoover, Address of May 12, 1926 (as reported in *The Memoirs*, vol. 2, p. 108).

58 Thomas Nixon Carver, *The Present Economic Revolution in the United States* (Boston: Little, Brown, 1925), pp. 261–62.

59 It was primarily with this thought in mind that he asked Wesley Mitchell to become the economic adviser to the Department of Commerce in July 1921. In Hoover's letter of invitation, he observed that "we have a myriad of problems on which I do not feel myself capable of passing" and that the Department of Commerce had "got to be stiffened up with stronger economic operators." (Hoover to Mitchell, July 29, 1921, Commerce Papers, HHPL.) When Mitchell declined the assignment, Julius Klein of the Harvard Business School was appointed to the post Hoover had in mind.

60 Wesley C. Mitchell, "A Review," in *Recent Economic Changes in the United States*, p. 861.

61 *Historical Statistics of the United States*, part 2, pp. 889, 898.

62 "Statement of the Bureau of Domestic and Foreign Commerce" in *Accomplishments of the Department of Commerce, 1921–28*, Commerce Papers, HHPL.

63 *Report of the Secretary of Commerce*, 1926, p. 34. Hoover offered the following explanation for this achievement: "Our work people have increased in education and skill. Above all they are largely free from the economic fallacy that restriction of individual effort increases the number of jobs. . . . Under the pressure of high wages we have ruthlessly revised our industry with every new invention. Beyond this there is great and cooperative movement in American industry and commerce for cutting out waste in a thousand directions through improved business practice, through simplification of processes and methods. Furthermore, we have had a great advantage which we must not deny, in that by volume production, made possible through a great domestic market, we have been able by repetitive processes to apply or focus every advance into standard commodities of high quality and low cost of production." (Ibid., p. 33.)

64 As quoted in a Department of Commerce Staff Paper, "Herbert Hoover's Fight against Foreign Raw-Material Monopolies," March 22, 1928, Commerce Papers, HHPL.

65 For a more extensive treatment of these episodes, see Joseph Brandes, *Herbert Hoover and Economic Diplomacy: Department of Commerce Policy,*

1921–1928 (Pittsburgh, Pa.: University of Pittsburgh Press, 1962).

66 Hoover to Everett Sanders, September 21, 1925, Commerce Papers, HHPL. (Sanders served as a White House aide to President Coolidge.)

67 Hoover to Sanders, January 12, 1928, Commerce Papers, HHPL.

68 Hoover's conception of the ideal tariff, it should be noted, had two additional features. It should leave room for flexibility to permit adjustments in schedules in response to changes in costs at home and abroad; and it should be "scientifically" managed – administered by a body of experts shielded from partisan and interest-group pressures.

69 Hoover to Secretary of States Charles E. Hughes, April 29, 1922, Commerce Papers, HHPL.

70 Ibid.

71 Ibid.

72 Benjamin Strong to Hughes, June 9, 1922, Commerce Papers, HHPL.

73 The aggregate values amounted to $576.6 million in 1921 and $1,724.7 million in 1927. (*Statistical Abstract of the United States, 1926*, p. 305, and *1934*, p. 278.)

74 Charles P. Kindleberger, *The World in Depression: 1929–1939* (Berkeley and Los Angeles: University of California Press, 1973), p. 56.

75 "Do Foreign Branch Plants Pay?" *The Business Week*, October 19, 1929 (as cited by Brandes, *Herbert Hoover and Economic Diplomacy*, p. 163).

76 More than two-fifths of these credits had been extended to Britain, about one-third to France, and about one-sixth to Italy (*Statistical Abstract of the United States, 1926*, p. 208).

77 *Statistical Abstract of the United States, 1934*, pp. 162–63.

78 As a member of the World War Foreign Debt Commission (created by Congress in 1922), Hoover had initially proposed that debts incurred before the Armistice be cancelled and that the Allies be held liable only for loans negotiated for postwar reconstruction. This disposition, he maintained, would strengthen the country's "moral position." He was persuaded by his fellow commissioners that this proposition was not politically viable. The practical problem thus became one of producing a formula that would "preserve the appearance of repayment of both principal and interest" but could be adapted to specific circumstances of debtor governments. (*Memoirs*, vol. 2, p. 178.)

79 Hoover to Adolph S. Ochs, of the *New York Times*, May 3, 1926, Commerce Papers, HHPL.

80 In his *Memoirs*, he wrote as follows: "The British and French officials, especially, inaugurated at once a propaganda for cancellation. We were Uncle Shylock. Many Americans who loved Europe more and America less took up this cry. Our international bankers agitated for cancellation night and day. They employed economists to prove that the debts never could be paid, that the debtors could not find international exchange to do it, and that anyway payment would hurt us worse than cancellation. These arguments, false in every particular, got under my economic skin." (Vol. 2, p. 179.)

81 Keynes, "Settlement of War Debts," *Sunday Times*, September 18, 1921 (as reprinted in *The Collected Writings*, vol. 17, pp. 272–78).

82 Calculated from the *Statistical Abstract of the United States, 1926*, pp. 162–63, 460–61.

83 Hoover gave a high priority to the preparation of reliable statistics covering transactions on the "invisible" account. This was a central consideration in the decision (taken in 1922) to commission John H. Williams of Harvard University to prepare balance-of-payments accounts for the United States. In the history of the statistical work of the federal government, this was a signal event. It marked the first occasion on which government itself generated the primary data, as opposed to relying on private organizations to supply them.

84 Hoover to Secretary of State Frank B. Kellogg, July 28, 1926, Commerce Papers, HHPL.

85 As Kindleberger has observed, the American portion of the Dawes loan ($100 million) was oversubscribed ten times and that "more than anything else, this was the spark that ignited foreign lending from New York, first to Germany, and shortly thereafter to Latin America and much of the rest of Europe." (*The World in Depression, 1929–1939*, p. 38.)

86 *Report of the Secretary of Commerce*, 1924, p. 7.

87 Keynes, "The End of Laissez-faire," in *Essays in Persuasion* (London: Rupert Hart-Davis, 1954), p. 318.

88 Ibid., p. 318.

89 Wesley C. Mitchell, "A Review," in *Recent Economic Changes in the United States*, p. 867.

2. Challenges to the new economics of the 1920s

1 Myron Watkins, "The Statistical Activities of Trade Associations," *American Economic Review Supplement*, 16 (March 1926), p. 231.

2 Throughout his career, Veblen was a vigorous critic of both the methods and the conclusions of neoclassical economics. At various times, he taught at the University of Chicago, the University of Missouri, Stanford University, and the New School for Social Research. Though he wrote prolifically, he was generally treated as an outcast by the establishment in academic economics.

3 Veblen (1857–1929) set out his thought in a series of books, most notably in *The Theory of the Leisure Class* (1899), *The Theory of Business Enterprise* (1904), *Engineers and the Price System* (1921), and *Absentee Ownership* (1923).

4 Stuart Chase, *The Tragedy of Waste* (New York: Macmillan, 1925), p. 270

5 Rexford Guy Tugwell, *Industry's Coming of Age* (New York: Harcourt, Brace, 1927), p. 218.

6 Veblen had drawn attention to the implications of absentee ownership in his writings in the 1920s. Two of Tugwell's colleagues at Columbia – A. A. Berle of the Law School and Gardiner C. Means in the Economics Department – were engaged in the first major empirical study of this issue, the find-

ings of which were published in *The Modern Corporation and Private Property* (New York: Columbia University Press, 1931).

7 Tugwell, *Industry's Coming of Age*, p. 232.

8 Ibid., p. 240.

9 Ibid., pp. 216–17.

10 Alvin H. Hansen, "Factors Affecting the Trend of Real Wages," *American Economic Review*, 15 (March 1925), p. 42

11 Paul H. Douglas, "The Movement of Real Wages and Its Economic Significance," *American Economic Review Supplement*, 16 (March 1926), p. 37.

12 Ibid., p. 48.

13 Alvin H. Hansen, "The Outlook for Wages and Employment," *American Economic Review Supplement*, 13 (March 1923), p. 37.

14 Ibid., p. 42.

15 Sumner Slichter, "Market Shifts, Price Movements, and Employment," *American Economic Review Supplement*, 19 (March 1929), p. 14n.

16 Ibid., p. 22.

17 Lawrence B. Mann, Acting Chief, Division of Statistical Research, to Julius Klein, February, 28, 1928, Commerce Papers, HHPL.

18 *Historical Statistics of the United States*, Part 1, pp. 483, 491.

19 It may be noted that the analysis offered by American agricultural economists in the 1920s anticipated the doctrines of Raoul Prebisch in the 1950s when he argued that the international terms of trade were biased against agricultural exporters and in favor of countries exporting manufactured goods.

20 Mordecai Ezekiel, "Studies of the Effectiveness of Individual Farm Enterprises," *Journal of Farm Economics*, 8 (January 1926), p. 101.

21 The first edition of their pamphlet, *Equality for Agriculture*, was published anonymously. Subsequent editions identified the authors.

22 Tugwell, "Reflections on Farm Relief," *Political Science Quarterly*, 43 (December 1928), p. 490.

23 Ibid., p. 493.

24 It was only later, however, that Ely worked out the details of what he had in mind. By December 1931 he was ready to argue that "English economic theory has in no small measure been responsible for this uncontrolled expansion and the plight of the farmer." The error arose from the absorption of Malthusian population doctrine and the Ricardian "law" of rent into American thinking. This implied that land values would always increase and that there could be no deficiency in demand for farm products. Ely held it to be "unfortunate" that American thinkers had not developed American economic theories." The nation was paying a high price for their failure to do so. A national land policy – one that could mandate that surplus crop acreage lie idle or be converted into pastures or forests – would be a step in the right direction. (Richard T. Ely, "Depression and the 150-year Plan" [abstract of a paper presented at the meetings of the American Economic Association, December 1931], reprinted in the *Congressional Record*, May 16, 1932, pp. 10317–19.)

25 Hoover described his cabinet colleague, Henry C. Wallace (who served as Secretary of Agriculture from 1921 until his death in 1924), as an "unwitting Fascist" for entertaining the McNary–Haugen proposal sympathetically. Ironically, it was Hoover himself who had pioneered the technique of price fixing for farm products in his capacity as War Food Administrator. But this episode could be dismissed as a regrettable necessity at a time when overriding national priorities called for maximizing production from the land.

26 Hoover to Everett Sanders, September 21, 1925, Commerce Papers, HHPL.

27 Ibid.

28 George F. Warren, "The Agricultural Depression," *The Quarterly Journal of Economics*, 38 (February 1924), p. 121.

29 The point principally at issue turned on the computation of a price index for goods purchased by farmers. The index did not include a number of manufactured products that had fallen considerably in price in the 1920s such as automobiles.

30 Frank M. Surface to Hoover, March 13, 1926, Commerce Papers, HHPL.

31 Slichter, "Market Shifts, Price Movements, and Unemployment," *American Economic Review Supplement*, 19 (March 1929), p. 22.

32 Foster and Catchings had been undergraduate classmates at Harvard, but had initially chosen quite divergent careers. Foster acquired a national reputation as an expert on debate, produced a number of well-regarded textbooks on forensics, and became the first president of Reed College. Catchings accumulated a considerable fortune as a partner in the investment banking house of Goldman–Sachs. As a member of the War Labor Board, his interest turned to questions of stabilization in employment and this experience inspired him to launch the Pollak Foundation, an economic research organization, which he supported from his private purse.

33 First prize was awarded to R. W. Souter of the University of Otago, New Zealand. The submissions of Alvin Hansen, then at the University of Minnesota, and of Calvin B. Hoover of Duke University received honorable mention. Four of the essays, along with a rebuttal prepared by Foster and Catchings, were published under the title *Pollak Prize Essays: Criticisms of Profits, A Book by William Trufant Foster and Waddill Catchings* (Newton, Mass.: Pollak Foundation for Economic Research, 1927).

34 Foster and Catchings, *The Road to Plenty* (Boston: Houghton Mifflin, 1928), p. 88.

35 From a later vantage point, it can be seen that Foster and Catchings were attempting to address the problem subsequently taken up by Roy Harrod and Evsey Domar when they specified the conditions required to sustain full employment in a growing economy.

36 Foster and Catchings, *Business without a Buyer*, 2nd ed. (Boston: Houghton Mifflin, 1928), p. 178.

37 Foster and Catchings, *The Road to Plenty*, p. 135.

38 Foster and Catchings, *Business without a Buyer*, p. 118.

39 Foster and Catchings, *The Road to Plenty*, p. 195.

40 Ibid., p. 200.

41 Ibid., pp. 202–3.

42 See Ralph Brewster, "Footprints on the Road to Plenty – A Three Billion Dollar Fund to Stabilize Business," in *Commerce and Finance*, November 28, 1928, p. 2527 (as reported by E. J. Howenstine, Jr., "Public Works Policy in the Twenties," *Social Research*, 13 [December 1946], p. 493).

43 Brewster to Hoover, January 2, 1929, Campaign and Transition Files, HHPL.

44 Foster and Catchings, "The New Attack on Poverty – Mr. Hoover's Plan: What It Is and What It Is Not," *The Review of Reviews*, 79 (April 1929), p. 78.

45 This was a recurrent theme, for example, in the voluminous correspondence between Benjamin Strong and Montagu Norman, governor of the Bank of England.

46 Membership in the system was required only for commercial banks operating with national charters. Banks chartered by state authorities, on the other hand, might elect to participate, but were not compelled to do so. Fewer than one-third of the 30,457 banks operating in 1921 were Federal Reserve members. While the total number of banks had fallen to under 26,000 by 1928, the membership ratio was still below 35 percent. Although it was true that Federal Reserve members commanded the bulk of the assets held by all commercial banks – some 70–73 percent of the total was held by member banks in the 1920s – there was still considerable slippage from the control network. (*Historical Statistics of the United States*, part 2, pp. 1021, 1023.)

47 Benjamin Strong, Hearings before the Committee on Banking and Currency, House of Representatives, April 8, 1926, p. 293.

48 In his presidential address to the American Economic Association in December 1926, Kemmerer observed that the governments of ten countries on five continents had sought his advice on steps required for their adoption of the gold standard. (See Edwin W. Kemmerer, "Economic Advisory Work for Governments," *American Economic Review*, 17 [March 1927], pp. 1–12.)

49 This was the position, for example, of Alvin Hansen in the early 1920s. See "The Outlook for Wages and Employment," *American Economic Review Supplement*, 13 (March 1923).

50 This was also the position taken by Keynes in his *Tract on Monetary Reform*.

51 Fisher, "Stabilizing the Dollar," in *The Stabilization of Business*, Lionel D. Edie, ed. (New York: Macmillan, 1923), p. 111.

52 Fisher did not restrict his lobbying work to American audiences. In 1927, he sought support for his ideas in Europe and, in that connection, had an audience with Mussolini in Rome.

53 Hoover was persuaded that the closeness of the relationship between Benjamin Strong and Montagu Norman, governor of the Bank of England, was a disservice to American interests. In his *Memoirs*, Hoover wrote with an overtone of conspiracy about this relationship.

54 *Historical Statistics of the United States,* part 2, p. 995.

55 Frank W. Taussig, *Free Trade, the Tariff and Reciprocity* (New York: Macmillan, 1924), p. 49.

56 Taussig, it should be noted, was displeased with the amendments in the Tariff Commission's authority produced by legislation in 1922. With presidential approval, the commission was then empowered to make changes in tariff schedules when deemed necessary to equalize costs of production at home and abroad. Taussig held this to be bad policy, both as a matter of principle and as a matter of procedure. (See Frank W. Taussig, "The United States Tariff Commission and the Tariff," *American Economic Review Supplement,* 16 [March 1926], pp. 171–81.)

3. The new economics at center stage in 1929

1 "Report of the Committee on Recent Economic Changes of the President's Conference on Unemployment," in *Recent Economic Changes in the United States,* p. xiv.

2 Ibid., p. xvii.

3 Willard L. Thorp, "The Changing Stucture of Industry," in *Recent Economic Changes,* pp. 184–85, 217.

4 William J. Cunningham, "Transportation: Part I – Railways," in *Recent Economic Changes,* p. 299.

5 "Report of the Committee on Recent Economic Changes," p. xxi.

6 O. M. W. Sprague and W. Randolph Burgess, "Money and Credit and Their Effect on Business," in *Recent Economic Changes,* p. 695.

7 "Report of the Committee on Recent Economic Changes," p. xii.

8 Sprague and Burgess, "Money and Credit," p. 682.

9 "Report of the Committee on Recent Economic Changes," p. xxi.

10 Ibid., pp. xx, xxii.

11 Hoover, Inaugural Address, March 4, 1929, *PPP, 1929,* pp. 5, 11.

12 Hoover, Annual Message to the Congress on the State of the Union, December 3, 1929, *PPP, 1929,* p. 423.

13 Hoover estimated that about 10 percent of the nation's electric power system was "of interstate character and beyond the jurisdiction of the States." (Ibid., p. 424.)

14 Irving Fisher had also urged this step on Hoover. "As one of your admirers and enthusiastic supporters," he wrote, "I sincerely hope you will seize the opportunity to secure a census of unemployment as a starting point for a monthly index number of unemployment." (Fisher to Hoover, April 24, 1929, Presidential Subject Files, HHPL.)

15 *Statistical Abstract of the United States, 1934,* p. 279.

16 Ibid., p. 278.

17 The Federal Reserve System's holdings of government securities at the end of 1928 had fallen to $228 million. This sum was trifling in relation to the magnitude of the problem that open-market sales might be expected to ad-

dress. In this connection, see John Kenneth Galbraith, *The Great Crash: 1929*, 3rd ed. (Boston: Houghton Mifflin, 1972), p. 35.

18 Hoover, *Memoirs*, vol. 3, p. 16.

19 As reported by Merlo J. Pusey, *Eugene Meyer* (New York: Knopf, 1974), pp. 201–2. According to this account, Hoover had discussed his concern about the speculative mania with Meyer who suggested that the president might appropriately assume the role of a stockbroker counseling his clients. Hoover preferred to have Mellon act on his behalf. The latter regarded this assignment as distasteful.

20 *New York Times*, Editorial, "Secretary Mellon's Advice," March 16, 1929.

21 Robinson, then chairman of the board of the Security First National Bank of Los Angeles, was to serve on numerous occasions as Hoover's contact with the financial community. His earlier public assignments had included membership of the Council of National Defense in 1917 and 1918 and of the Supreme Economic Council at the Paris Peace Conference in 1919. He had also served as chairman of the American delegation to the International Economic Conference in 1922 and as a member of the Dawes Plan Committee in 1924.

22 Thomas W. Lamont (no kin of Robert P. Lamont, secretary of commerce) had spent most of his career in investment banking. His public duties included participation in the Paris Peace Conference as a U.S. Treasury representative and service as an alternate delegate on the Committee of Experts on German Reparations in 1929.

23 Thomas W. Lamont to Hoover, October 19, 1929, President's Personal Files, HHPL.

24 Ibid.

25 Ibid. In a penciled notation inscribed some years later on the first page of this eighteen-page memorandum, Hoover wrote: "This document is fairly amazing in light of two years after."

26 William Trufant Foster and Waddill Catchings, "Is the Reserve Board Keeping Faith?" *The Atlantic Monthly*, 144 (July 1929), p. 94.

27 Ibid., p. 95.

28 Ibid., p. 101.

29 Ibid., p. 102.

30 As quoted by John Kenneth Galbraith, *The Great Crash: 1929*, p. 75.

4. Activating the stabilization model in late 1929 and 1930

1 This remark was reported in a memorandum from Martin Egan, a member of the staff of J. P. Morgan and Company, to Thomas W. Lamont. Egan had met with the president at the White House, though the precise timing of their conversation is obscure. Lamont's memorandum of October 19 was obviously available at the time of this meeting. Egan's report to Lamont is dated October 23, 1929. Hoover, however, was then on a trip in the Midwest. See Egan to Lamont, President's Personal Files, HHPL.

2 Henry M. Robinson to Hoover, October 25, 1929, Presidential Subject Files, HHPL.

3 Hoover, Statement on the National Business and Economic Situation, October 25, 1929, *PPP, 1929*, p. 356.

4 Hoover, News Conference, November 5, 1929, *PPP, 1929*, pp. 366–68.

5 Lamont to Hoover, November 15, 1929, Presidential Subject Files, HHPL.

6 Hoover, Statement Announcing a Series of Conferences with Representatives of Business, Industry, Agriculture, and Labor, November 15, 1929, *PPP, 1929*, pp. 384–85.

7 Hoover to Secretary of State Stimson, November 18, 1929, Presidential Subject Files, HHPL. An identical memorandum was sent to all cabinet officers.

8 Hoover, Telegrams to Governors Urging Stimulation of Public Works to Aid the Economy, November 23, 1929, *PPP, 1929*, p. 397.

9 Ibid.

10 White House Statement, November 25, 1929, *PPP, 1929*, p. 398.

11 Message to the president on the Chicago Meeting of Railway Executives, November 22, 1929, *PPP, 1929*, p. 392.

12 Hoover to Julius Barnes, December 7, 1929, Presidential Subject Files, HHPL.

13 As Albert U. Romasco has pointed out, there were some precedents for presidential intervention in the responses of the White House to the banking panic of 1907 (Theodore Roosevelt), the recession of 1914 (Woodrow Wilson), and the recession of 1921 (Warren Harding). Hoover's activism in 1929 was still distinctive in two respects: (1) by its magnitude; and (2) by the fact that it was executed in accordance with a preconceived plan. See Romasco, "Herbert Hoover's Policies for Dealing with the Great Depression: The End of the Old Order or the Beginning of the New?" in *Herbert Hoover Reassessed*, Mark Hatfield, organizer (Washington, D.C.: U.S. Government Printing Office, 1981), pp. 292–309.

14 Hoover, *Memoirs*, vol. 3, p. 30.

15 *Survey of Current Business*, December 1929 (as quoted by Joseph W. Duncan and William C. Shelton, *Revolution in United States Government Statistics, 1926–1976*, U.S. Department of Commerce, 1978, p. 23).

16 Hoover, News Conference, November 19, 1929, *PPP, 1929*, p. 387.

17 Ibid., p. 388.

18 Hoover, News Conference, November 29, 1929, *PPP, 1929*, p. 401.

19 P. J. Croghan, Division of Current Information, Department of Commerce, to Secretary Lamont, April 26, 1930, Presidential Subject Files, HHPL.

20 Hoover to Lamont, April 26, 1930, Presidential Subject Files, HHPL.

21 Hoover, Address to the United States Chamber of Commerce, May 1, 1930, *PPP, 1930*, pp. 171, 173, 174. The latter statement is as close as Hoover came to saying that "prosperity is just around the corner." In fact, he never used those words, though they have frequently been attributed to him.

22 Hoover, Address to the American Bankers' Association, October 2, 1930, *PPP, 1930*, pp. 393, 396.

23 Ibid., p. 400.
24 Hoover, Address to the United States Chamber of Commerce, May 1, 1930, *PPP, 1930*, p. 174.
25 This finding was reported at the 1931 convention of the American Federation of Labor, as cited by Hoover, *Memoirs*, vol. 3, p. 46.
26 Hoover, Statement on the Tariff Bill, June 16, 1930, *PPP, 1930*, pp. 231, 232. On the basis of estimates prepared by the Tariff Commission, Hoover maintained that the Smoot–Hawley Tariff would raise the average level of duties on the value of all imports (free and dutiable) from about 13.8 percent to roughly 16 percent. In fact, however, the average rate of duty on the value of all imports (both free and dutiable) turned out to be higher than these calculations suggested. In 1931 – the first year in which the full impact of the new tariff was felt – the ratio was 17.75 percent and it rose to nearly 20 percent in 1932. For dutiable items alone, the ratio of duties to imports (which was about 40 percent in 1929) exceeded 59 percent by 1932. (*Historical Statistics of the United States*, part 2, p. 888.)
27 Hoover, Annual Budget Message to Congress, December 4, 1929, *PPP, 1929*, p. 449.
28 *Economic Report of the President, 1982*, p. 320.
29 *Annual Report of the Secretary of the Treasury on the State of the Finances for the Fiscal Year Ended June 30, 1929*, p. 22.
30 Undersecretary of the Treasury Ogden L. Mills, Memorandum of November 13, 1929, Presidential Subject Files, HHPL. Mills believed it desirable for the executive branch to be given scope to make year-to-year changes in tax schedules. His argument for administrative discretion, however, was substantially different from the one that was to be advanced in later decades. Mills was concerned primarily with avoiding a deficit in light of the problematic nature of forecasting revenues for more than one year ahead. The latter-day case for discretionary authority over tax rates has instead emphasized the potential usefulness of this tool in stabilizing the economy.
31 Wesley C. Mitchell, "Are There Practicable Steps toward an Industrial Equilibrium?" (paper presented before a meeting of the Taylor Society, New York, December 4, 1929), *Bulletin of the Taylor Society*, 15 (February 1930), p. 6.
32 William Trufant Foster and Waddill Catchings, "Mr. Hoover's Road to Prosperity," *The Review of Reviews*, 81 (January 1930), p. 51.
33 Ibid., p. 52.
34 Irving Fisher, *The Stock Market Crash – and After*, (New York: Macmillan, 1930), p. 269.
35 Ibid., pp. 268–269.
36 John Maurice Clark, "Public Works and Unemployment" (paper presented at the American Economic Association meetings of December 1929), *American Economic Review Supplement*, 20, (March 1930), pp. 15, 19.
37 Ibid., p. 17.
38 Ibid., p. 18.
39 Ibid., p. 20.

40 Frank G. Dickinson, "Public Works and Unemployment" (paper presented at the American Economic Association meetings of December 1929), *American Economic Review Supplement*, 20 (March 1930), pp. 24, 25. This session of the annual gathering of the AEA was held in Washington. Hoover's appointment calendar indicates that Dickinson met with him at the White House on December 31, 1929. (*PPP, 1930*, p. 706.)

41 Rexford Guy Tugwell, "Hunger, Cold and Candidates," *The New Republic*, 54 (May 2, 1928), pp. 323–24.

42 As reported in *The Review of Reviews*, 81 (June 1930), p. 23.

43 During his campaign for the presidency in 1932, Franklin D. Roosevelt refered to this episode, observing that he had been told that "never before in history have so many economists been able to agree upon anything." In campaign style, he asked: "Would [Hoover] have ignored a warning by a thousand engineers that a bridge which the national Government was building was unsafe?" (*The Public Papers and Addresses of Franklin D. Roosevelt*, vol. 1, [New York: Random House, 1938], p. 637, reproducing a speech delivered at St. Paul, Minnesota, April 18, 1932.)

5. Preliminary readings of the results of the stabilization strategy

1 Hoover to Secretary of Commerce Lamont, October 1, 1930, Presidential Subject Files, HHPL.

2 As calculated from data in the *Historical Statistics of the United States*, part 2, pp. 620–21.

3 Ibid., p. 618.

4 Ibid., p. 618.

5 Hoover, Annual Message to the Congress on the State of the Union, December 2, 1930, *PPP, 1930*, p. 513.

6 J. M. Clark and Sumner Slichter were among the technical advisers engaged to assist the advisory committee.

7 Joseph H. Willits, chairman of the Advisory Committee on Employment Statistics, to Hoover, February 9, 1931, Presidential Subject Files, HHPL.

8 Paul H. Douglas and Aaron Director, *The Problem of Unemployment* (New York: Macmillan, 1931), p. 17. Even this estimate was held to be a conservative statement of the overall problem. Their calculations referred to the numbers who were completely without work and thus took no account of those who held a job but with shortened hours.

9 In April 1931, for example, Hoover observed to the secretary of Commerce that "we are in need of a definition or nomenclature in connection with unemployment in order that we may carry less confusion to the public in the various statistical and official statements." He suggested that data be prepared which would distinguish between three types of unemployment: (1) "normal" (i.e., transitional); (2) "seasonal"; (3) "abnormal." The final category, he noted, was the important one and "our statistics should be arranged if possible to express this number after deducting the two above

mentioned categories." (Hoover to Lamont, April 2, 1931, Presidential Subject Files, HHPL.)

10 *Historical Statistics of the United States*, part 1, p. 244. These data indicate the following changes: (1) reductions in nominal GNP: between 1930 and 1929 – 12.3 percent: between 1921 and 1922 – 23.9 percent; (2) reductions in real GNP (measured at 1958 prices): between 1930 and 1929 – 9.9 percent; between 1921 and 1920 – 8.7 percent.

11 Hoover, Address to the American Bankers Association, October 2, 1930, *PPP, 1930*, pp. 392, 396.

12 Hoover to Roy A. Young, governor of the Federal Reserve Board, March 24, 1930, Presidential Subject Files, HHPL.

13 Ibid.

14 A. E. Goldenweiser to Young, April 11, 1930, Presidential Subject Files, HHPL.

15 The details of this proposal were as follows: no credit would be allowed for investment less than or equal to one-third of the sums spent in 1929; a credit of 10 percent would be awarded on the second third; a credit of 15 percent would be awarded on capital spending in excess of two-thirds of the 1929 volume. No more than half of the normal tax obligation, however, could be so written off.

16 Ogden L. Mills, undersecretary of the Treasury to Hoover, December 8, 1930, Presidential Subject Files, HHPL.

17 Eugene Meyer, governor of the Federal Reserve Board, to Hoover, October 22, 1930, Presidential Subject Files, HHPL.

18 See, for example, Milton Friedman and Anna Jacobson Schwartz, *The Great Contraction, 1929–1933* (Princeton, N.J.: Princeton University Press, 1965), p. 44. By their measure, the money stock declined by 2.6 percent between August 1929 and October 1930.

19 Hoover, News Conference, May 15, 1931, *PPP, 1931*, p. 225.

20 Foster and Catchings, "Riotous Saving," *The Atlantic Monthly*, 146 (November 1930), pp. 667–68.

21 Foster and Catchings, "Must We Reduce Our Standard of Living?" *The Forum*, 85 (February 1931), p. 79.

22 Wesley C. Mitchell, "Causes of Depression" (discussion at the meeting of the Academy of Political Science, April 24, 1931), *Proceedings of the Academy of Political Science*, 14 (June 1931), p. 72.

23 Josef Schumpeter, "The Present World Depression: A Tentative Diagnosis" (paper presented at the meetings of the American Economic Association, December 1930), *American Economic Review Supplement*, 21 (March 1931), pp. 179–80.

24 Alvin H. Hansen, "The Business Depression of 1930: Discussion" (comments on Schumpeter's paper to the American Economic Association Meetings, December 1930), *American Economic Review Supplement*, 21 (March 1931), p. 201.

25 Hansen, "The Decline of Laissez Faire: Discussion" (comments at the American Economic Association Meetings, December 1930), *American Economic Review Supplement*, 21 (March 1931), p. 8.

26 Sumner Slichter, "Doles for Employers," *The New Republic*, 65 (December, 31, 1930), pp. 181–83.

6. The unraveling of the first official model in 1931

 1 Hoover, Annual Budget Message to Congress, Fiscal Year, 1932, December 3, 1930, *PPP, 1930*, pp. 540–41.

 2 These studies, prepared by J. F. Dewhurst, offered the following conclusion: "Judged by the course of business recovery in five major depressions during the past 50 years, it appears likely –
(a) that business volume, now 34 per cent below normal, is virtually at bottom;
(b) that business will continue close to the present levels for 2 or 3 months longer;
(c) that recovery should get well under way in the last half of this year;
(d) that business volume will most probably return to normal during the last half of 1932." (J. F. Dewhurst to Klein, March 19, 1931, Presidential Subject Files, HHPL.)

 3 Hoover, News Conference, December 5, 1930, *PPP, 1930*, p. 553.

 4 L. W. Wallace to Lawrence Richey, Secretary to the President, January 21, 1931, Presidential Subject Files, HHPL.

 5 "Emergency Measures and the Present Depression," Statement Adopted by the American Engineering Council, January 16, 1931. This statement was transmitted to the White House on January 21, 1931.

 6 Hoover, News Conference, January 2, 1931, *PPP, 1931*, pp. 1–3.

 7 Hoover, News Conference, February 10, 1931, *PPP, 1931*, p. 67. On this occasion, Hoover paid special tribute to the work of two men, Edward Eyre Hunt and Otto Mallery. They had, he noted, "first proposed this sort of set-up for advance planning of public works against depression in the unemployment conference of 1921. And they were members of two subsequent committees that were appointed to investigate it, and as a result it was placed before Congress at various times, but it takes a depression in order to bring home the utility of such proposals." (Ibid., pp. 67–68.)

 8 D. H. Sawyer, Director, Federal Employment Stabilization Board, to Roy D. Chapin, Secretary of Commerce and Chairman, Federal Employment Stabilization Board, October 21, 1932, Presidential Subject Files, HHPL.

 9 Raymond Clapper to Walter H. Newton, secretary to the president, March 2, 1931 (with an enclosed draft of a column on an interview with the president). Clapper requested White House authorization, which was denied, to publish this account. (Presidential Subject Files, HHPL.)

10 Hoover, Veto of the Muscle Shoals Resolution, March 3, 1931, *PPP, 1931*, pp. 120–29.

11 Walter S. Gifford, director of the President's Organization on Unemployment Relief, Hearings before the Subcommittee of the Committee on Manu-
factures, Senate, January 8, 1932, p. 313.

12 E. Cary Brown, "Fiscal Policy in the Thirties: A Reappraisal," *American
Economic Review*, 46 (December 1956), pp. 857–79.

13 Secretary of the Treasury A. W. Mellon to Senator Arthur H. Vandenberg,
December 4, 1930 (reprinted as Exhibit 78 in the *Annual Report of the
Treasury, 1931*, p. 387).

14 Hoover, Veto of the Emergency Adjusted Compensation Bill, February 26,
1931, *PPP, 1931*, p. 106.

15 Frank T. Hines, administrator of veterans' affairs, to the president, February 26, 1931 (as reprinted in *PPP, 1931*, p. 112).

16 "What President Hoover Has Done in the Relief of Unemployment during
the Depression from November, 1930 to September, 1931," undated memorandum, Presidential Subject Files, HHPL.

17 *Historical Statistics of the United States*, part 2, p. 1038.

18 Of the 1,352 banks that suspended operations in 1930, only 161 held national charters and but 188 were members of the Federal Reserve System.
(Ibid., p. 1038.)

19 Hoover's position on this point, it may be noted, was in accord with the
view of Foster and Catchings who had chastized bankers for tolerating statements from leading members of their fraternity suggesting that the country's
standard of living was already too high and that a period of austerity was
in order.

20 Fisher was here referring to a banking convention which was to persist in
many smaller communities until the mid-1970s: that is, the "3-6-3 rule"
(pay 3 percent on savings, lend at 6 percent, and be on the golf course at
3:00 P.M.).

21 Irving Fisher to Hoover, May 9, 1931, Presidential Subject Files, HHPL.
Some of Meyer's skepticism about the willingness of bankers to cooperate
was conveyed in a memorandum he prepared for Hoover in October 1930.
The Federal Reserve System, he insisted, was trying to force interest rates
lower, but it had "received many requests from the banks to use its influence
to raise the level of rates, as the banks find it difficult to earn their expenses
in the existing circumstances." (Meyer to Hoover, October 22, 1930, Presidential Subject Files, HHPL.)

22 *Historical Statistics of the United States*, part 2, p. 1021.

23 On August 26, 1931, Hoover asked the Justice Department to consider
whether such power could be legally acquired. The attorney-general reported
negatively on this proposition. In his opinion, the Constitution did not em-
power Congress to regulate commercial banking as such, nor could a bank
be regarded as engaging in interstate commerce "when it purchases for investment or sells securities that are transmitted to it from another State or
by it to another State." And further: "even if it be assumed that an important part of a bank's business may be in interstate commerce, this fact

does not authorize Congress to regulate its entire business, intrastate as well as interstate." (Attorney-General William D. Mitchell to Hoover, December 1, 1931, Presidential Subject Files, HHPL.)

24 Hoover to Secretary of the Treasury Mellon, August 31, 1931, Presidential Subject Files, HHPL.

25 Hoover to Secretary of Commerce Lamont, April 15, 1931, Presidential Subject Files, HHPL.

26 James Harvey Rogers, "Foreign Markets and Foreign Credits," in *Recent Economic Changes in the United States*, pp. 754–55.

27 Hoover, Message to Senator Arthur Capper about the Domestic Impact of the European Economic Crisis, July 18, 1931, *PPP, 1931*, pp. 357–58.

28 James Harvey Rogers, *America Weighs Her Gold* (New Haven, Conn.: Yale University Press, 1931), p. 209.

29 For a more extended itemization of proposals in circulation at the time, see Herbert Stein, *The Fiscal Revolution in America* (Chicago: University of Chicago Press, 1969), p. 23.

30 Report of the Committee on Program of Federal Public Works of the President's Organization on Unemployment Relief, December 16, 1931, Presidential Subject Files, HHPL. The membership of this committee (which was chaired by James R. Garfield, Chairman of the Midland Bank of Cleveland) was dominated by bankers. One academic economist – Professor Jacob S. Hollander of the John Hopkins University – and Matthew Woll, vice-president of the American Federation of Labor, participated.

31 Ibid.

32 Ibid.

33 Swope had joined the War Industries Board as a replacement for General Hugh S. Johnson, who had sought relief from desk duties in order to serve in France.

34 The text of Swope's address was published as the "Plan for Stabilization of Industry by the President of the General Electric Company," *Monthly Labor Review*, 33 (November 1931), pp. 1049–57.

35 William Starr Myers and Walter H. Newton, *The Hoover Administration: A Documented Narrative* (New York: C. Scribner's Sons, 1936), p. 119.

36 Hoover to Solicitor General Thomas D. Thatcher, September 12, 1931, Presidential Subject Files, HHPL.

37 Henry I. Harriman, "The Stabilization of Business and Employment" (paper presented to the meetings of the American Economic Association, December 1931), *American Economic Review Supplement*, 22 (March 1932), p. 67.

38 Rexford Guy Tugwell, "The Principle of Planning and the Institution of Laissez-faire" (paper presented to the meetings of the American Economic Association, December 1931), *American Economic Review Supplement*, 22 (March 1932), pp. 89–90.

39 "Long-Range Planning for the Regularization of Industry: the Report of a Subcommittee of the Committee on Unemployment and Industrial Stabilization of the National Progressive Conference," J. M. Clark, Chairman,

January 13, 1932, pp. 11, 13, 15. This report was published as a supplement to *The New Republic* of that date and was also signed by its editor, George Soule.

40 Hoover, Annual Message to the Congress on the State of the Union, December 8, 1931, *PPP, 1931*, p. 584. The surgeon general's report on the effect of the depression on health conditions had been transmitted to Hoover on August 18, 1931. (Ibid., pp. 393–98.)

7. Shifting course in late 1931 and early 1932

1 Studies by A. E. Goldenweiser of the Research Division of the Federal Reserve Board (which were transmitted to the White House on September 14, 1931) indicated that the net volume of "currency in circulation" as measured in the monetary aggregates had increased by about $400 million in the preceding twelve months. He noted, however, that "this increase ... represents hoarding rather than circulation," adding that this estimate was a "rock bottom minimum figure." If adjustments were made for reductions in payrolls and in retail trade (where the major claims on cash were typically made), the actual volume of hoarding was more likely to be of the order of $700 million. (Goldenweiser to Governor Meyer, September 14, 1931, Presidential Subject Files, HHPL.)

2 Hoover to Eugene Meyer, September 8, 1931, Presidential Subject Files, HHPL.

3 For that matter, President Franklin D. Roosevelt had no enthusiasm for federal guarantees for bank deposits when he inherited a banking crisis of still larger proportions in 1933. He went along with legislation creating a Federal Deposit Insurance Corporation which was packaged as part of the program for reopening banks following the "bank holiday" he had ordered in the first days of his administration.

4 Myers and Newton, *The Hoover Administration: a Documented Narrative*, p. 121.

5 Hoover spelled out the force of this consideration most fully in a campaign address in October 1932 in these words: "Going off the gold standard in the United States would have been a most crushing blow to most of those with savings and those who owed money and it was these we were fighting to protect. . . . In our country, largely as a result of fears generated by the experience after the Civil War and by the Democratic free-silver campaign in 1896, our people have long insisted upon writing a large part of their long-term debtor documents as payable in gold. A considerable part of farm mortgages, most of our industrial and all of our Government, most of our state and municipal bonds, and most other long-term obligations are written as payable in gold. . . . [I]f the United States had been forced off the gold standard, you in this city would have sold your produce for depreciated currency. . . . [B]ut you would have to pay a premium on such of your debts as are written in gold. The Federal Government, many of the States, the municipalities, to meet their obligations, would either need to

increase taxes which are payable in currency, or alternatively, to have re-
pudiated their obligations." (Hoover, Address at the Coliseum in Des
Moines, Iowa, October 4, 1932, *PPP, 1932–1933*, pp. 467–68.)

6 As Friedman and Schwartz have pointed out, the erosion in bond values
was not uniformly distributed. The lower quality corporate issues were off-
loaded first and their prices deteriorated substantially more than did those
of U.S. Treasury issues. (See Milton Friedman and Anna Jacobson Schwartz,
The Great Contraction, 1929–1933, p. 16.)

7 Hoover, Statement on Financial and Economic Problems to New York Bankers at the Home of Secretary of the Treasury Mellon, October 4, 1931, Presidential Subject Files, HHPL.

8 Hoover, Statement on Financial and Economic Problems, October 7, 1931,
PPP, 1931, p. 467.

9 George L. Harrison, governor of the Federal Reserve Bank of New York, to
Hoover, October 7, 1931, *PPP, 1931*, pp. 457–58.

10 Ibid., p. 456.

11 On these points, see James Stuart Olson, *Herbert Hoover and the Reconstruction Finance Corporation, 1931–1933* (Ames: Iowa State University
Press, 1977), pp. 30–31.

12 In 1931 some nineteen railway corporations failed and, by the end of the
year, the quoted prices of bonds issued by the survivors had collapsed. (Ibid.,
p. 30.)

13 George L. Harrison, Hearings before a Subcommittee of the Committee
on Banking and Currency, Senate, December 18, 1931, p. 773.

14 Though the RFC was held to be important in this undertaking, the administration recognized that it could not do all that was needed. Ultimately,
the debt-servicing capacity of the railroads would have to be restored by
improving their earning power. Hoover urged again that the Interstate
Commerce Commission expedite railroad consolidations, and that it should
review its policies on rate schedules in light of the industry's need to enhance its revenues. And – in a further retreat from a principle of "new era"
doctrine – he conceded that wage cuts by the railroads would be a necessary
part of a program of cost reduction. In addition, he called upon the industry to form a voluntary credit pool through which the resources of the
stronger carriers could be brought to the assistance of the weaker ones.

15 Hoover, Annual Message to the Congress of the State of the Union, December 8, 1931, *PPP, 1931*, p. 590.

16 Undersecretary of the Treasury Ogden L. Mills, Hearings before a Subcommittee of the Committee on Banking and Currency, Senate, December 18,
1931, p. 50.

17 Ibid., p. 50.

18 The tone of opposing congressional sentiment can be captured in the remarks of Representative Fiorello La Guardia of New York who characterized
the bill as "a millionaire's dole. . . . It is a subsidy for broken bankers – a
subsidy for bankrupt railroads – a reward for speculation and unscrupulous
bond pluggers." (*Congressional Record*, January 11, 1932, as quoted by

Olson, *Herbert Hoover and the Reconstruction Finance Corporation*, p. 35.)

19 Hoover, Annual Budget Message to the Congress, Fiscal Year, 1932, December 3, 1930, *PPP, 1930*, p. 540.

20 Hoover, News Conference, September 1, 1931, *PPP, 1931*, pp. 403–5.

21 Hoover had believed this matter to be of such urgency that he made an air trip to Detroit, Michigan on September 21, 1931 to argue against a resolution before the American Legion Convention which called for a second bonus payment. He would have preferred to stay in Washington to cope with the fall-out of Britain's departure from gold (which had been announced the preceding day), but this exercise took precedence. Even though he won the convention's support for this position, the issue was back on the congressional agenda in 1932 and very much on the minds of veterans who encamped in Washington – with tragic consequences – in July 1932.

22 This complication turned on the rules then governing the backing of Federal Reserve notes. Commercial bills and gold were required for this purpose, but government securities were not permissible as substitutes. For reasons which will be discussed in greater detail in Chapter 8, the Federal Reserve could not in late 1931 have absorbed any significant quantity of new Treasury securities. These conditions were relaxed with the passage of the Glass–Steagall Act of February, 1932. By then, however, the administration was already committed to a different strategy.

23 Hoover, Annual Message to Congress, Fiscal Year 1933, December 9, 1931, *PPP, 1931*, p. 601.

24 As calculated ibid., p. 599.

25 It will be recalled that the Treasury's acquisition of the capital stock of the corporation was treated as a budget expenditure. But this was to be a once-and-for-all transaction that would appear in the accounts of fiscal year 1932 when all hope of avoiding a sizable deficit had already been written off. The goal of "balance" (as redefined) referred to fiscal year 1933.

26 Hoover to Secretary of Commerce Lamont, January 25, 1932, Presidential Subject Files, HHPL.

8. Renewing the offensive in February and March 1932

1 As Ogden L. Mills (who had become secretary of the Treasury with Andrew Mellon's departure to become ambassador to Great Britain) described the situation: "The Federal Reserve Act clearly contemplates that a 40 per cent gold reserve is adequate behind the note issues of the system, but we find ourselves where, because of peculiar circumstances, we are obliged to mobilize not 40 per cent of gold, but approximately 80 per cent of gold." (Mills, Hearings before the Committee on Banking and Currency, House of Representatives, February 12, 1932, p. 24.)

2 Hoover, Statement on Signing the Federal Reserve Act Amendments, February 27, 1932, *PPP, 1932–1933*, pp. 80–81.

3 Eugene Meyer, Hearings before the Committee on Banking and Currency,

House of Representatives, February 12, 1932, p. 13.

4 Lester V. Chandler, *America's Greatest Depression, 1929–1941* (New York: Harper & Row, 1970), p. 118.

5 He had made that distinction in a message marking "National Thrift Week" in January 1932. Presidents on such occasions are usually expected to produce ritual statements extolling the virtues of thriftiness. Hoover instead put the issue as follows: "Thrift is not hoarding. It is the wise provision against future needs. Provision against future needs involves savings and wise spending for insurance, home ownership and many other constructive, sensible and discriminating actions." (Hoover, Message on National Thrift Week, January 17, 1932, *PPP, 1932–1933*, p. 24.)

6 Hoover, Statement on the Hoarding of Currency, February 3, 1932, *PPP, 1932–1933*, pp. 38–39.

7 Knox was later to be the Republican nominee for vice-president (on the ticket headed by Alfred M. Landon in 1936) and to serve as secretary of the navy under President Franklin D. Roosevelt during World War II.

8 White House Statement about the Conference on the Hoarding of Currency, February 6, 1932, *PPP, 1932–1933*, p. 45.

9 Hoover, News Conference, March 11, 1932, *PPP, 1932–1933*, p. 104.

10 Lawrence Richey, secretary to the president, to Knox, March 1, 1932, Presidential Subject Files, HHPL.

11 Knox to Hoover, March 9, 1932, Presidential Subject Files, HHPL.

12 Hoover, Statement on New Car Sales, April 1, 1932, *PPP, 1932–1933*, p. 131.

13 This estimate was prepared by A. E. Goldenweiser of the research division of the Federal Reserve Board; Goldenweiser to Joslin, June 23, 1932, Presidential Subject Files, HHPL.

14 Hoover to Harrison, April 26, 1932, Presidential Subject Files, HHPL.

15 W. W. Finney, president of the Emporia Telephone Company and chairman of the Anti-Hoarding Campaign in Kansas, to Senator Arthur Capper of Kansas, April 20, 1932, Presidential Subject Files, HHPL. Capper forwarded this correspondence to Hoover, who in turn shared it with Harrison.

16 Hoover to Thomas W. Lamont, April 2, 1932, Presidential Subject Files, HHPL.

17 Thomas W. Lamont to Hoover, April 8, 1932, Presidential Subject Files, HHPL.

18 Knox to Lawrence Richey, June 6, 1932, Presidential Subject Files, HHPL.

19 F. J. Stippe, The Chicago Wire Iron and Brass Works, to Richey, May 26, 1932, Presidential Subject Files, HHPL. The White House referred this letter to the secretary of the Treasury for reply.

20 In July 1932 Harrison calculated that the increases in the Federal Reserve's holdings of government securities since this program was launched in late February came to $1,060 million. The potential expansionary effect of these transactions on the lending capacity of banks had been offset to the extent of $403 million by heavy losses of gold. (Harrison to All Federal Reserve District Bank Governors, July 5, 1932, Presidential Subject Files, HHPL.)

9. The economists and their views on policy for 1932

1 This telegram, sent to the White House on January 31, 1932 was signed by the following: Irving Fisher (Yale University); Alvin H. Hansen and Arthur W. Marget of the University of Minnesota; Henry Schultz, Jacob Viner, Garfield V. Cox, Frank H. Knight, John H. Cover, Chester W. Wright, Harry D. Gideonse, Theodore O. Yntema, Harry A. Millis, Lloyd W. Mints, Aaron Director, and Henry C. Simons (all of the University of Chicago); Charles O. Hardy and Harold G. Moulton (the Brookings Institution, Washington, D.C.); John H. Williams (Harvard); Ivan Wright (University of Illinois); Max Handman (University of Michigan); Frank H. Streightoff and Thomas S. Luck (Indiana University); N. J. Ware and C. O. Fisher (Wesleyan University); Ernest M. Patterson (University of Pennsylvania); James W. Angell (Columbia University); Charles S. Tippitts (University of Buffalo); and Chester A. Phillips (University of Iowa). (Fisher et al., to Hoover, January 31, 1932, Presidential Subject Files, HHPL, and J. Ronnie Davis, *The New Economics and the Old Economists* [Ames: Iowa State University Press, 1971], pp. 155–56.)

2 Among those endorsing this position were Irving Fisher (Yale), John R. Commons (University of Wisconsin); John Maurice Clark and Edwin R. A. Seligman (Columbia); Frank W. Taussig and Thomas Nixon Carver (Harvard); Paul H. Douglas (University of Chicago); Jacob Hollander (Johns Hopkins); and Edwin W. Kemmerer (Princeton). (*New York Times*, January 16, 1932, as reported by Joseph Dorfman, *The Economic Mind and American Civilization*, vol. 5 [New York: Viking Press, 1959], pp. 675–76.)

3 M. S. Rukeyser to William Randolph Hearst, letter transmitting "The Economists' Plan for Accelerating Public Works in 1932," as reprinted in the *Congressional Record*, January 15, 1932, p. 2001.

4 The full list of signers was as follows: Thomas N. Carver (Harvard University); Paul H. Douglas (University of Chicago); W. N. Loucks (University of Pennsylvania); James C. Bonbright, Paul H. Brissenden, R. M. MacIver, Merryle Stanley Rukeyser (Columbia University); Willard L. Thorp, George R. Taylor, and Phillips Bradley (Amherst College); William T. Foster (Pollak Foundation); Arthur Evans Wood (University of Michigan); John Ise and Seba Eldridge (University of Kansas); Arthur Gayer (Barnard College); Gordon B. Hancock (Virginia Union University); H. H. McCarty (University of Iowa); LeRoy E. Bowman (The National Community Center Association); Edwin A. Elliott (Texas Christian University); David D. Vaughan (Boston University); Everett W. Goodhue (Dartmouth College); Edward Berman (University of Illinois); C. W. Doten (Massachusetts Institute of Technology); Truman C. Bigham and Walter J. Matherly (University of Florida); John E. Brindley (Iowa State College); and Jacob E. LeRossignol (University of Nebraska).

5 "Economists' Plan for Accelerating Public Works in 1932," *Congressional Record*, January 15, 1932, pp. 2001–02.

6 Arthur D. Gayer, Hearings before a Subcommittee of the Committee on Education and Labor, Senate, March 11, 1932, p. 107.

7 Gayer, ibid., p. 110.

8 Merryle Stanley Rukeyser, Hearings before a Subcommittee of the Committe on Education and Labor, Senate, March 10, 1932, p. 68.

9 Willard L. Thorp, Hearings before a Subcommittee of the Committee on Education and Labor, Senate, March 9, 1932, p. 21.

10 William T. Foster, Hearings before the Committee on Banking and Currency, Senate, June 2, 1932, p. 61.

11 Ibid., p. 62.

12 Gayer, Hearings before a Subcommitte of the Committee on Education and Labor, Senate, March 11, 1932, p. 112.

13 Rukeyser, Hearings before a Subcommittee of the Committee on Education and Labor, Senate, March 11, 1932, p. 60.

14 Senator Robert F. Wagner, Congressional Record, May 16, 1932, p. 10309.

15 Ibid., p. 10320.

16 Ibid., p. 10319.

17 Ibid., p. 10316.

18 Ibid., pp. 10319–20.

19 Ibid., p. 10337.

20 Ibid., p. 10338.

21 Ibid., p. 10338.

22 Ibid., p. 10338.

23 Ibid., p. 10336.

24 Ibid., pp. 10317–19.

25 Ibid., pp. 10328–29.

26 Ibid., p. 10330.

27 Ibid., p. 10334.

28 One of the strong voices of the 1920s, that of Wesley C. Mitchell (AEA president, 1924), was publicly silent during the sampling of professional opinion initiated by members of Congress in the spring of 1932. Mitchell was then in England as a visiting professor at the University of Oxford. In correspondence with his wife, he assessed the situation at that time as follows: "Now as to the business outlook: I feel sure that Americans are as emotionally unbalanced at present as they were at the top of the stock-market boom in 1929. Then I expected the delusion to pass a year or more before it did. Now I expect a turn for the better; but the fact that there is no economic justification for the present depression aside from the almost universal discouragement may not prevent the depression from running on for another year. I don't think it will; but the wise course is to prepare for that contingency." (As quoted by Lucy Sprague Mitchell, Two Lives: the Story of Wesley Clair Mitchell and Myself [New York: Simon and Schuster, 1953], p. 338.)

29 The positions of the profession's future "elder statesmen" (those who would subsequently have the presidency of the American Economic Association conferred upon them) are also worth noting:

John Maurice Clark (Columbia University, 1935), as an early supporter of the strategy of countercyclical public works, endorsed this approach to a "depression of moderate severity." The existing situation, however, was different in view of "the danger to public confidence and governmental credit, the danger of lowering security values in a way that may further undermine shaky collateral values on which bank credit rests." A $1 billion bond issue would have to avoid these risks and also make sure that a "forced contraction of private credit" did not result. Whether this was possible or not, he did not know. (Ibid., p. 10314.)

Alvin H. Hansen (University of Minnesota, 1938, who was later at Harvard University) registered his disapproval of the Wagner proposal with the observation that "this is not an advantageous time to engage in public works on the scale which is suggested in your bill." (Ibid., p. 10338.)

Sumner Slichter (Harvard University, 1940) recorded his enthusiastic support for the principles of deficit spending for public works, noting (1) that the action of the Federal Reserve in promoting easier credit conditions needed reinforcement in borrowing and spending which was not likely to be forthcoming promptly from business, (2) that the administration's program to reduce government expenditures was misguided because more spending – not less – was needed, and (3) that "the theory that public borrowing would divert funds from private industry overlooks the fact that money borrowed by the Government would be used to buy goods and hence would increase orders and profits." (Ibid., p. 10329.)

Frank H. Knight (University of Chicago, 1950), though unwilling to regard himself as an "expert" on the practical details of the proposition in question, agreed in principle that "the Government should spend as much and tax as little as possible, at a time such as this." (Ibid., p. 10323.)

Edwin E. Witte (the Wisconsin Free Library Commission, 1956, who was later at the University of Wisconsin) adjudged the Wagner approach "well worth trying." There appeared to be "no prospect of a boom in any industry. Public works alone hold promise of giving the necessary impetus to industry for a general recovery." (Ibid., p. 10336.)

30 Memorandum of University of Chicago economists to Representative Samuel B. Pettengill, April 26, 1932, Hearings before the Committee on Ways and Means, House of Representatives, April 25, 1932, pp. 524–27. The signers of this memorandum were Garfield V. Cox, Aaron Director, Paul H. Douglas, Harry D. Gideonse, Frank H. Knight, Harry A. Millis, Lloyd W. Mints, Henry Schultz, Henry C. Simons, Jacob Viner, Chester W. Wright, and Theodore O. Yntema.

31 Ibid., p. 524.

32 Ibid., p. 524.

33 Edwin W. Kemmerer, Hearings before the Committee on Ways and Means, House of Representatives, April 21, 1932, p. 399.

34 Ibid., pp. 399–400.

35 Ibid., p. 400.

36 Ibid., p. 422.

37 Ibid., pp. 422–23.

38 Ibid., p. 437. Hoover had sought Kemmerer's views in the autumn of 1931

about the feasibility of calling an International Monetary Conference. Kemmerer then held, and continued to do so, that the crux of international reconstruction was "the perfection of the gold standard, or, more correctly, its improvement." The best way to achieve this was through "frequent informal conferences among the officials of the world's central banks." In such a setting, the problem could be "discussed by qualified men in a serious way." He hesitated to endorse an International Monetary Conference at that time "when two years of world depression have been letting loose all the radical and half-baked monetary plans that such a period always brings to the fore." But, though nothing of a "constructive character" could be expected from such a gathering, it might still have something to recommend it "on the grounds that it would afford an opportunity to various dangerous groups to 'blow off steam' . . . [and] divert the attention of agitators for the time being from a national to an international field." (Kemmerer to Hoover, November 7, 1931, Presidential Subject Files, HHPL.)

39 Irving Fisher, Hearings before the Committee on Ways and Means, House of Representatives, April 29, 1932, p. 686.

40 Ibid., p. 689.

41 The diagnosis of the "diseases" which Fisher presented in official Washington in the spring of 1932 later emerged as "The Debt-Deflation Theory of Great Depressions," in *Econometrica*, 1 (October 1933), and in *Booms and Depressions* (New York: Adelphi, 1932).

42 Fisher to Senator Frederic D. Walcott, May 4, 1932, Presidential Subject Files, HHPL.

43 Fisher, Hearings before the Committee on Ways and Means, House of Representatives, April 29, 1932, p. 693.

44 Fisher, Hearings before the Committee on Banking and Currency, House of Representatives, March 30, 1932, p. 144.

45 Fisher to Senator Robert F. Wagner, July 13, 1932, Presidential Subject Files, HHPL. Versions of this scheme were also brought to Hoover's attention, both by Fisher and by Congressman James A. Frear of Wisconsin, who had been in correspondence with Barker. Hoover appears not to have understood this proposal fully, but indicated that he would give it "further study." (Hoover to Frear, July 21, 1932, Presidential Subject Files, HHPL.)

46 Fisher to Frederic D. Walcott, May 4, 1932.

47 Hansen heavily criticized the *General Theory* when it first appeared. The concluding paragraph of his 1936 review observed: "The book under review is not a landmark in the sense that it lays a foundation for a 'new economics'. . . . The book is more a symptom of economic trends than a foundation stone upon which a science can be built." (Hansen, "Mr. Keynes on Underemployment Equilibrium," *Journal of Political Economy*, 44 [October 1936], p. 686.) These sentences were deleted when Hansen reprinted his review in a collection of essays published in 1938. See Hansen, *Full Recovery or Stagnation?* (New York: Norton, 1938), p. 34.

48 Alvin H. Hansen, *Economic Stabilization in an Unbalanced World* (New York: Harcourt, Brace, 1932), p. 366.

49 Ibid., p. 189.

50 Ibid., pp. 389, 389n.

51 Frank A Fetter, "The Economists' Committee on Anti-Trust Law Policy," *American Economic Review*, 22 (September 1932), p. 465.

52 "Statement," ibid., p. 468.

53 In addition to Fetter, signers who had been accorded this honor were John Bates Clark (Columbia University, 1894–95); David Kinley (University of Illinois, 1913); John R. Commons (University of Wisconsin, 1917); Fred M. Taylor (University of Michigan, 1928); M. B. Hammond (Ohio State University, 1930); and E. L. Bogart (University of Illinois, 1931).

54 Those in this group were Willard L. Thorp (Amherst College); Clyde Olin Fisher (Wesleyan University); Carroll W. Doten (Massachusetts Institute of Technology); Paul Douglas (University of Chicago); and James C. Bonbright (Columbia University).

55 Members of the Chicago School who signed both this statement and the memorandum to Congressman Pettengill were the following: Paul Douglas, Jacob Viner, Henry Schultz, H. A. Millis, and Chester W. Wright.

56 The absence of John Maurice Clark from the list of signers is noteworthy. His father, John Bates Clark, was one of the signators; the son must surely have been aware of the existence of the petition.

10. Official model II as shaped in May 1932 and the aftermath

1 John Maynard Keynes, "The World's Economic Outlook," *The Atlantic Monthly*, 149 (May 1932), p. 521.

2 Hoover, Statement on the Economic Recovery Program, May 12, 1932, *PPP, 1932–1933*, pp. 211–12.

3 Ibid., p. 212.

4 It will be recalled that RFC's total lending capacity was defined as the $500 endowment initially subscribed by the Treasury plus the funds it was entitled to raise by issuing debt instruments in its own name.

5 C. F. Childs and Company, Government Bond Brokers, Chicago, to the Secretary of the Treasury, January 27, 1932, Records of the Department of the Treasury, Office of the Secretary, Box 118, NA.

6 Solicitor of the Treasury to Undersecretary A. A. Ballantine, March 5, 1932, Records of the Department of the Treasury, Office of the Secretary, Box 118, NA.

7 Henry J. Allen, Reconstruction Finance Corporation, to A. A. Ballantine, Undersecretary of the Treasury, March 4, 1932, Records of the Department of the Treasury, Office of the Secretary, Box 118, NA.

8 Treasury Department Comments on H.R. 7360, as Reported to the House on January 9, 1932, Records of the Department of the Treasury, Office of the Secretary, Box 118, NA.

9 Mills to the Editor of the *New York Evening Post*, July 11, 1932.

10 Hoover, Statement on the Economic Recovery Program, May 12, 1932, *PPP, 1932–1933*, p. 211.

11 Secretary of the Treasury Ogden L. Mills, Hearings before the Committee on Banking and Currency, Senate, June 7, 1932, pp. 107–8.

12 Ibid., p. 97.

13 Mills, Hearings before the Committee on Banking and Currency, Senate, June 2, 1932, p. 39.

14 Mills, Hearings before the Committee on Banking and Currency, Senate, June 7, 1932, p. 96.

15 Mills, Hearings before the Committee on Ways and Means, House of Representatives, June 2, 1932, p. 264.

16 Hoover, Statement on Emergency Relief and Construction Legislation, July 6, 1932, *PPP, 1932–1933*, p. 296.

17 Mills tried to clarify this point for the benefit of a Congressional interrogator:

Congressman Ragon: "I may not get the distinction, but when you resolve it down, I do not see but what the Reconstruction Finance Corporation is doing business now in competition with the banks."

Secretary Mills: "No, no; it loans to banks. It is not doing a banking business. . . . [W]e are not set up to run a bank; we really are not." (Hearings before the Committee on Ways and Means, House of Representatives, May 31, 1932, p. 32.)

18 John Nance Garner, Speaker of the House of Representatives, Hearings before the Committee on Ways and Means, House of Representatives, May 31, 1932, p. 32.

19 Hoover to Herbert S. Crocker, President of the American Society of Civil Engineers, May 21, 1932, Presidential Subject Files, HHPL. This letter, which was released to the press, was the administration's response to the endorsement of a $3 billion public works program by the executive committe of the American Society of Civil Engineers. This document is the most comprehensive single statement of the new approach to spending on public works.

20 Ibid.

21 Thomas MacDonald, chief of the Bureau of Public Roads, to George A. Hastings, administrative assistant to the president, July 31, 1932, Presidential Subject Files, HHPL.

22 Hoover to Crocker, May 21, 1932, Presidential Subject Files, HHPL.

23 Hoover, Statement About Signing the Federal Home Loan Bank Act, July 22, 1932, *PPP, 1932–1933,* p. 333.

24 Hoover, Statement about Signing the Emergency Relief and Construction Act of 1932, July 17, 1932, *PPP, 1932–1933*, p. 323.

25 Hoover to Governor Eugene Meyer, Federal Reserve Board, July 23, 1932, Presidential Subject Files, HHPL.

26 Meyer to Hoover, July 26, 1932, Presidential Subject Files, HHPL.

27 D. H. Sawyer, director of the Federal Employment Stabilization Board, to Julius Klein, May 20, 1932, Presidential Subject Files, HHPL.

28 William Trufant Foster was more explicit than were most others in this camp in arguing that a force outside the profit system was required to

spur the spending necessary for recovery. By mid-1932 he denounced Hoover for his failure to keep faith with the spirit of the program presented at the Governor's Conference in 1928. At the same time he argued in favor of "federal financing of sound private corporations which ordinarily would pay for expansion of plant with new bond issues, but which now postpone expansion solely because they cannot sell the bonds" and for the provision of federal monies for "self-liquidating projects" undertaken by state and local governments. The latter two points were precisely what Hoover had in mind in his proposed redesign of RFC. (Foster, "Better than the Bonus: Why Not Self-liquidating Relief?" *The Forum*, 88 [August 1932], pp. 88–92.)

29 Atlee Pomerene, chairman of the RFC, Radio Address of September 10, 1932, Records of the Department of the Treasury, Office of the Secretary, Box 119, NA.

30 In 1932 the RFC's base lending rates were as follows: to financial institutions in business as going concerns: 5½ percent; to railroads: 6 percent; "relief loans" to states: 3 percent. Most loans for "self-liquidating projects" were in the range of 5½ to 6½ percent, and a few were negotiated at 5 percent. Meanwhile, the notes issued by the RFC (which were absorbed in their entirety by the Treasury) carried a nominal interest rate of 3½ percent. (*Quarterly Report of the Reconstruction Finance Corporation to the Congress Covering the Corporation's Operations for the Periods October 1 to December 31, 1932 Inclusive and February 2 to December 31, 1932 Inclusive* [Washington, D.C.: U.S. Government Printing Office, 1933].) In September 1932 the Treasury placed an issue of $400 million in one-year certificates at 1¼ percent (an issue that was oversubscribed nearly eightfold). In mid-October 1932 it offered $450 million in 3 percent notes with a maturity of 4½ years and this issue was oversubscribed by nearly 20 times. (Arthur A. Ballantine, undersecretary of the Treasury, Address to the 21st Annual Convention of the Investment Bankers Association of America, October 26, 1932, Records of the Department of the Treasury, Office of the Secretary, Box 120. NA.)

31 *Quarterly Report of the Reconstruction Finance Corporation to the Congress Covering the Corporation's Operations for the Periods October 1 to December 31, 1932 Inclusive and February 2 to December 31, 1932 Inclusive.*

32 Ibid.

33 D. H. Sawyer, director, Federal Employment Stabilization Board, to Secretary of Commerce Roy D. Chapin (with attached report by Corrington Gill, chief economist), October 21, 1932, Presidential Subject Files, HHPL.

34 Hoover, News Conference, September 9, 1932, *PPP, 1932–1933*, pp. 404–5.

35 Hoover and officials of the RFC were outraged by what they took to be a breach of faith on this point and did their best to minimize its impact. The law was understood to mean that the reporting requirement applied only to loans negotiated after the enactment of the Emergency Relief and Construction Bill in July and that it was not retroactive. With the aid of a ruling from the corporation's general counsel, Martin G. Bogue, the RFC direc-

tors took the position that renewals of loans extended before the passage of the act did not have to be reported under the publicity provision. (Bogue to the Board of Directors, Reconstruction Finance Corporation, August 23, 1932, Records of the Department of the Treasury, Office of the Secretary, Box 1991, NA.)
36 As reported by James Stuart Olson, *Herbert Hoover and the Reconstruction Finance Corporation, 1931–1933*, p. 104.
37 Hoover to the Governors and Members of the Federal Reserve Board, February 22, 1933, Presidential Subject Files, HHPL.
38 Hoover to James H. Rand, Jr., Remington-Rand, New York, February 28, 1933, Presidential Subject Files, HHPL. Tugwell later disputed the accuracy of the views attributed to him by Rand in the latter's report to the White House of their conversation. In Tugwell's account, Rand had tried to "pump" him about "likely Roosevelt policies," but Tugwell had "put him off with generalities and jests." (Tugwell, "The New Deal: the Contributions of Herbert Hoover, p. 34, n.d. Tugwell Papers, FDRPL.)
39 Meyer to Hoover, March 2, 1933, Presidential Subject Files, HHPL.
40 Meyer to Hoover, March 3, 1933, Presidential Subject Files, HHPL.
41 Hoover to Meyer, March 4, 1933, Presidential Subject Files, HHPL.

Epilogue: transition to the New Deal — continuities and discontinuities

1 Rexford Guy Tugwell, "The New Deal: The Contributions of Herbert Hoover," unpublished manuscript, n.d., Tugwell Papers, FDRPL, pp. 30, 36, 61.
2 Ibid., p. 65.

Selected bibliography

The primary materials essential for the study of Hoover's thinking about economic problems are to be found in the holdings of the Herbert Hoover Presidential Library, in the National Archives, and in the documents assembled in the *Public Papers of the Presidents, 1929–1933.* For insight into the positions of economists on the central issues of the period considered in this study, the most important sources are the words of contemporary economists themselves, as recorded in their contributions to professional journals, in their books, and in the transcripts of their testimony and other submissions to congressional committees.

Recent scholarship has produced a rich array of studies treating various aspects of the problems considered in this book. A select list of works that are particularly rewarding follows.

Arnold, Peri. 1972. "Herbert Hoover and the Continuity of American Public Policy." *Public Policy* 20:525–44.

Best, Gary Dean, 1975. *The Politics of American Individualism: Herbert Hoover in Transition, 1918–1921.* Westport, Conn.: Greenwood Press.

Brandes, Joseph. 1962. *Herbert Hoover and Economic Diplomacy: Department of Commerce Policy, 1921–1928.* Pittsburgh, Pa.: University of Pittsburgh Press.

Burner, David. 1979. *Herbert Hoover: The Public Life.* New York: Knopf.

Chandler, Lester V. 1970. *America's Greatest Depression, 1929–1941.* New York: Harper & Row.

Davis, J. Ronnie. 1971. *The New Economics and the Old Economists.* Ames: Iowa State University Press.

Degler, Carl. 1963. "The Ordeal of Herbert Hoover," *Yale Review* 52:563–83.

Dorfman, Joseph. 1959. *The Economic Mind and American Civilization,* vols. 4, 5. New York: Viking Press.

Fausold, Martin L., and George T. Mazuzan, (eds.). 1974. *The Hoover Presidency: a Reappraisal.* Albany: State University of New York Press.

Friedman, Milton, and Anna Jacobson Schwartz. 1965. *The Great Contraction, 1929–1933.* Princeton, N.J.: Princeton University Press.

Galbraith, John Kenneth. 1972. *The Great Crash: 1929,* 3rd ed. Boston: Houghton Mifflin.

Hatfield, Mark O. (organizer). 1981. *Herbert Hoover Reassessed: Essays Com-*

memorating the Fiftieth Anniversary of the Inauguration of Our Thirty-First President. Washington, D.C.: U.S. Government Printing Office.

Hawley, Ellis W. (ed.). 1981. *Herbert Hoover as Secretary of Commerce: Studies in the New Era Thought and Practice.* Iowa City: University of Iowa Press.

1974. "Herbert Hoover, The Commerce Secretariat, and the Vision of an 'Associative State,' 1921–1928." *Journal of American History* 61:116–40.

Himmelberg, Robert H. 1976. *The Origins of the National Recovery Administration: Business, Government and the Trade Association Issue, 1921–1933.* New York: Fordham University Press.

Huthmacher, J. Joseph, and Warren I. Sussman (eds.). 1973. *Herbert Hoover and the Crisis of American Capitalism.* Cambridge: Schenkman.

Karl, Barry D. 1969. "Presidential Planning and Social Science Research." *Perspectives in American History* 3:347–409.

Kindleberger, Charles P. 1973. *The World in Depression: 1929–1939.* Berkeley and Los Angeles: University of California Press.

Metcalf, Evan B. 1975. "Secretary Hoover and the Emergence of Macroeconomic Management." *Business History Review* 49:60–80.

Nash, George H. 1983. *The Life of Herbert Hoover,* vol. 1. New York: Norton.

Olson, James S. 1977, *Herbert Hoover and the Reconstruction Finance Corporation, 1931–1933.* Ames: Iowa State University Press.

New York: Oxford University Press.

Romasco, Albert U. 1965. *The Poverty of Abundance: Hoover, the Nation, and the Depression.* New York: Oxford University Press.

Rosen, Elliot A. 1977. *Hoover, Roosevelt, and the Brains Trust: From Depression to the New Deal.* New York: Columbia University Press.

Schwarz, Jordan A. 1970. *The Interregnum of Despair: Hoover, Congress and the Depression.* Urbana: University of Illinois Press.

Stein, Herbert. 1969. *The Fiscal Revolution in America.* Chicago: University of Chicago Press.

Wilson, Joan Hoff. 1971. *American Business and Foreign Policy, 1920–1933.* Lexington: University Press of Kentucky.

1975. *Herbert Hoover: Forgotten Progressive.* Boston: Little, Brown.

Ziegler, Robert H. 1969. *Republicans and Labor, 1919–1929.* Lexington: University Press of Kentucky.

1965. "Herbert Hoover: A Reinterpretation." *American Historical Review* 81:800–810.

Index

233